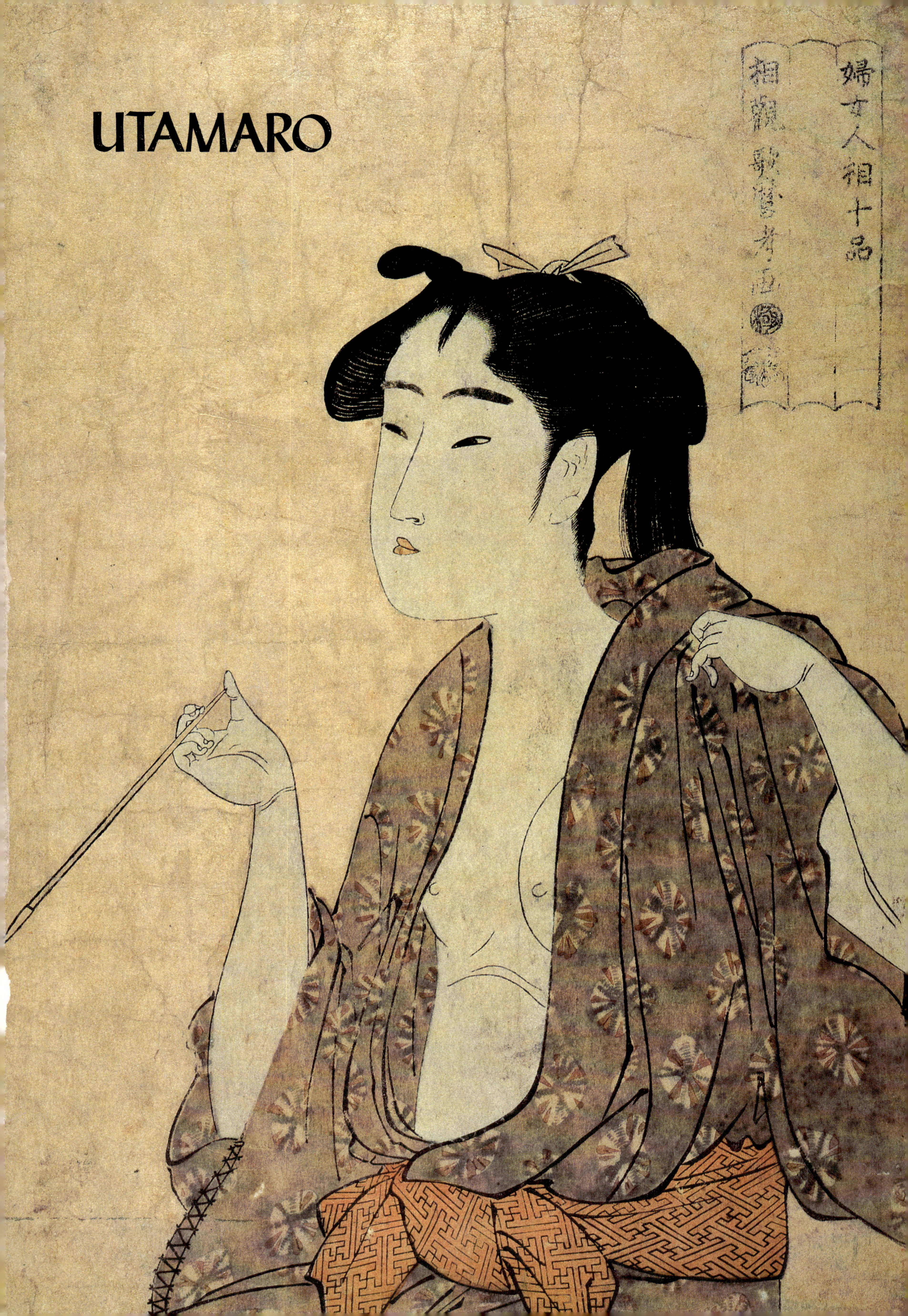

UTAMARO

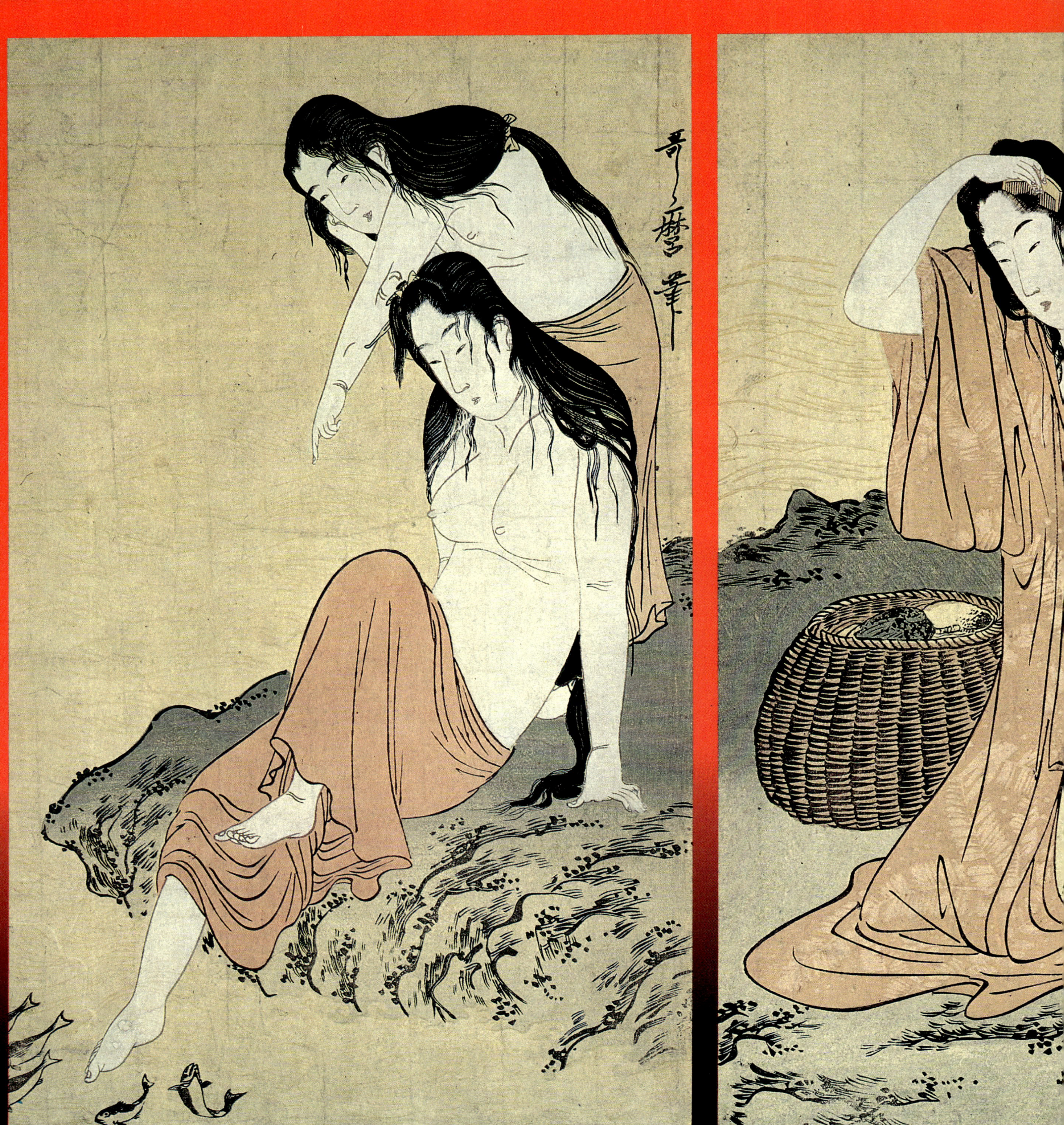

歌麿筆

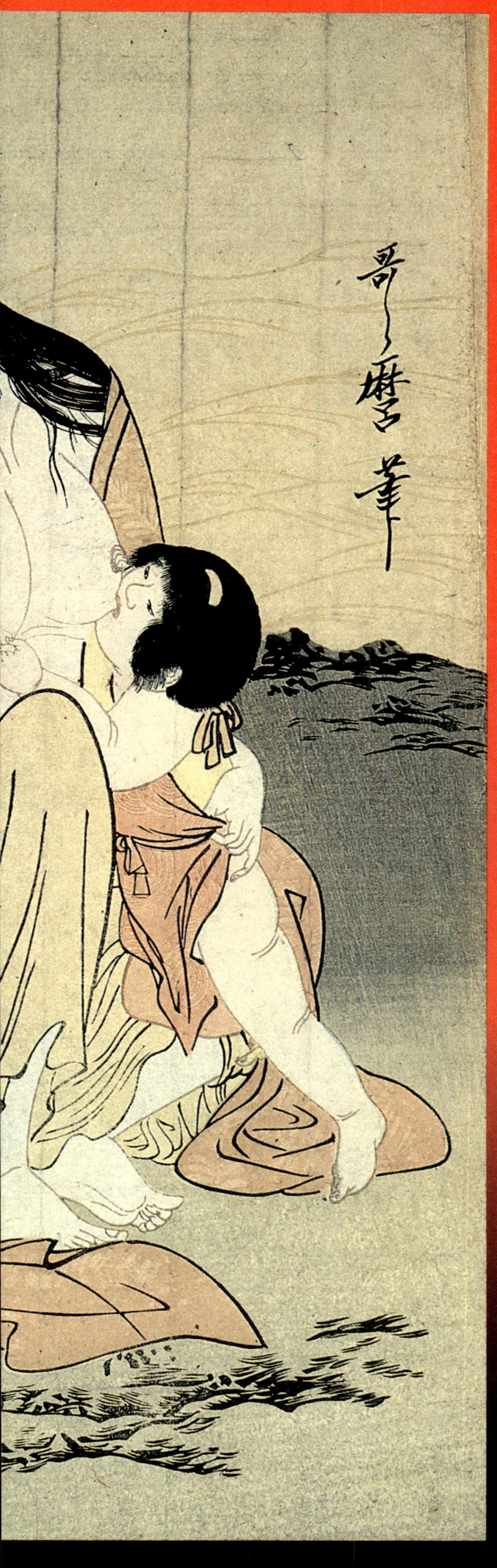

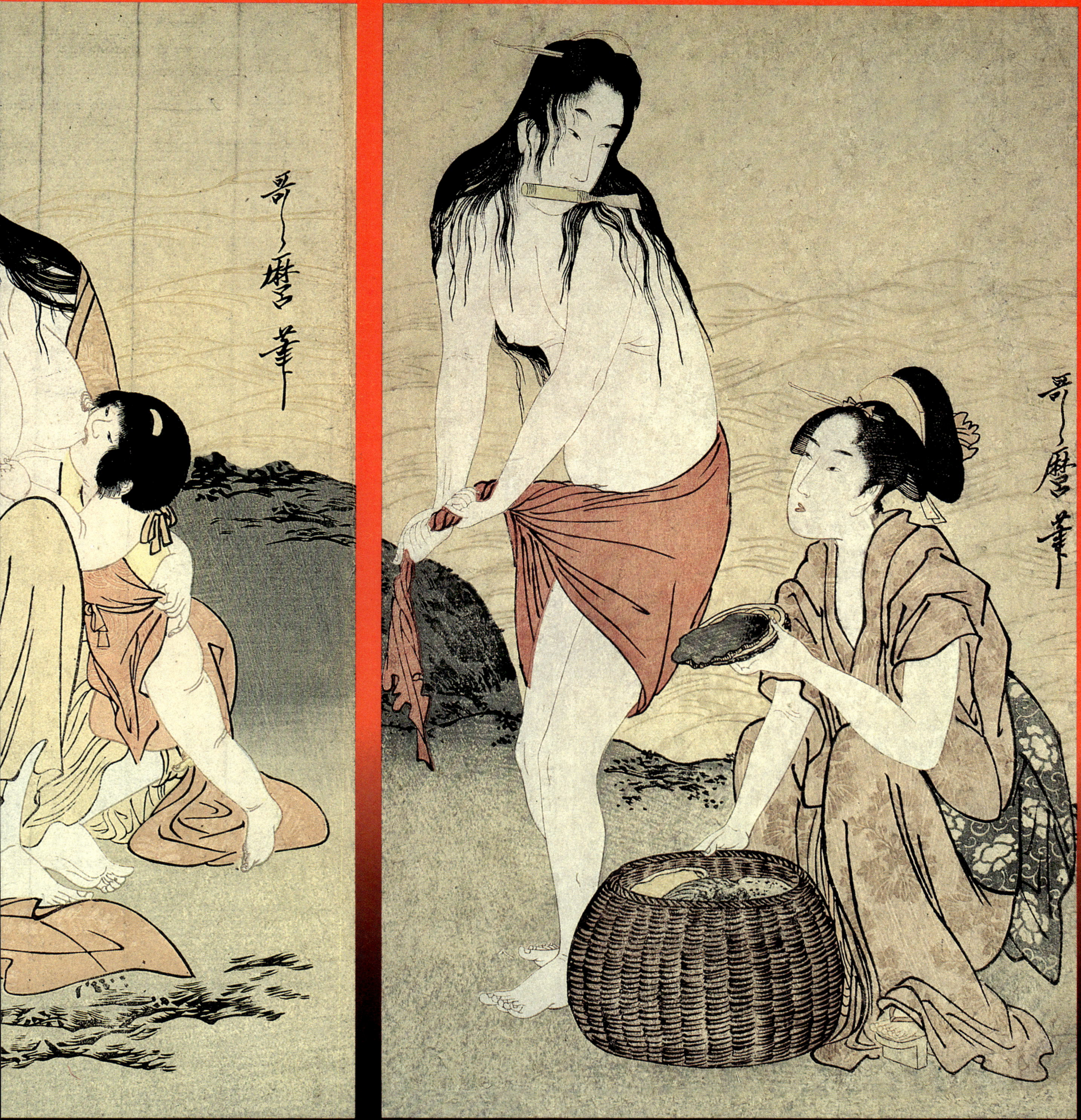

UTAMARO

Tadashi Kobayashi

Half-title page. *Woman Smoking a Pipe:* "Ten Studies in Female Physiognomy."
Title pages. *Abalone Divers.*

Note to the Reader: Japanese names are given in the customary Japanese order, surname preceding given name.

Published with the cooperation of Kodansha International Ltd. and distributed in Great Britain and Europe by Robert G Sawers Publishing, PO Box 4QA, London W1A 4QA, England.

Originally published and distributed throughout the rest of the world by Kodansha International Ltd., 12-21, Otowa 2-chome, Bunkyo-ku, Tokyo 112, Japan and Kodansha International/USA Ltd., 10 East 53rd Street, New York 10022 and 44 Montgomery Street, San Francisco, California 94104.

Printed in Japan.

ISBN 0-903697-16-5 (Robert G Sawers Publishing)

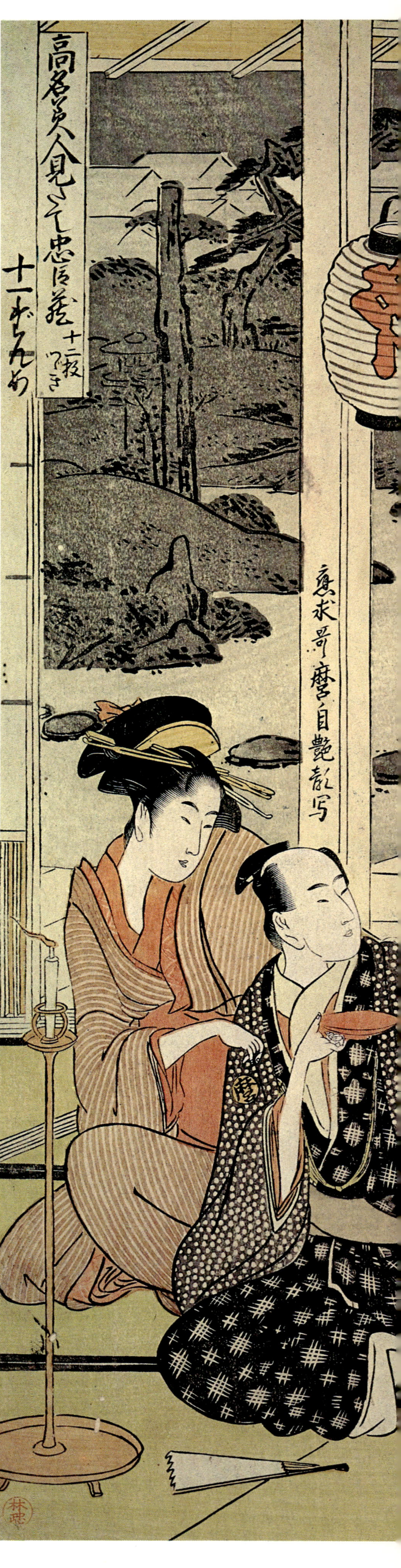

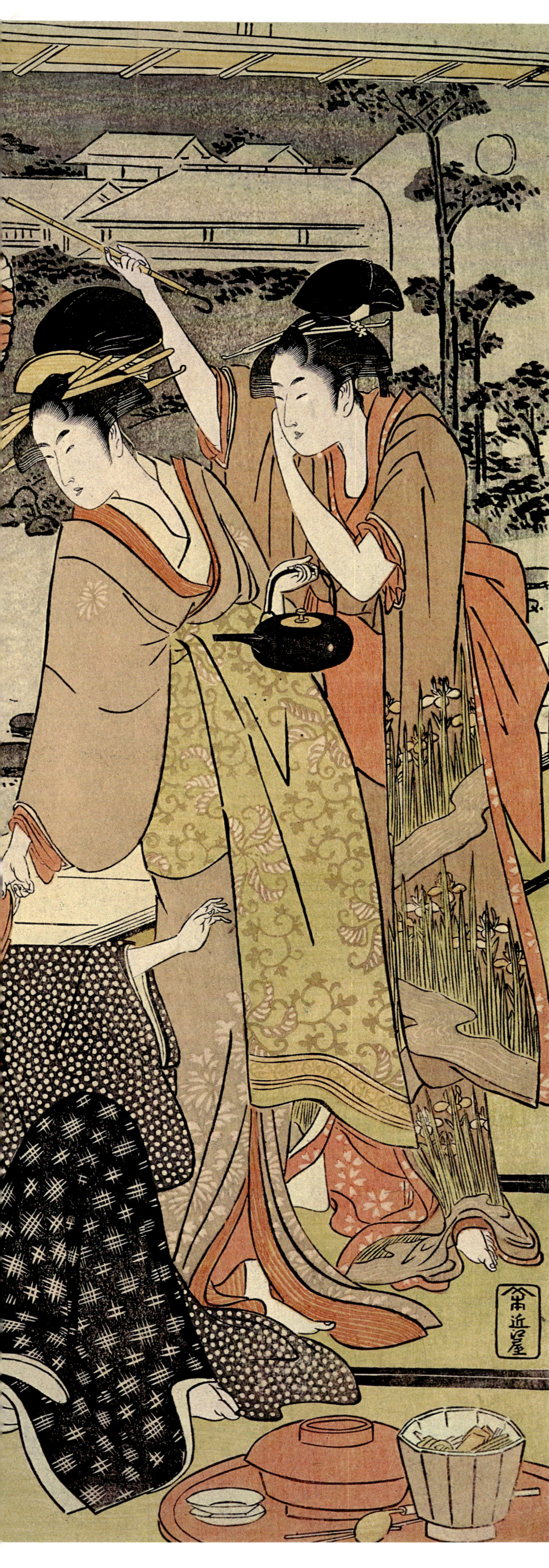

Contents

Scene Eleven: "Famous Beauties in the Role of *Chūshingura*."
On the column behind the seated figure, Utamaro has written,
"In response to popular demand I have portrayed my own
handsome face and figure."

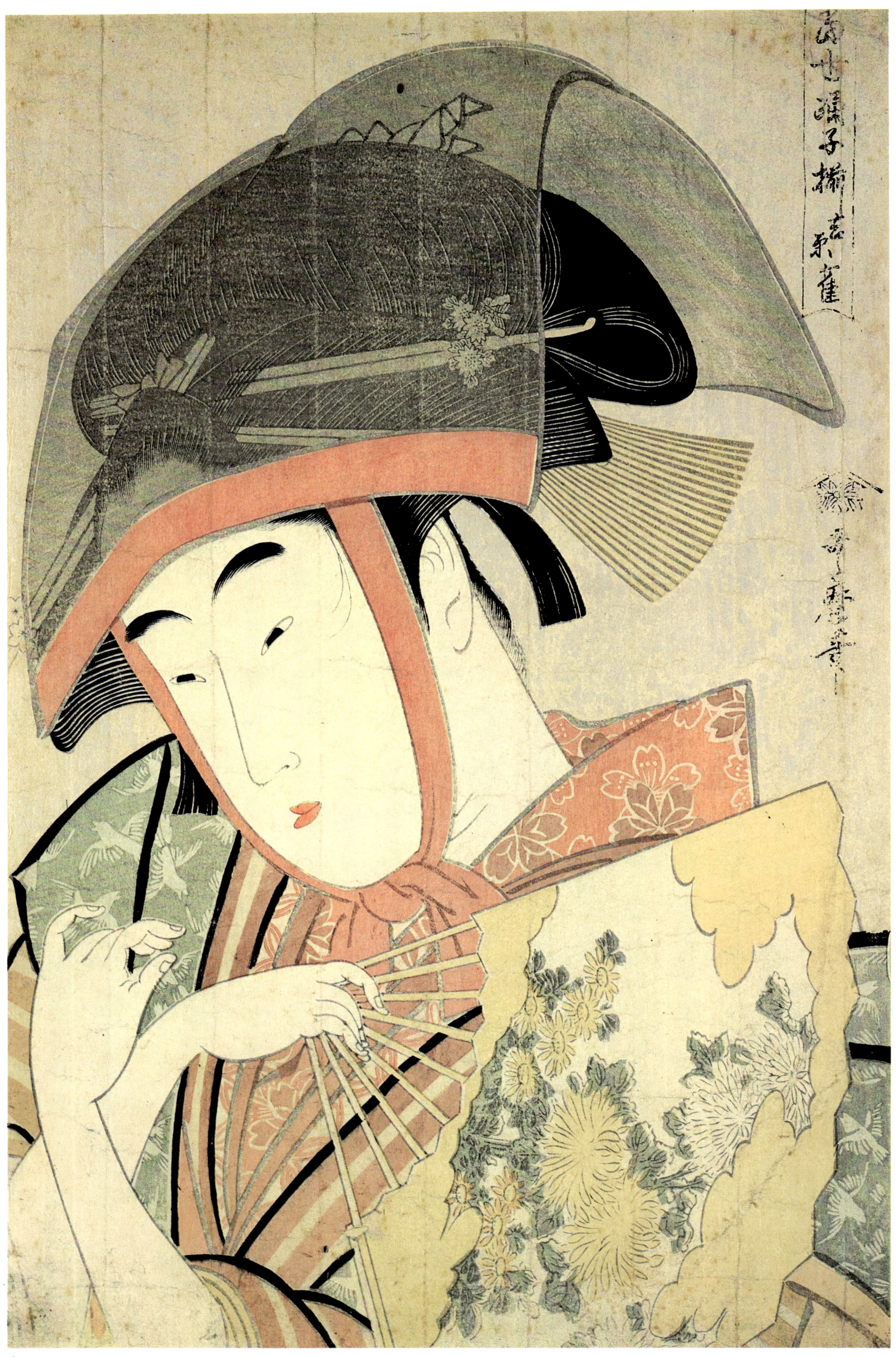

1. *The Yoshiwara Sparrow Dance*: "Contemporary Edo Dancers Arrayed for the Yoshiwara Niwaka Festival."

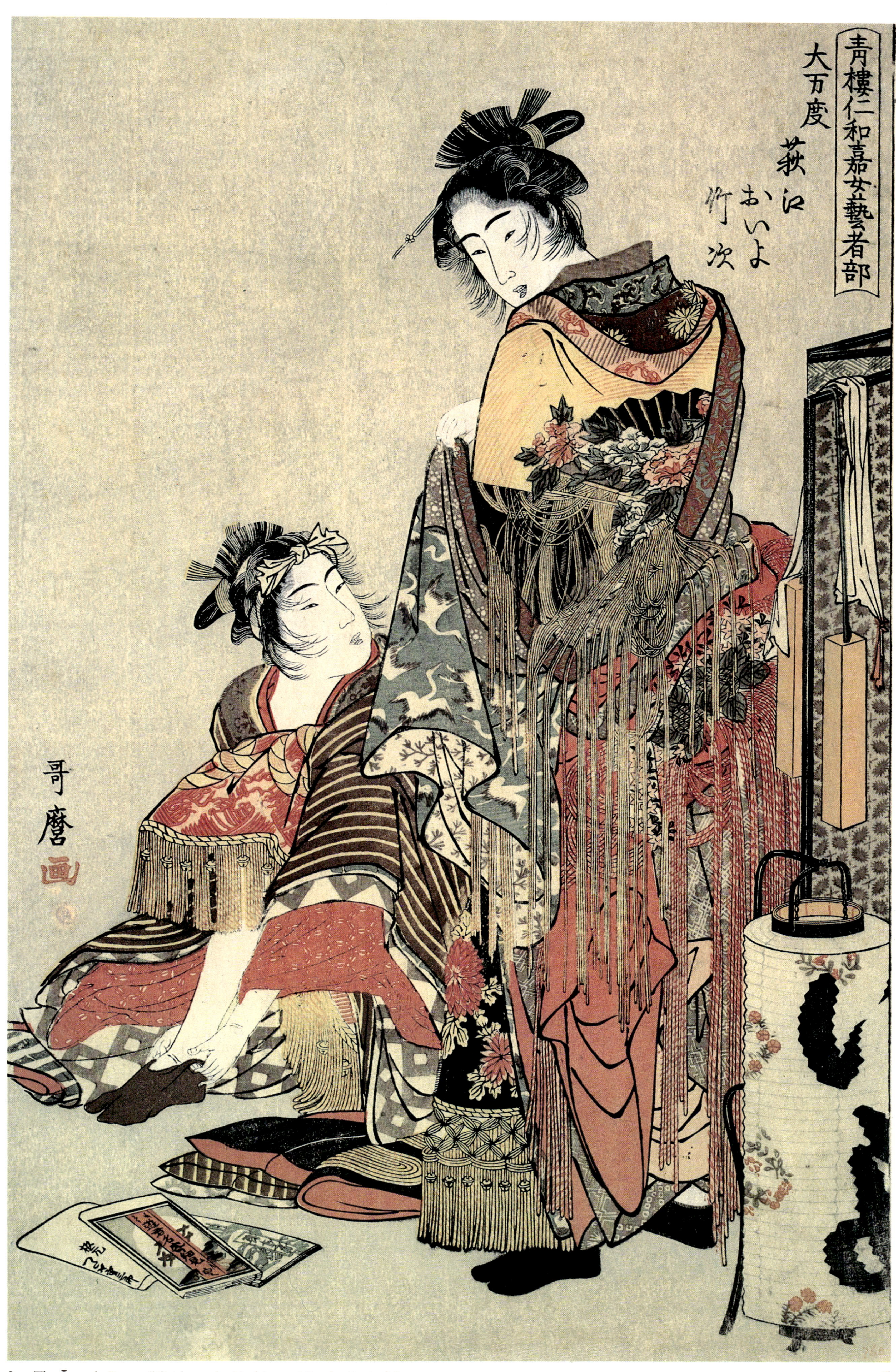

2. *The Ōmando Dance*: "*Geisha at the Yoshiwara Niwaka Festival.*"

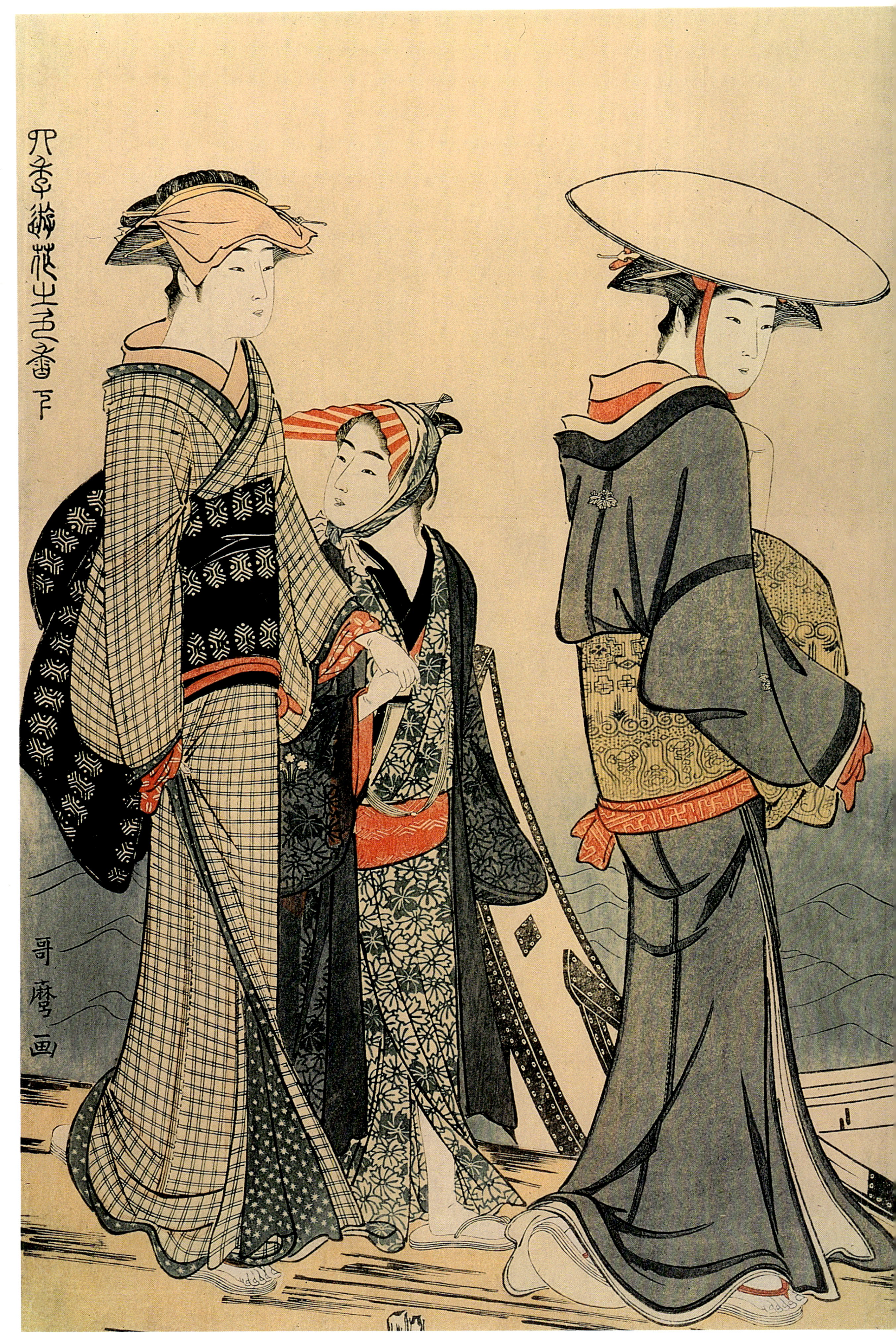

   3. *Stylish Amusements of the Four Seasons.*

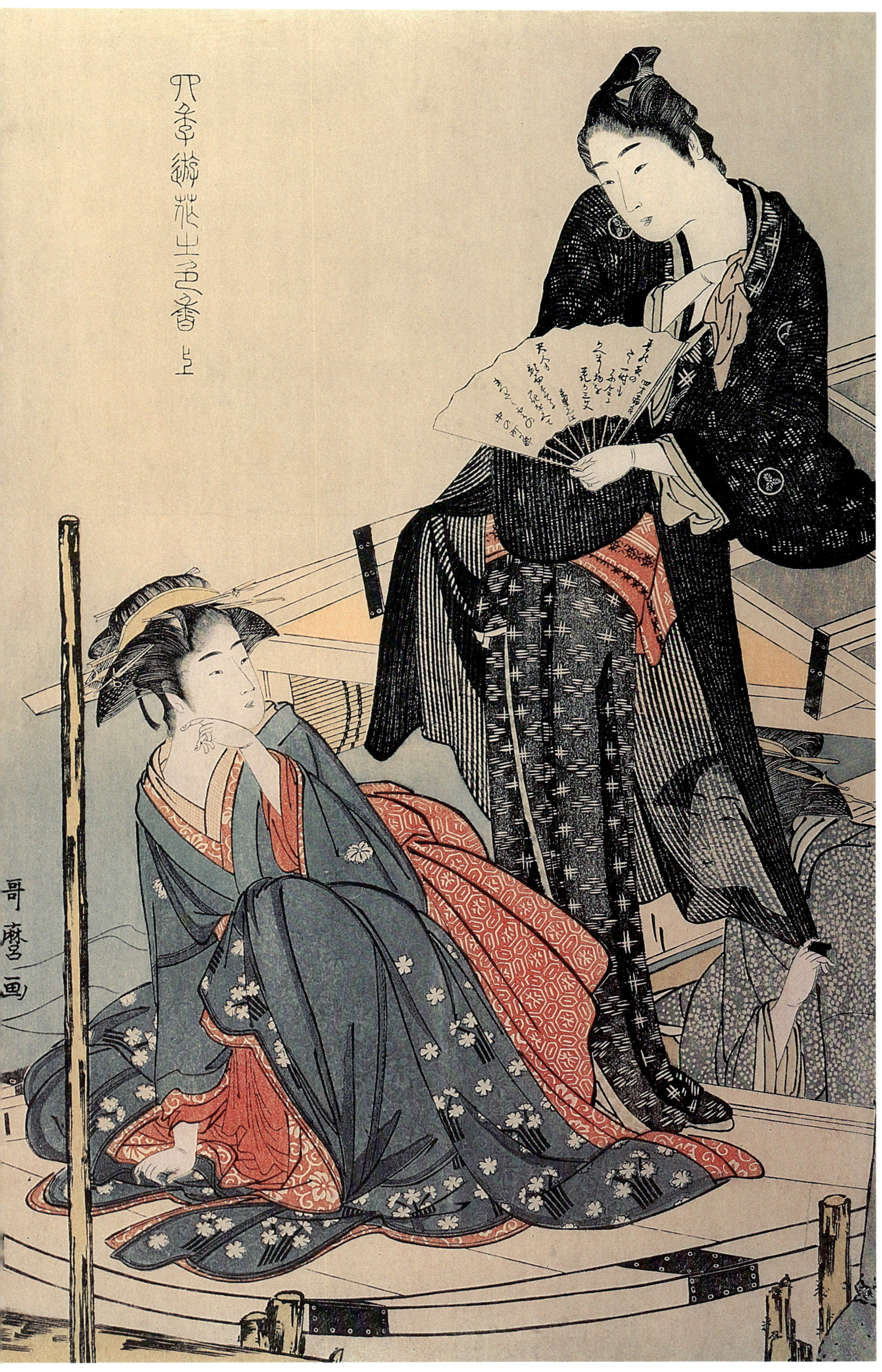

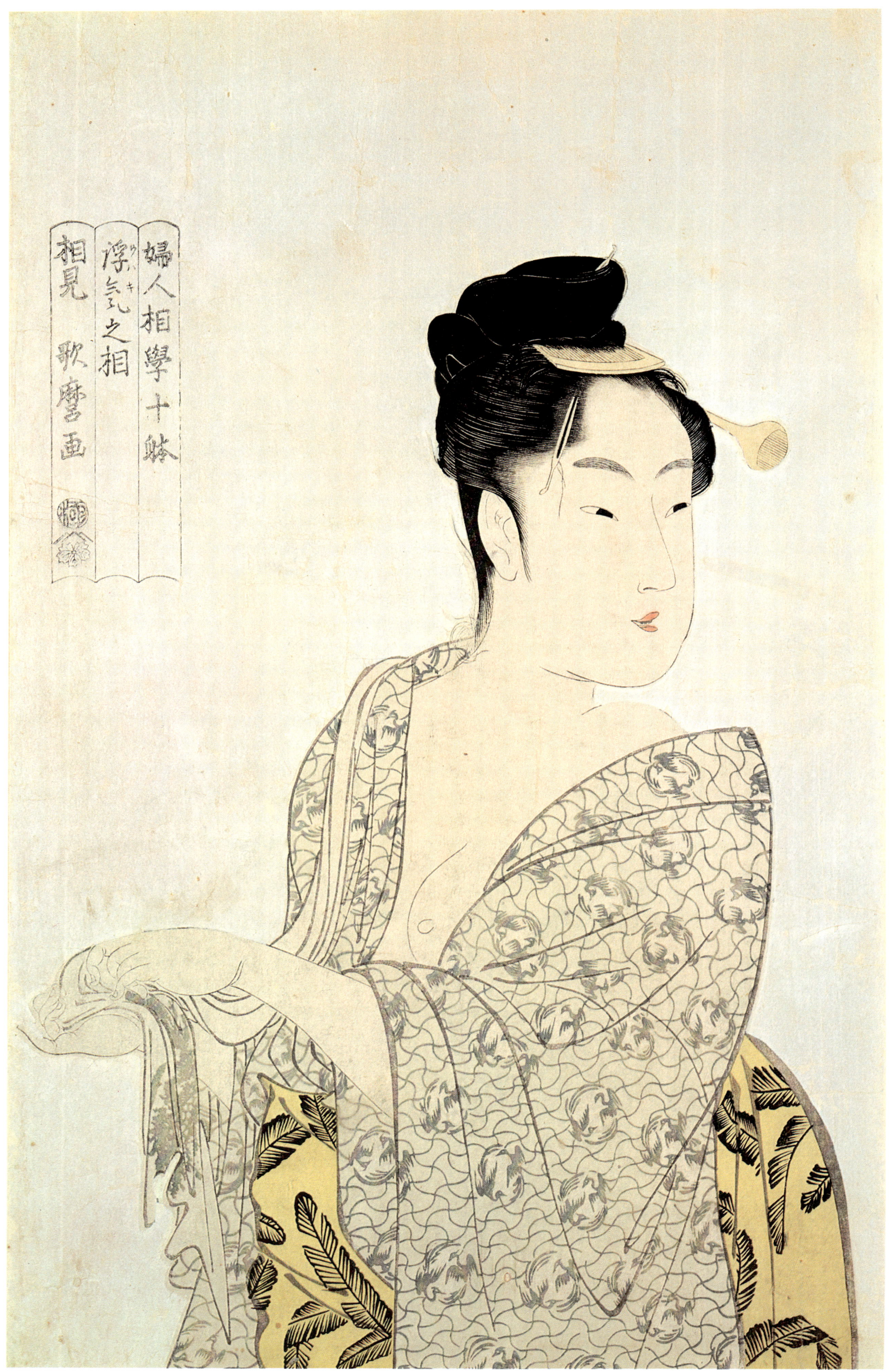

4. *The Hedonist*: "Ten Studies in Female Physiognomy."

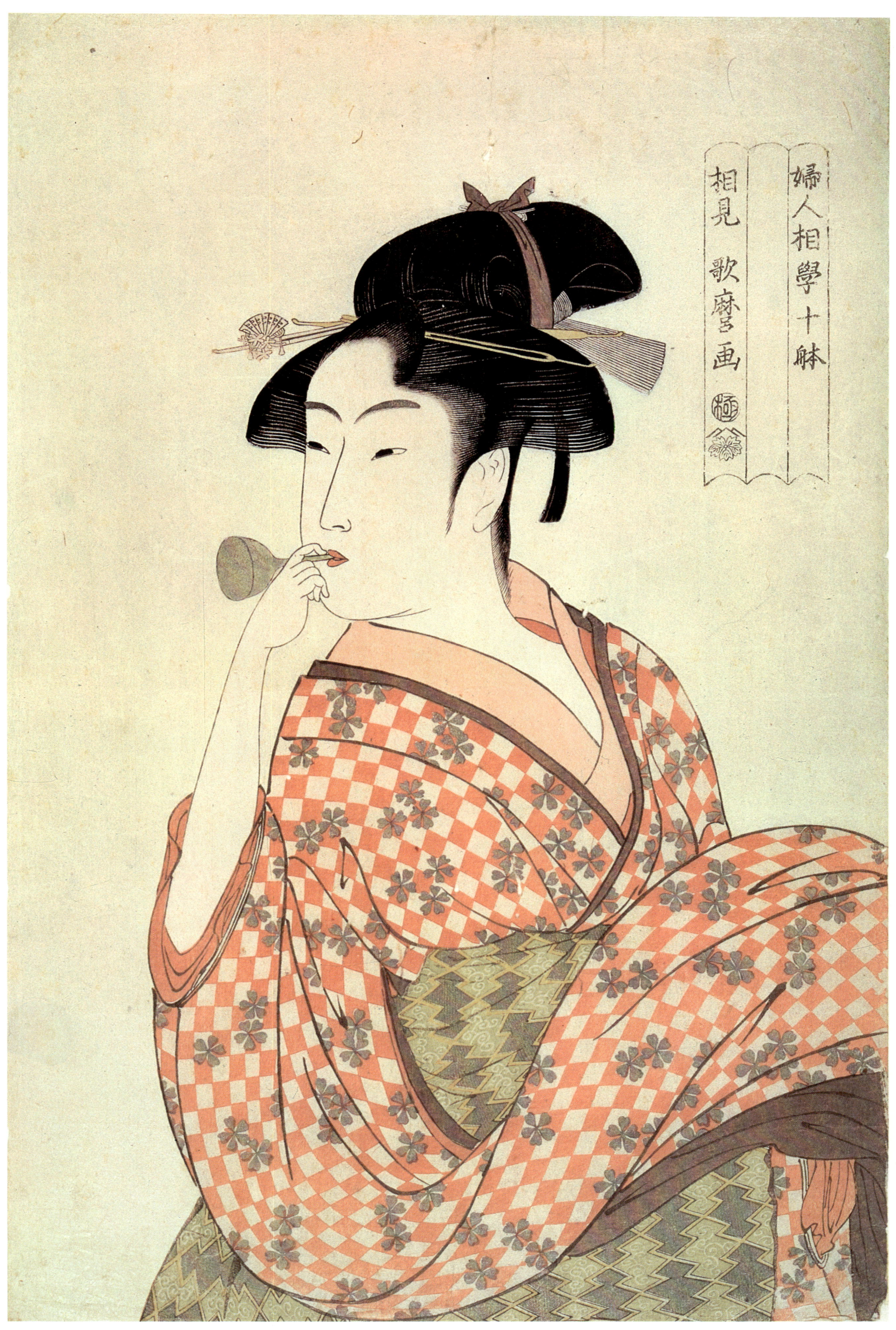

5. *A Woman Playing a Poppin*: "Ten Studies in Female Physiognomy."

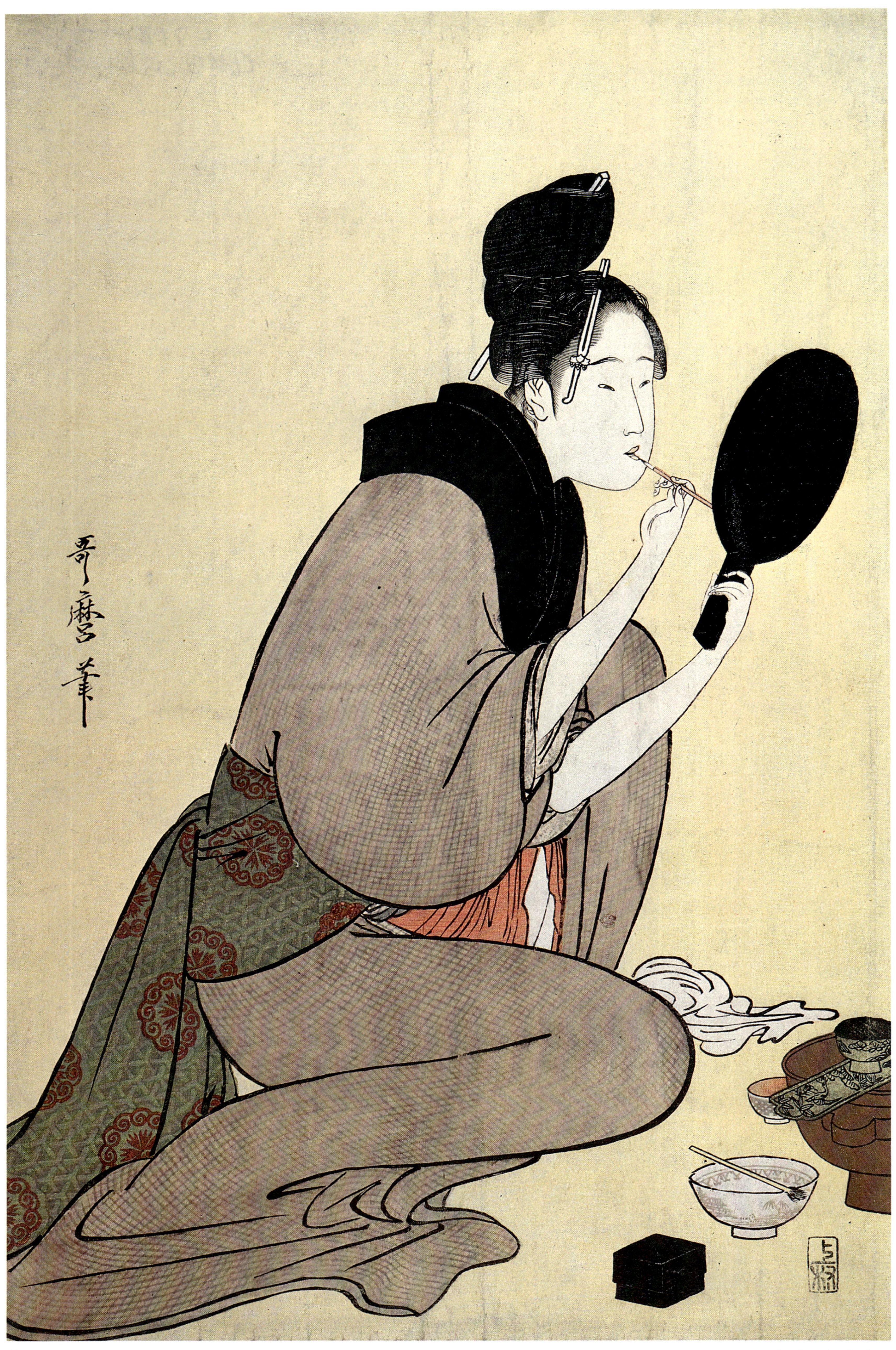

6. *Painting the Lips.*

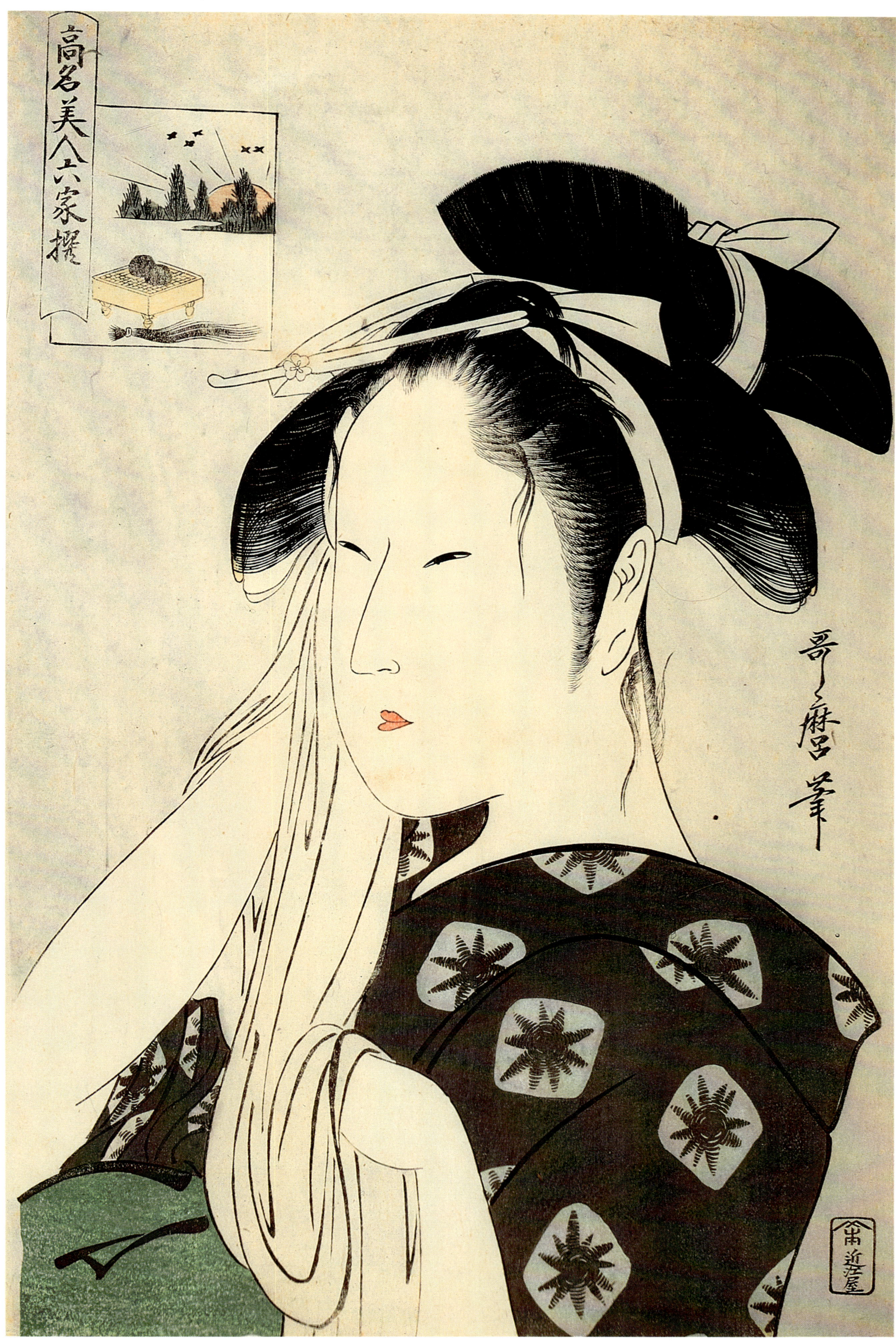

7. *The Widow of Hinodeya:* "Six Famous Beauties Challenge the Magnificence of the Six Poetic Geniuses."

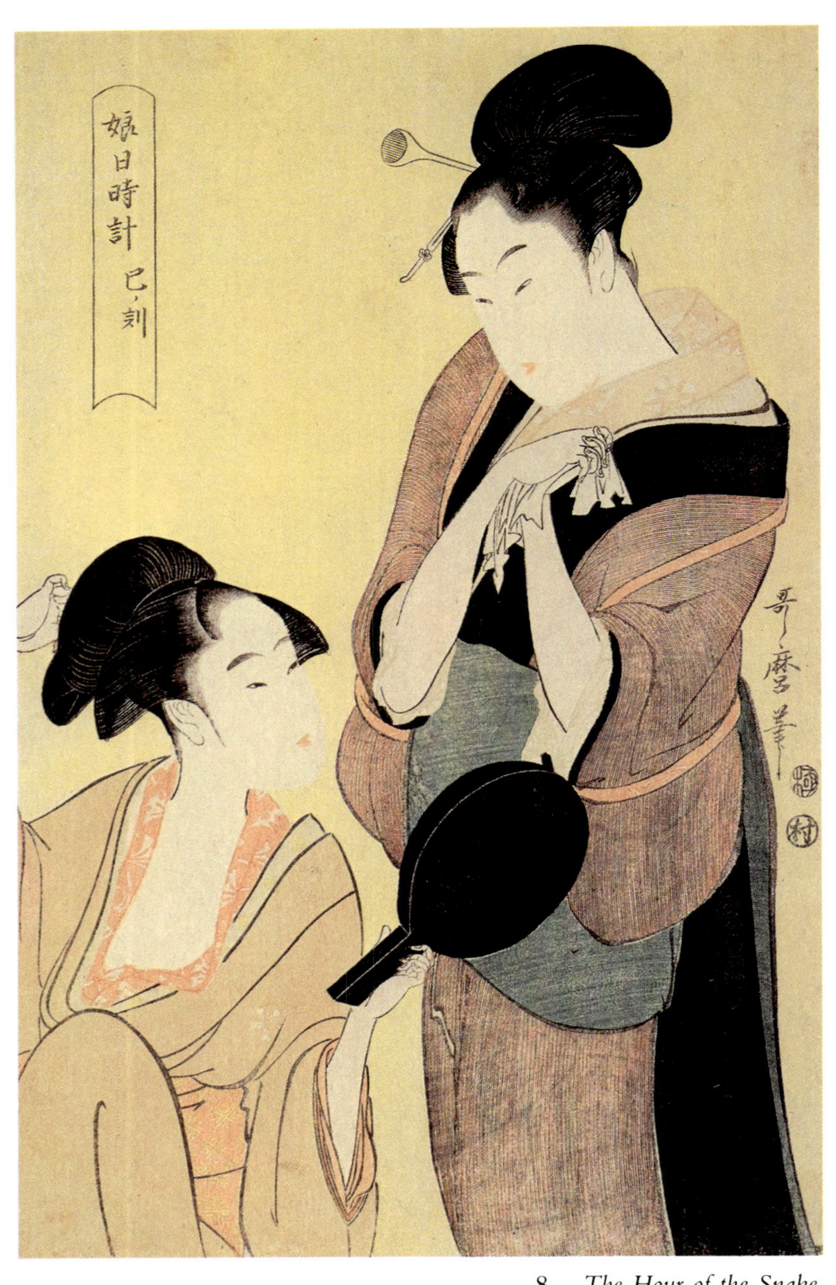

8. *The Hour of the Snake.*

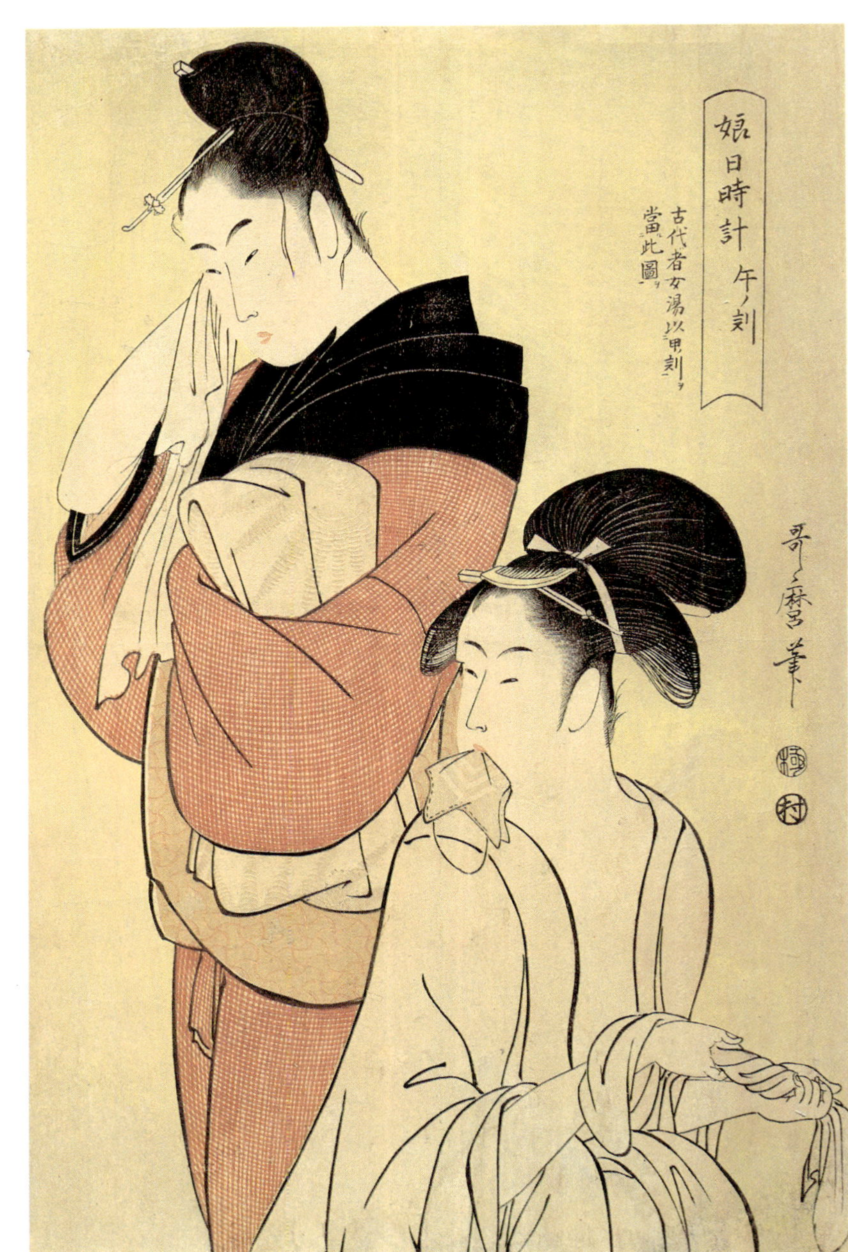

9. *The Hour of the Horse.*

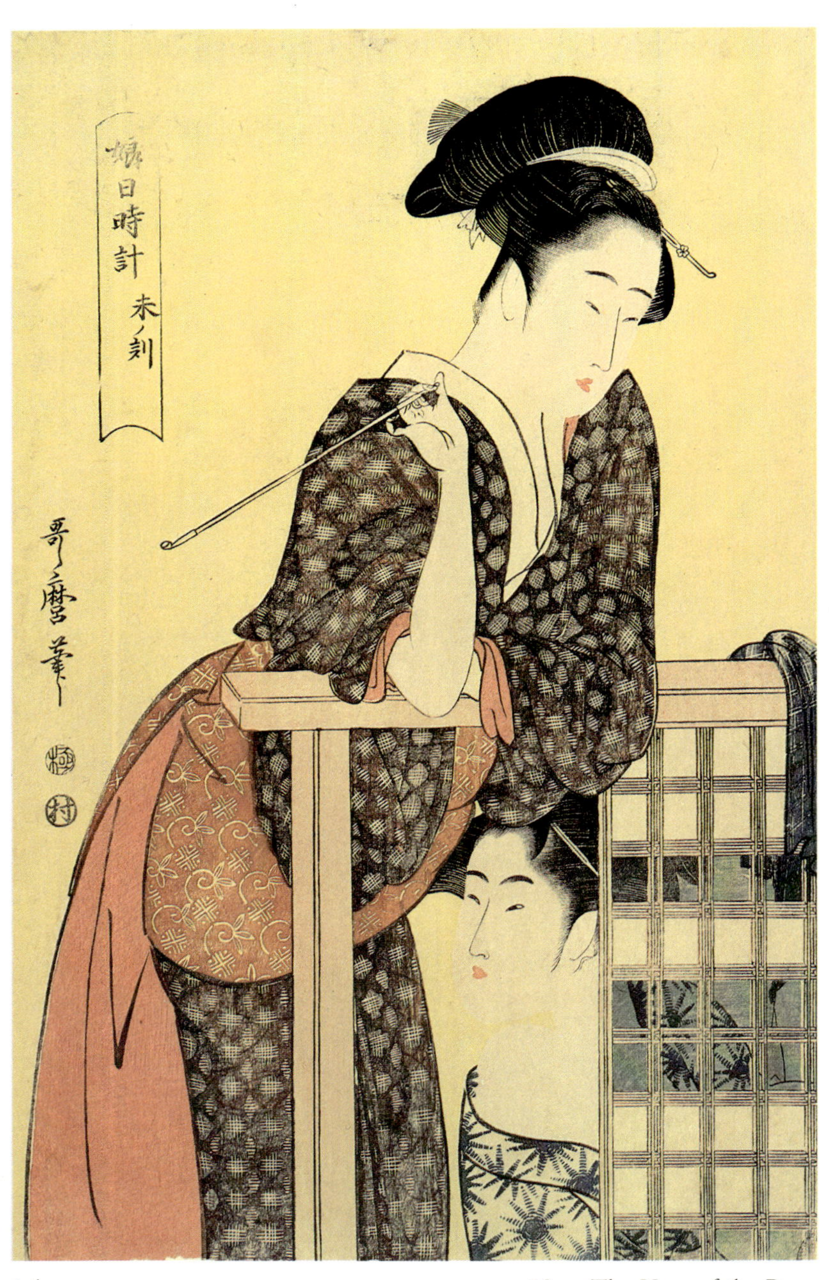

10. *The Hour of the Ram.*

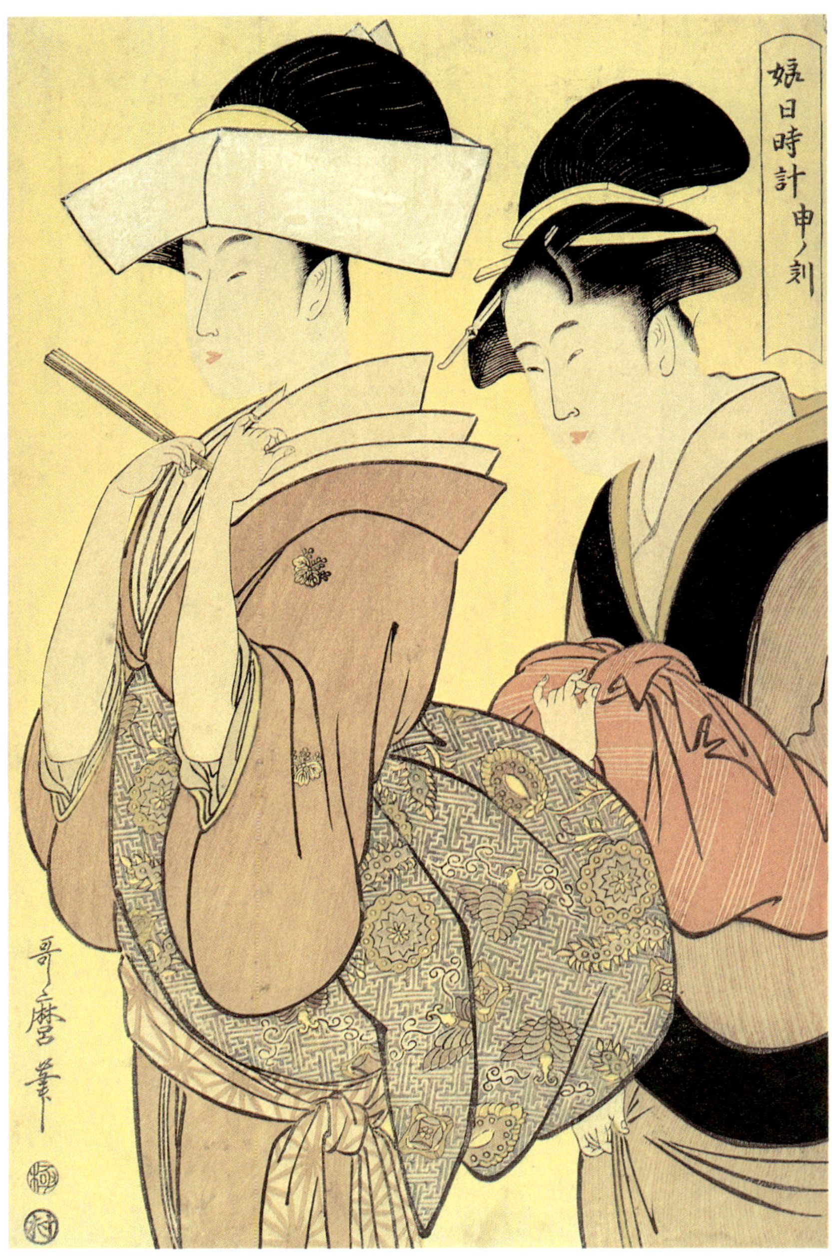

11. *The Hour of the Monkey.*

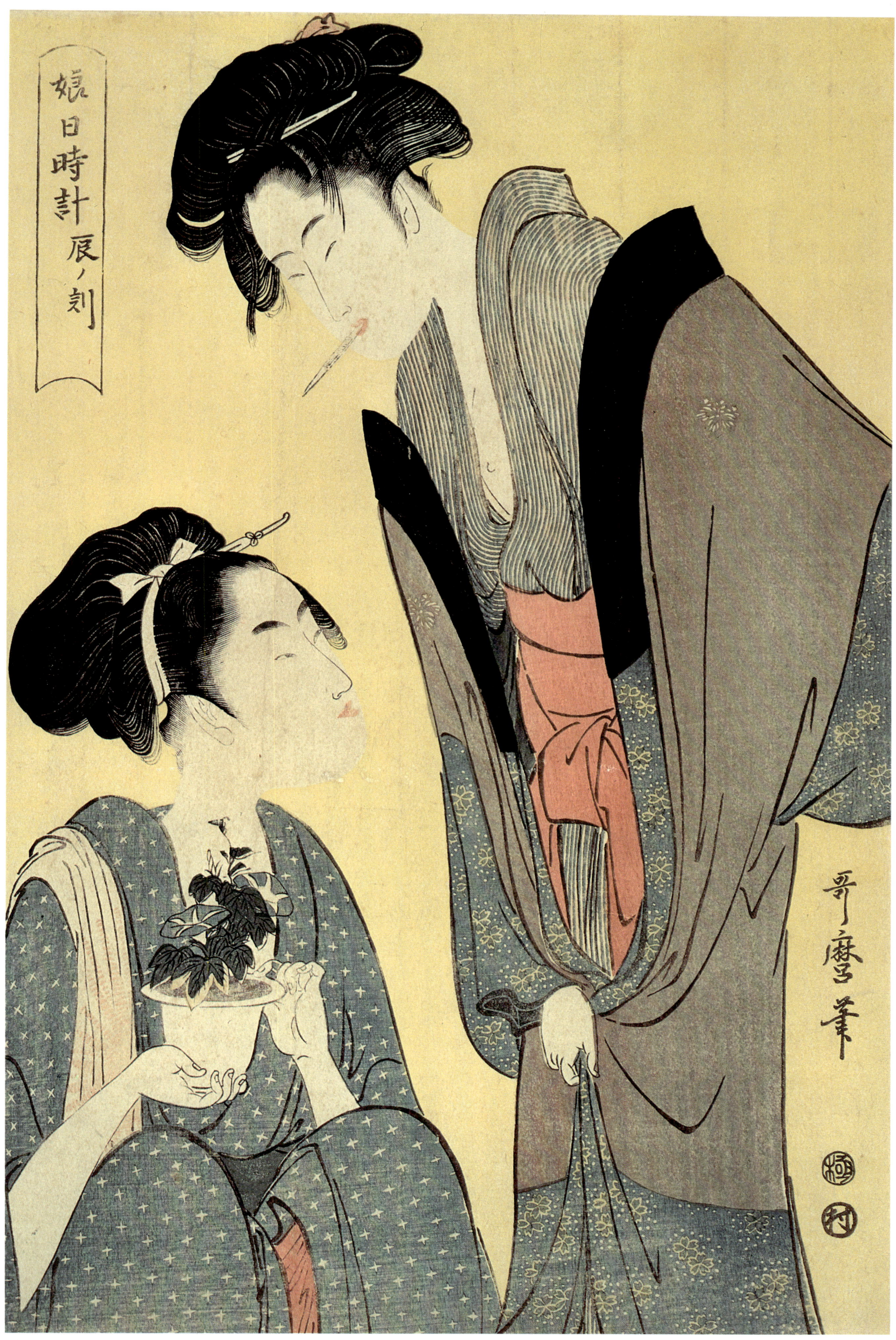

12.   *The Hour of the Dragon.*   8–12.   The series "A Sundial of Maidens."   15

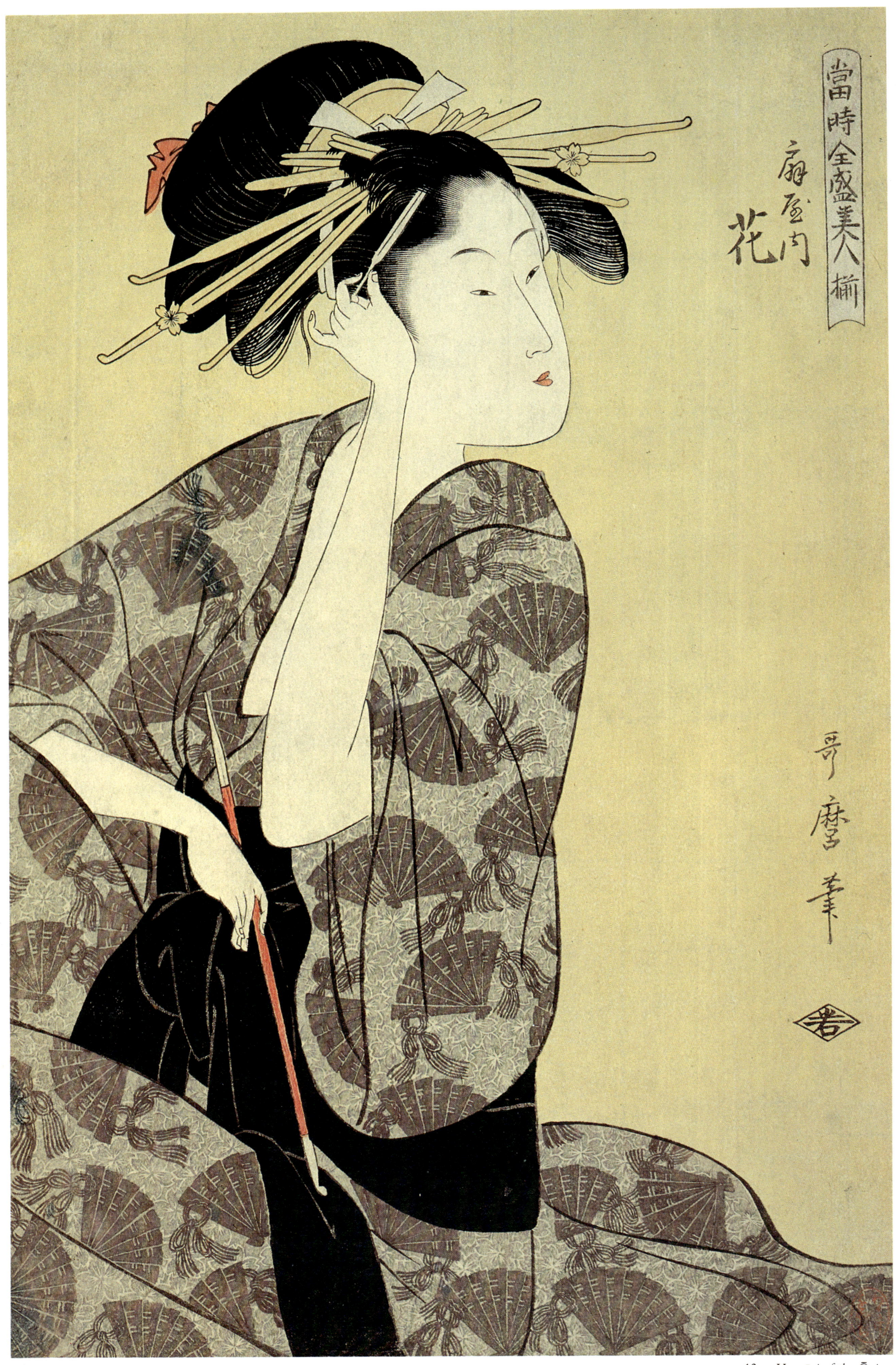

13. *Hanaōgi of the Ōgiya.*

13–16. From the series "A Collection of Reigning Beauties."

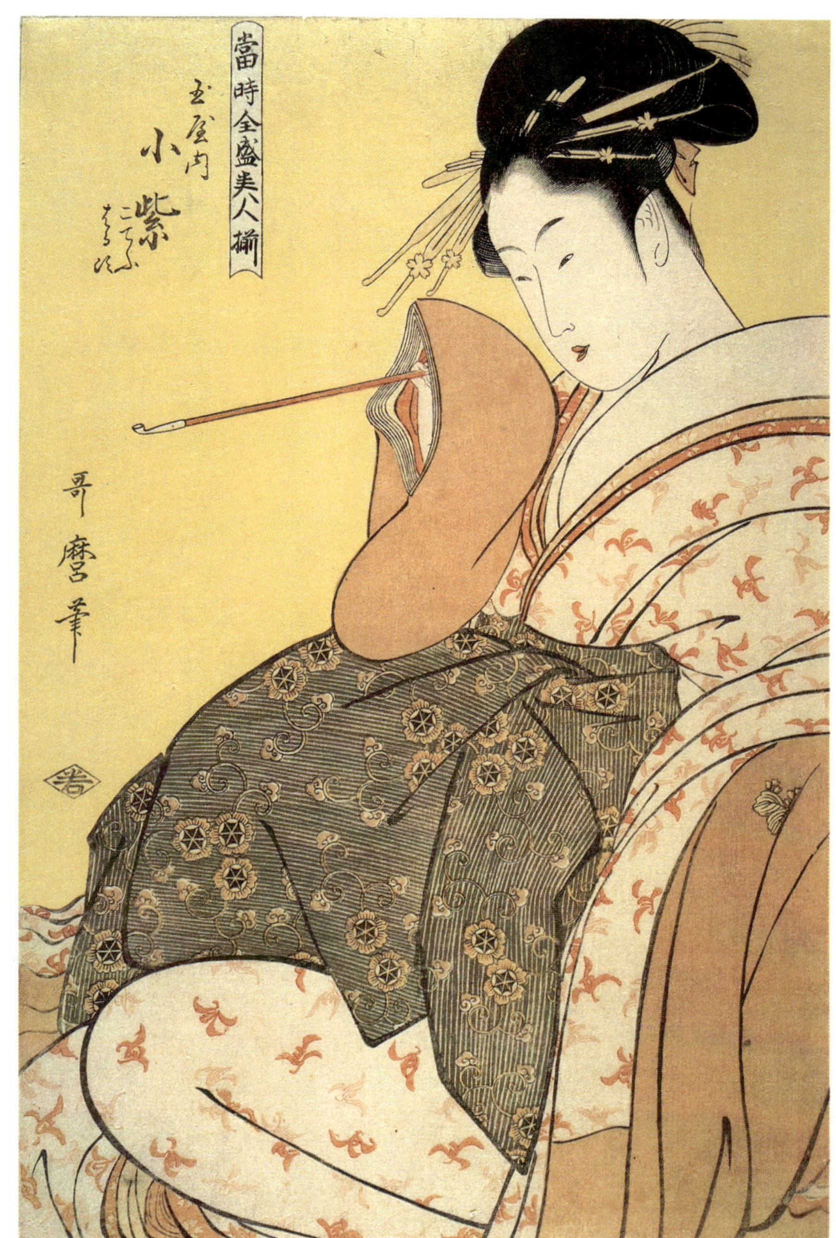

15. *Komurasaki of the Tamaya.*

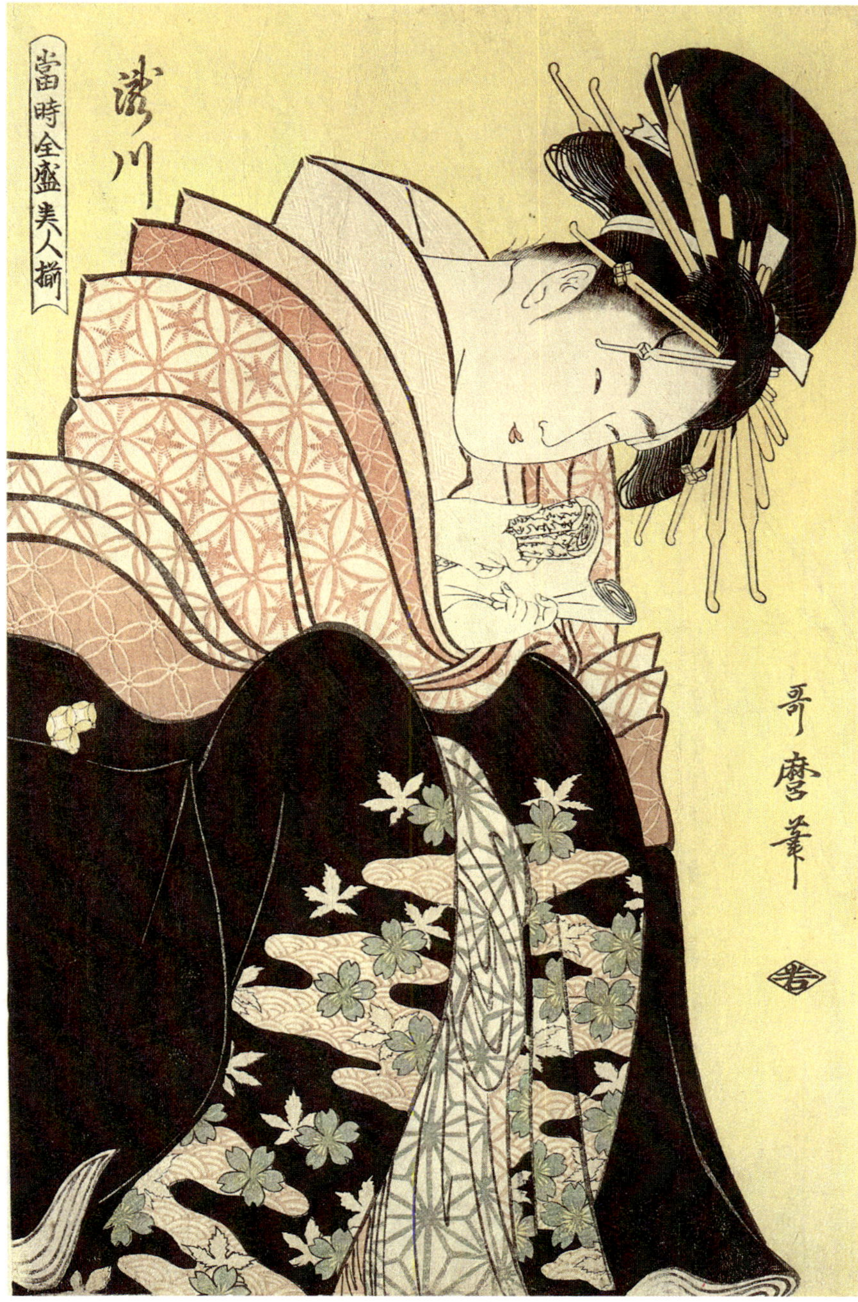

14. *Takigawa of the Ōgiya.*

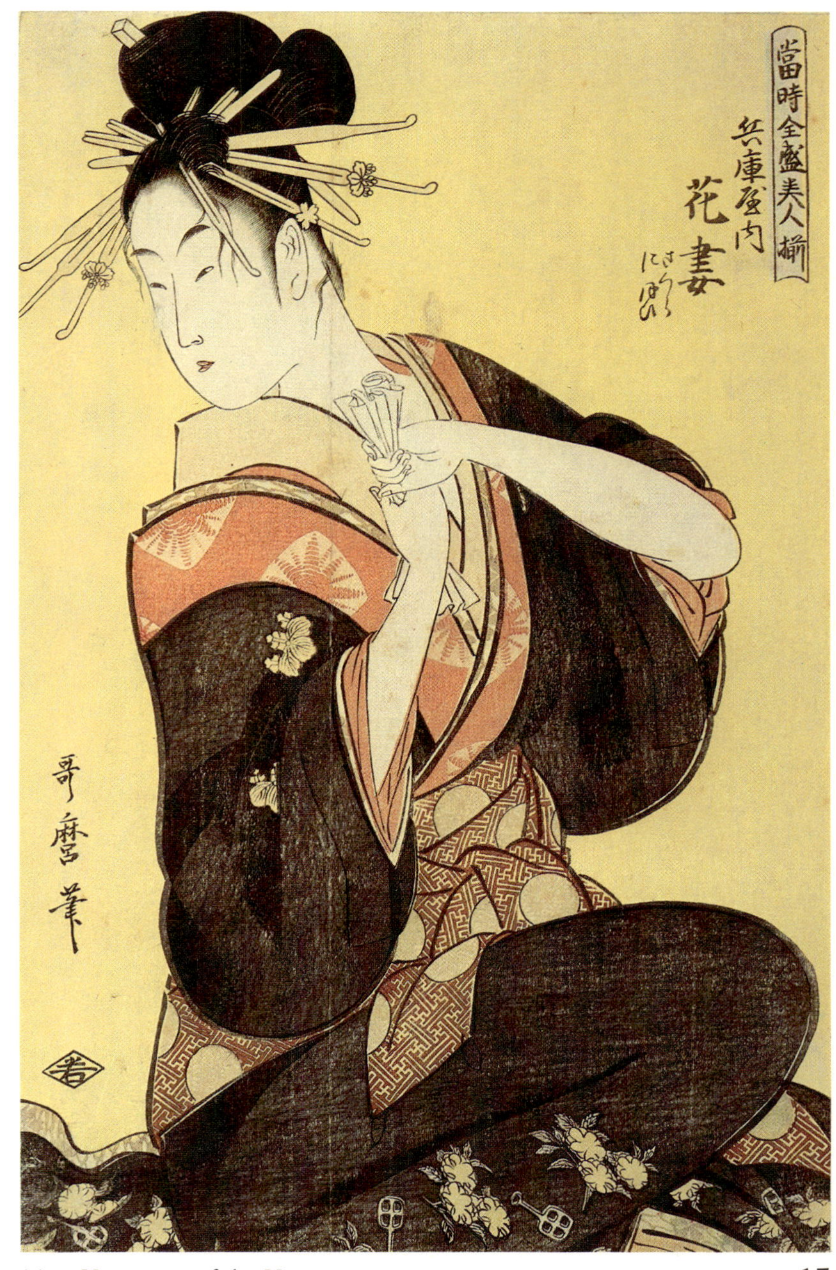

16. *Hanazuma of the Hyōgoya.*

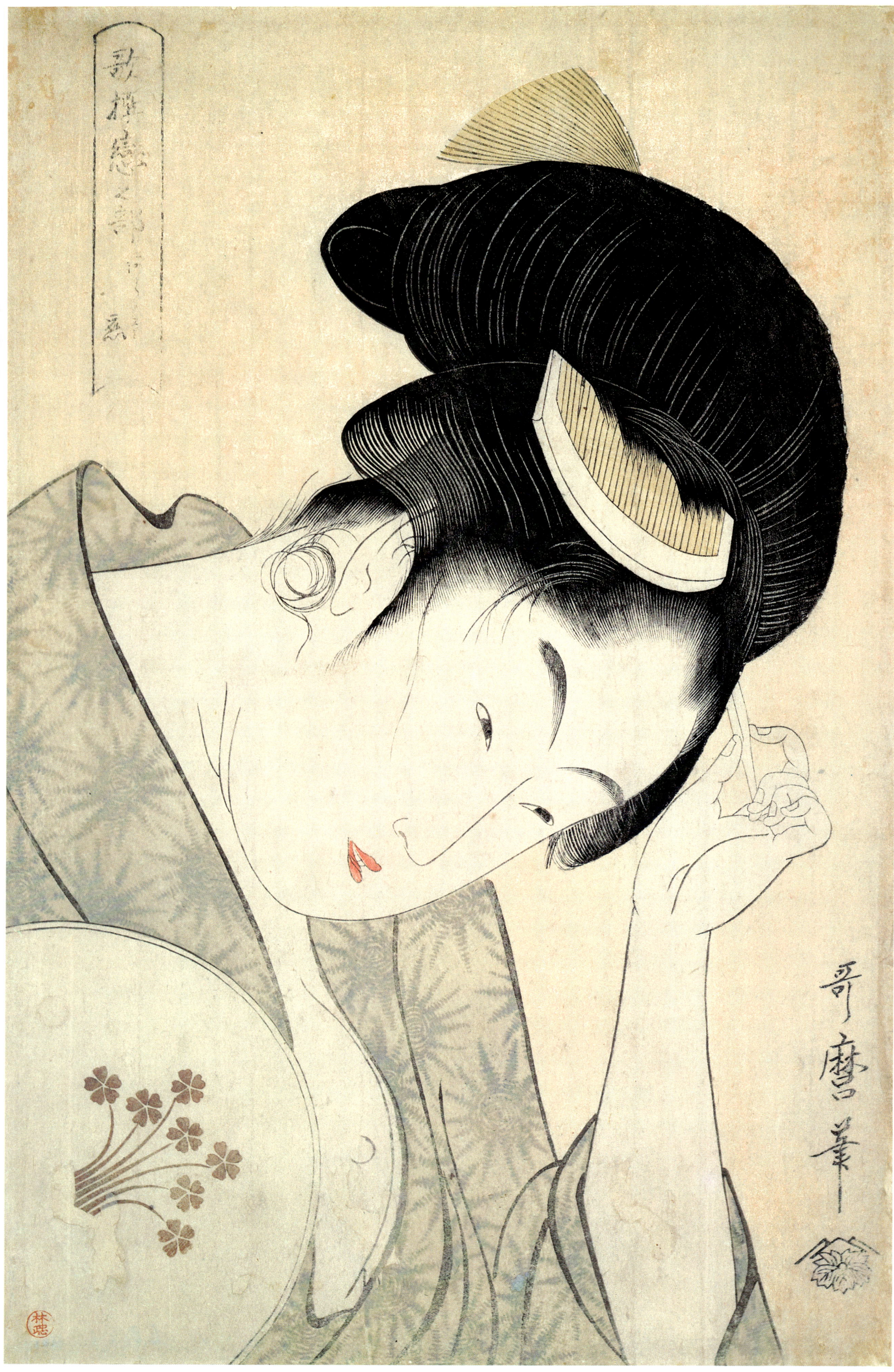

17.   *Revealed Love:* "Great Love Themes of Classical Poetry."

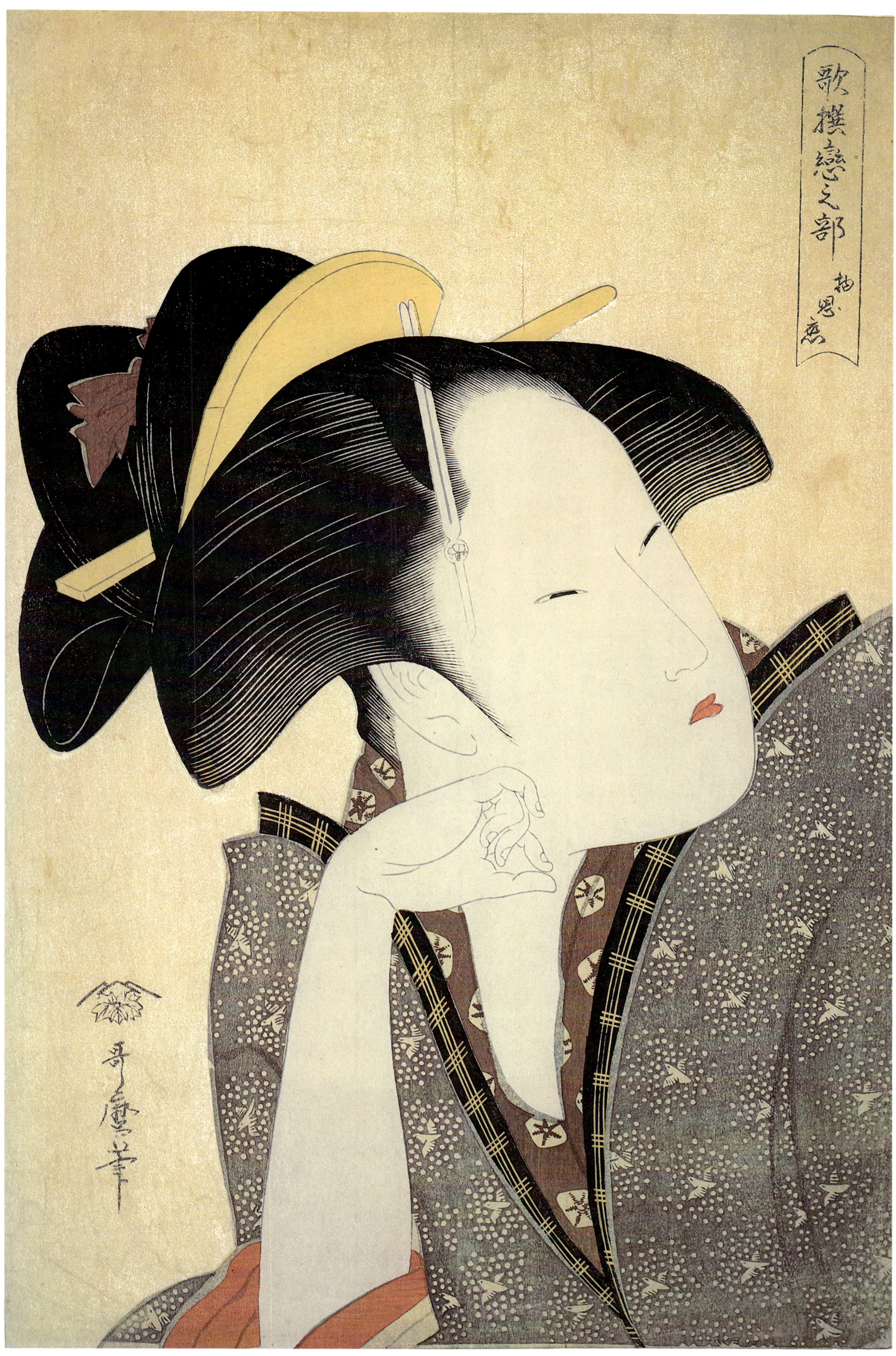

18. *Contemplative Love*: "Great Love Themes of Classical Poetry."

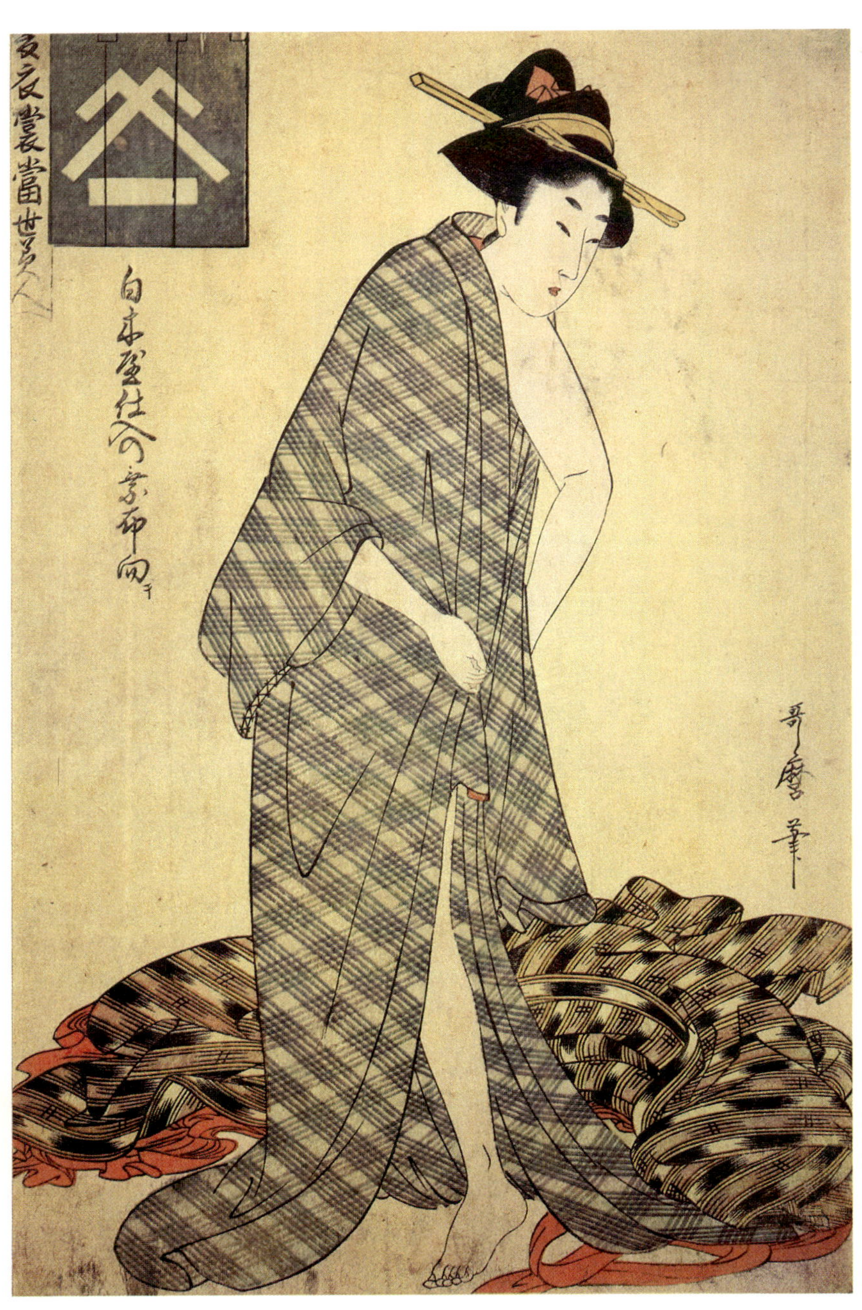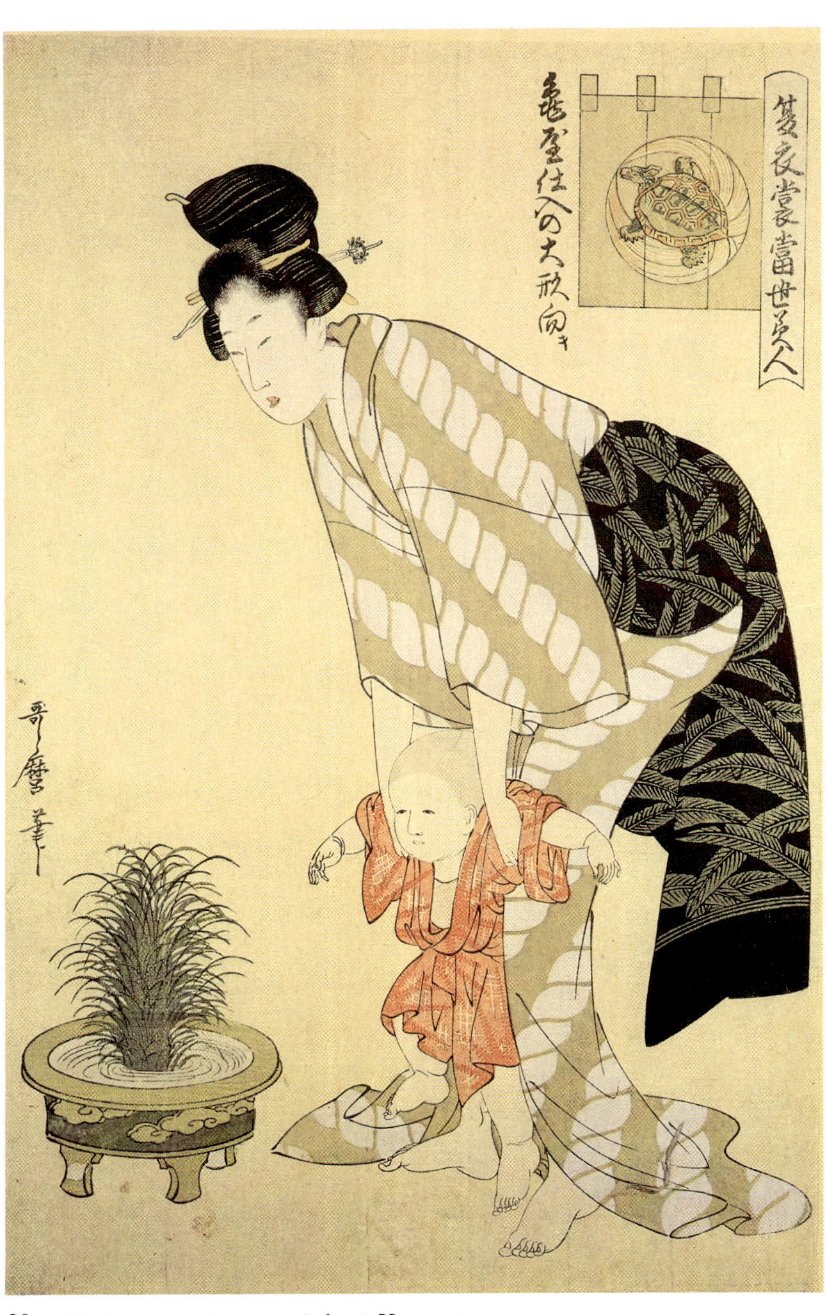

19–20. From the series "Modern Beauties in Summer Kimono."

19. *Flower-patterned Cottons at Shirokiya.*

20. *Bold Patterns Now on Sale at Kameya.*

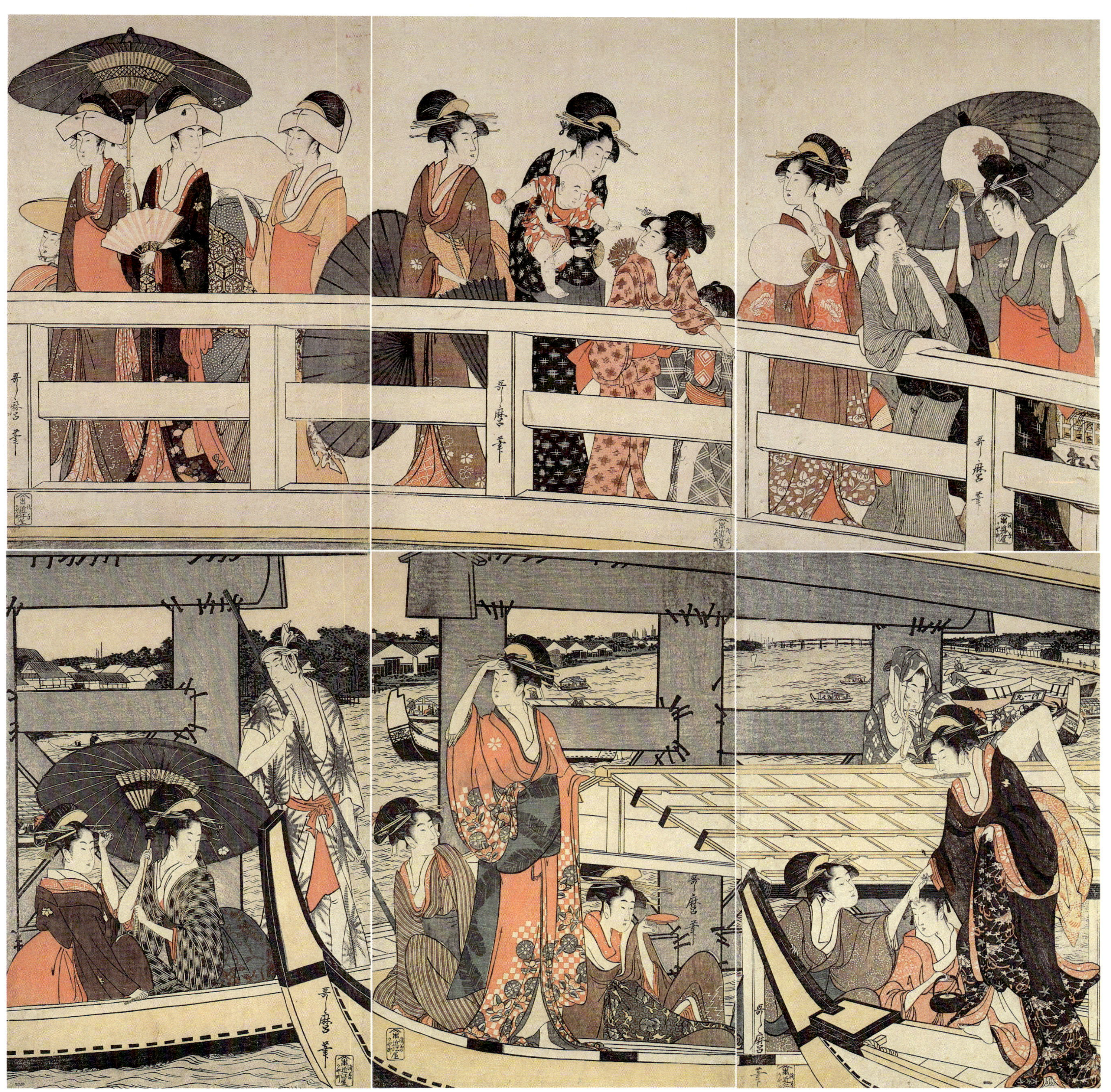

21. *A Scene on the Bridge and Below It.*

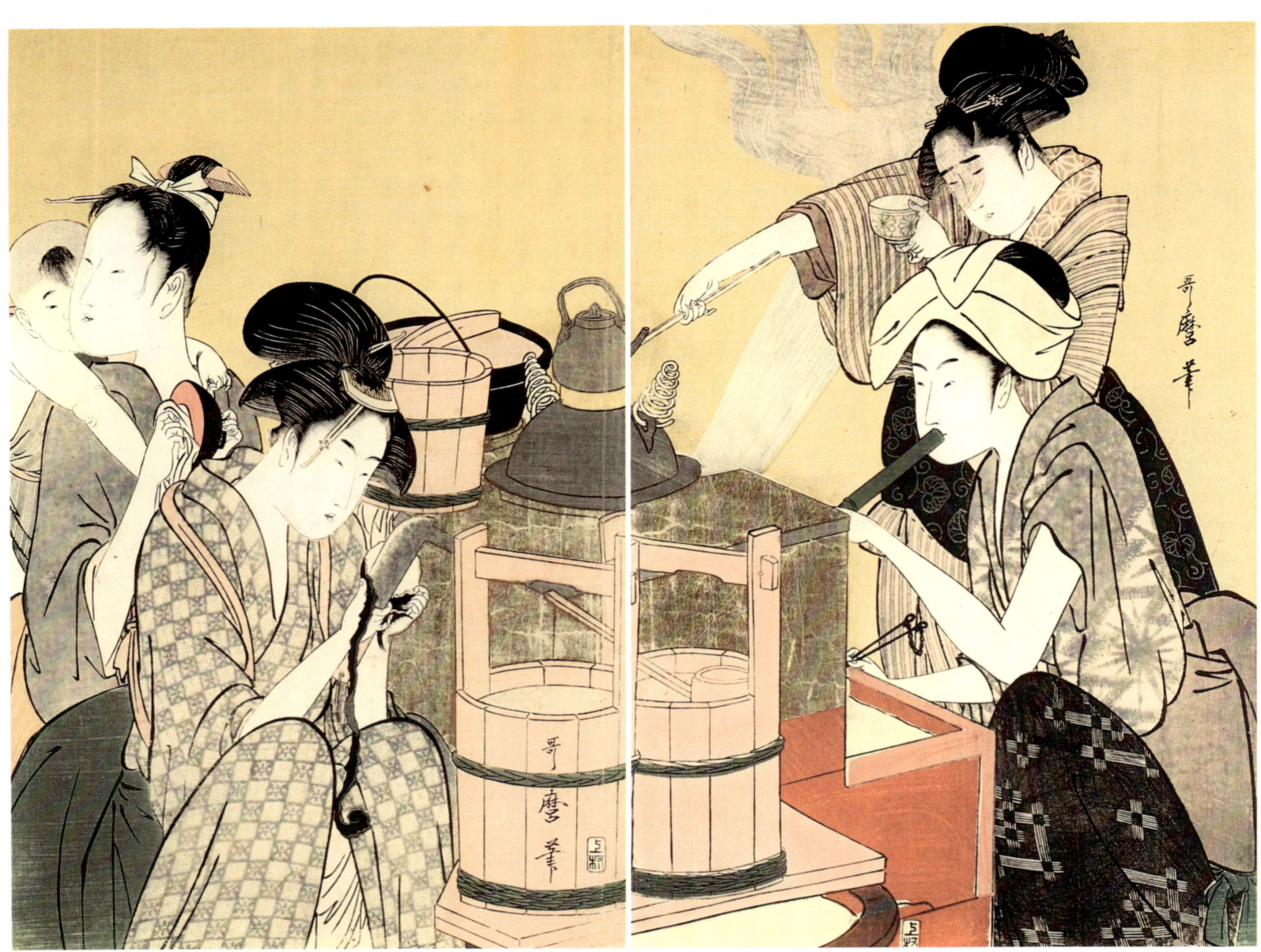

22. *Beauties in the Kitchen.*

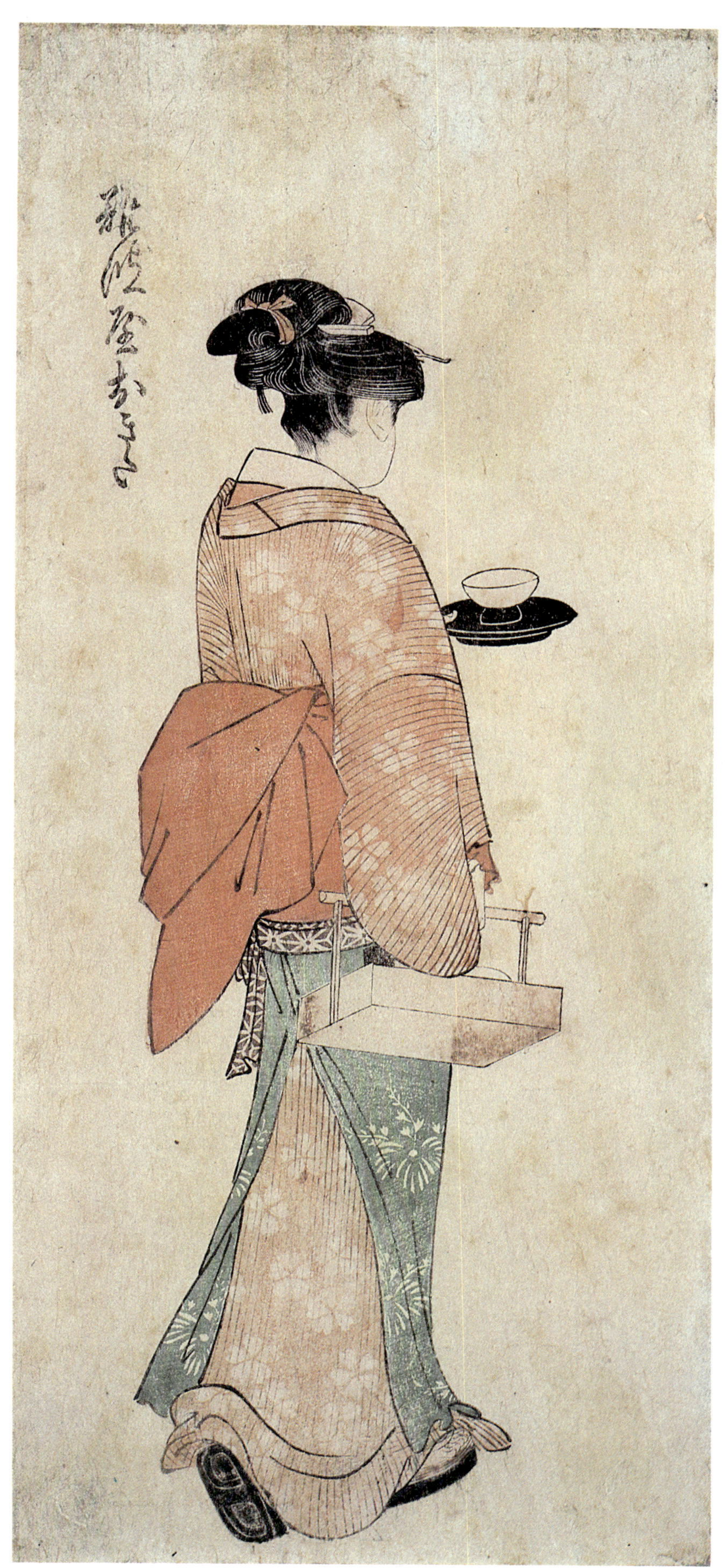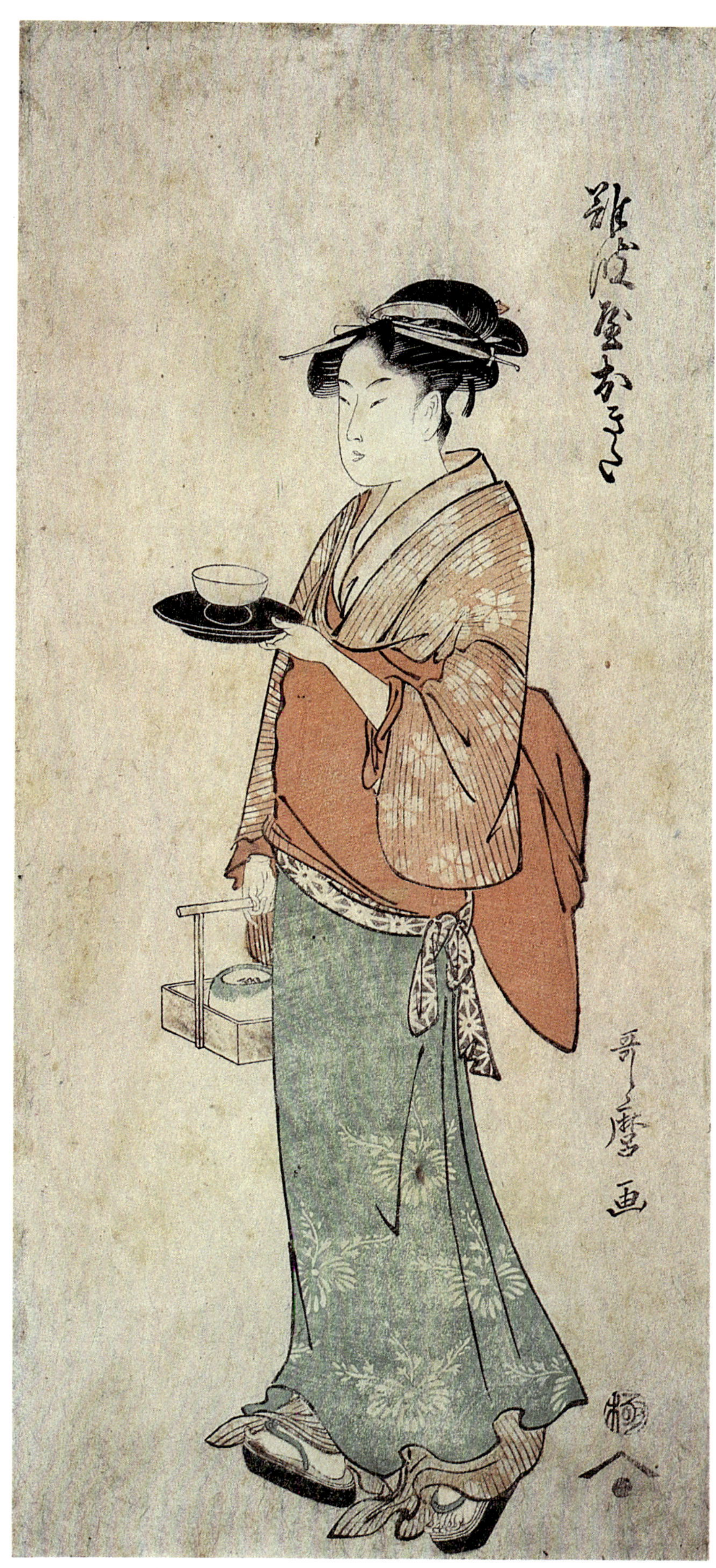

23. *Okita, the Teahouse Girl at the Naniwaya*, two sides of one print.

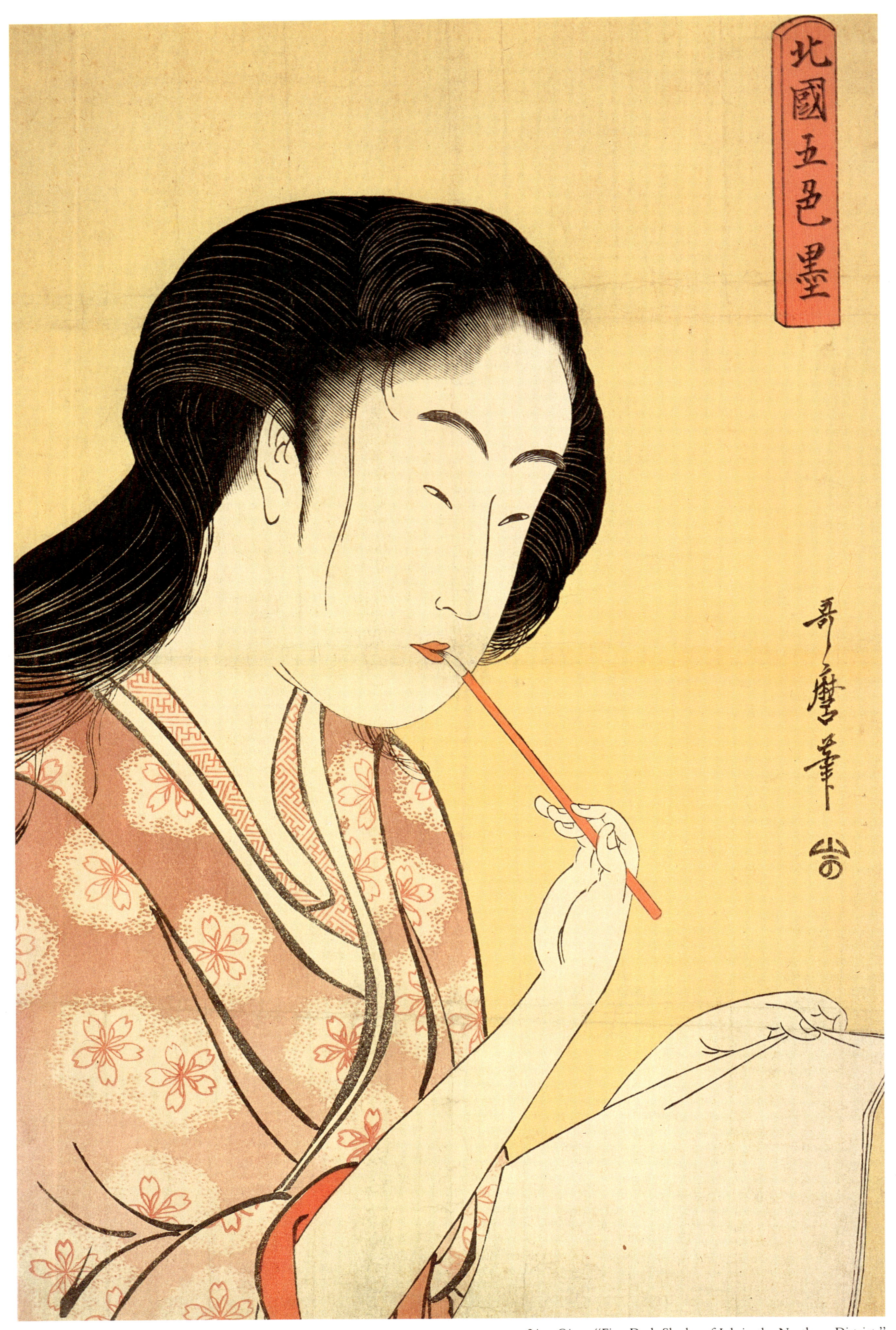

24. *Oiran:* "Five Dark Shades of Ink in the Northern District."

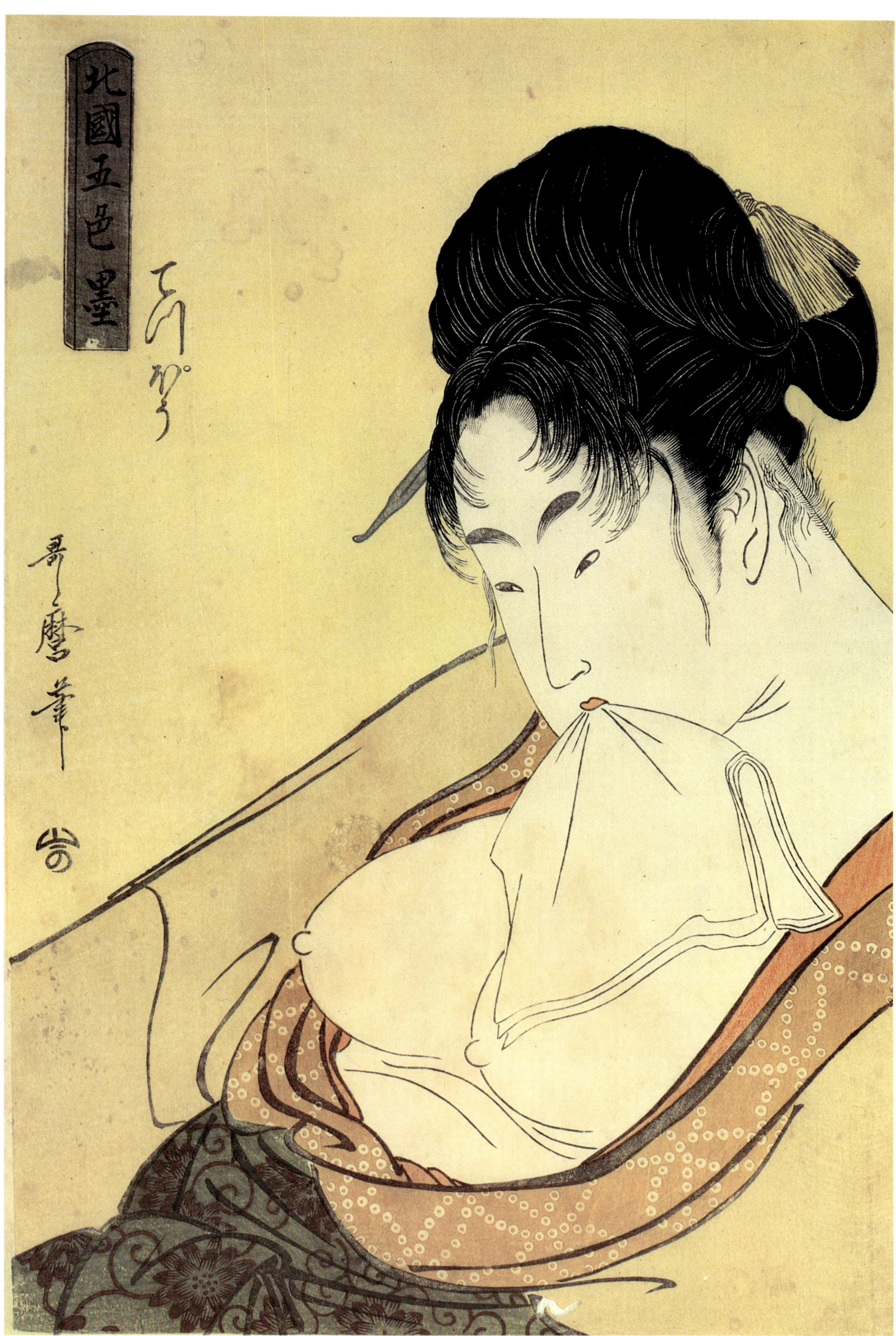

25.   *Teppō*: "Five Dark Shades of Ink in the Northern District."

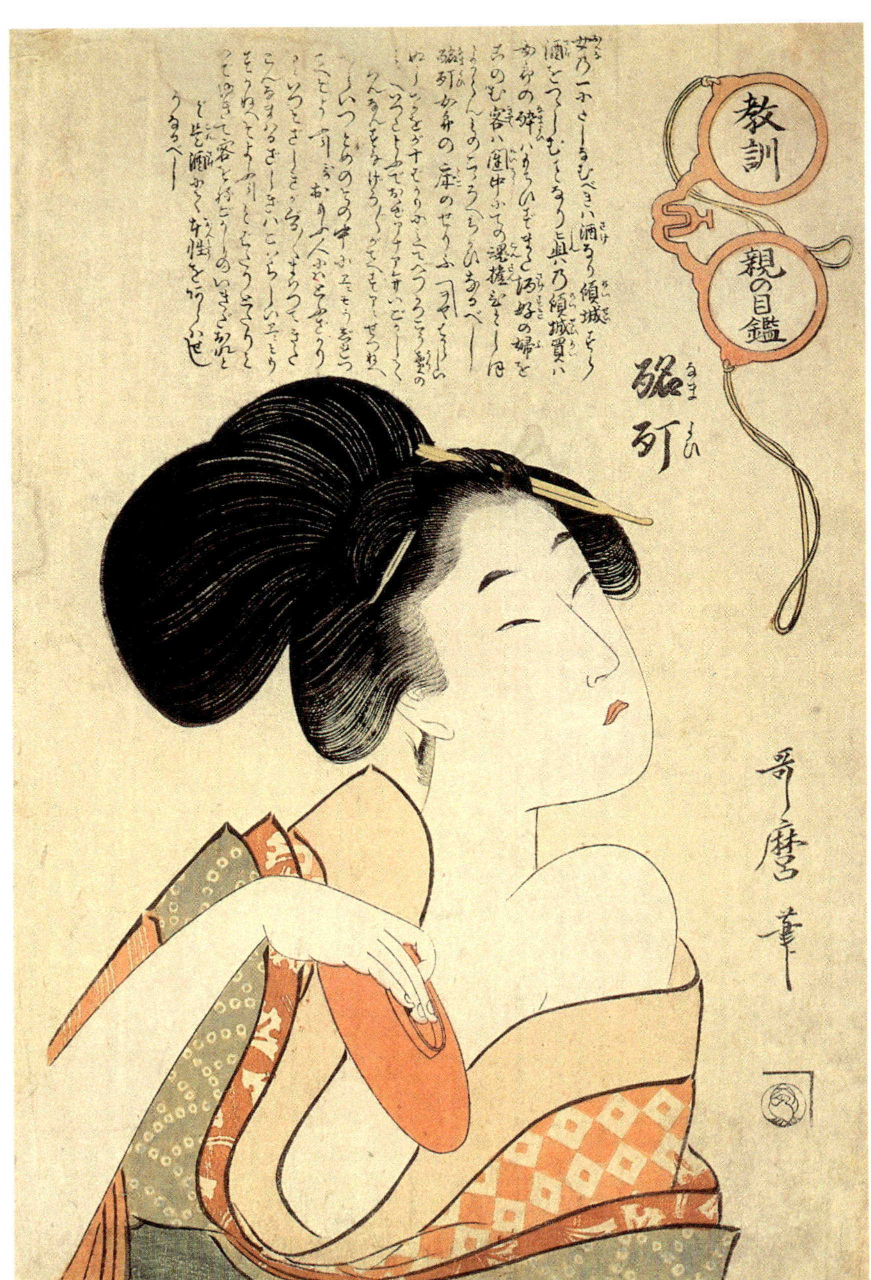

26. *The Drunken Courtesan.*

26–28. From the series "The Eyeglasses of a Watchful Parent."

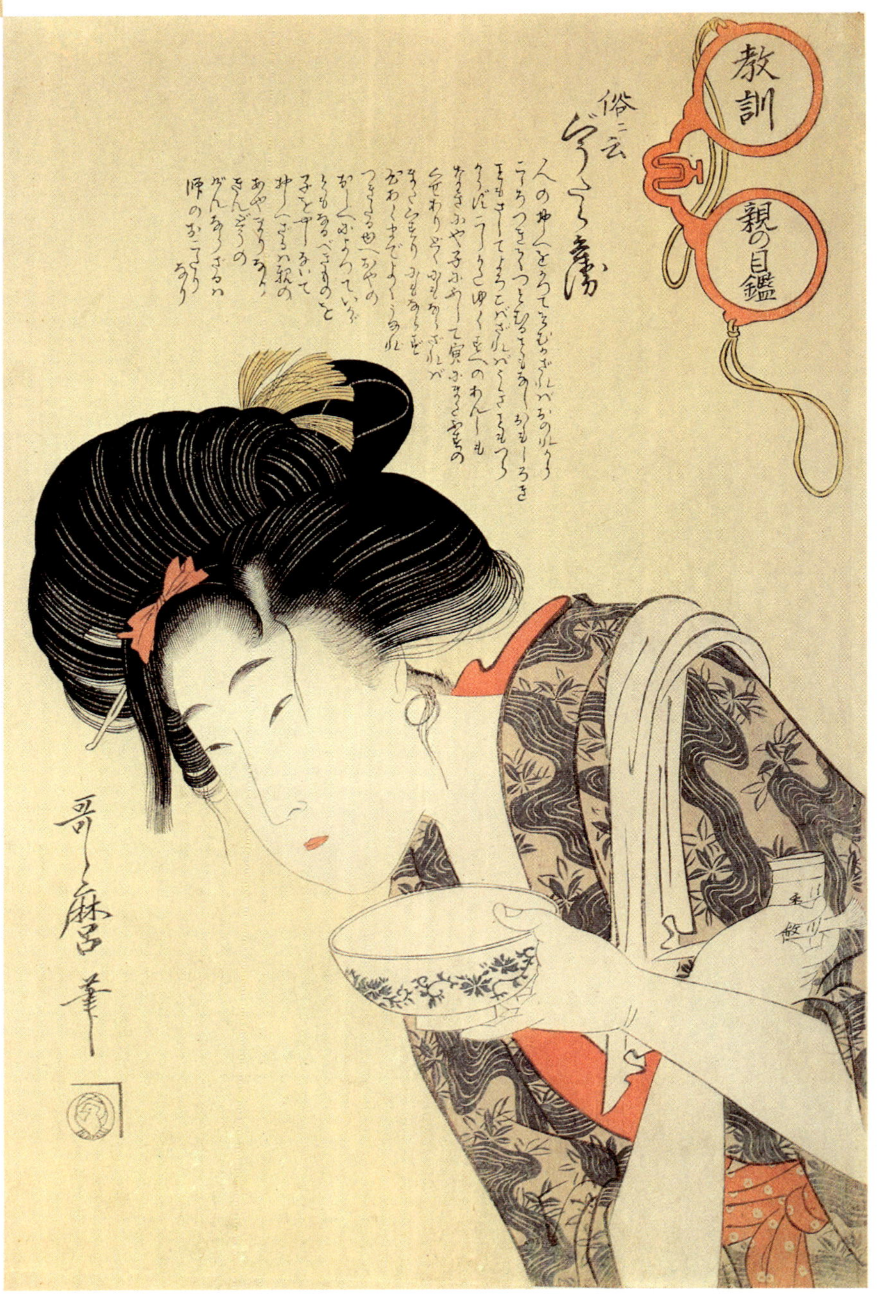

27. *The Lazybones.*

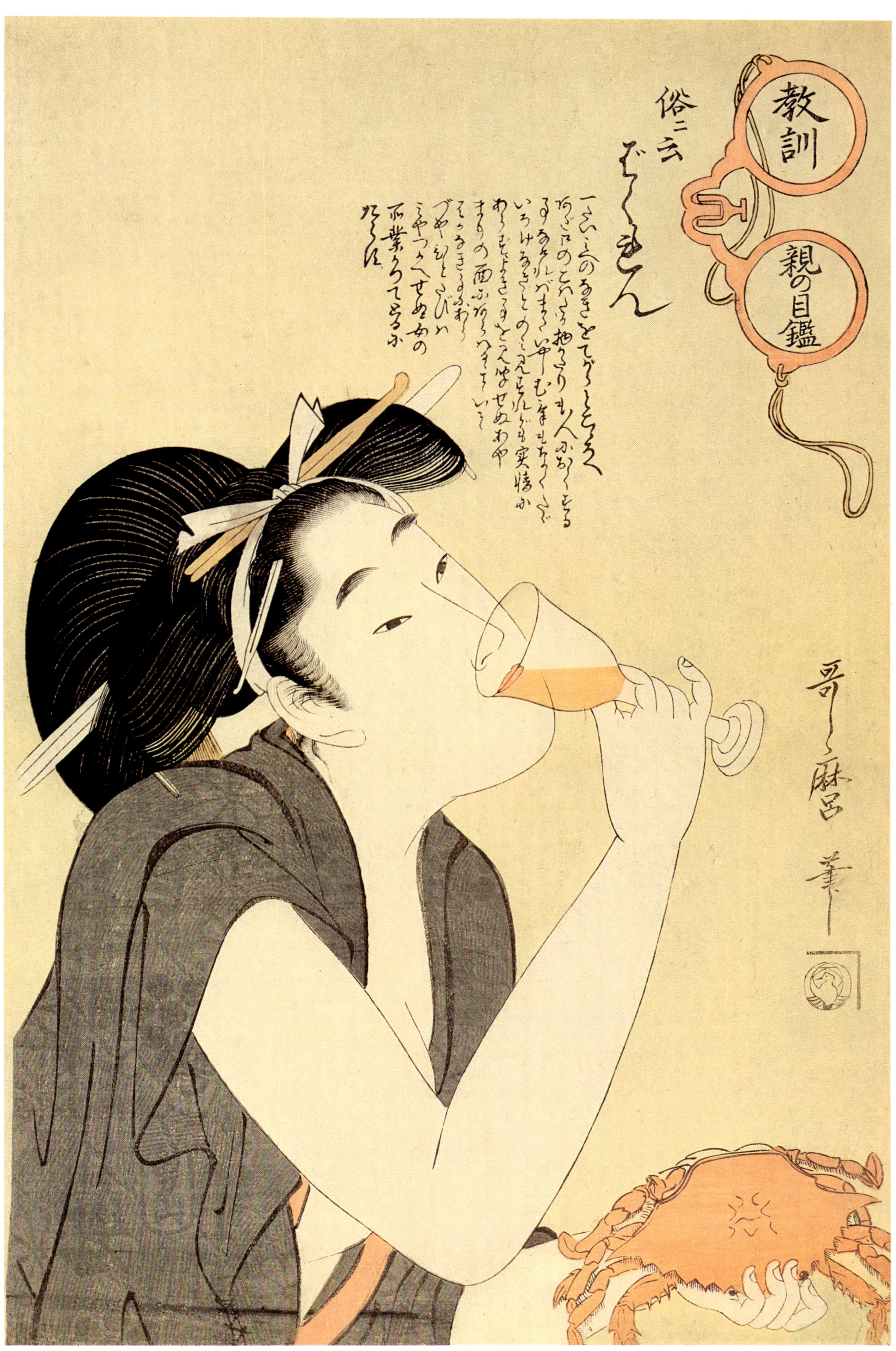

28. *The Hussy.*

27

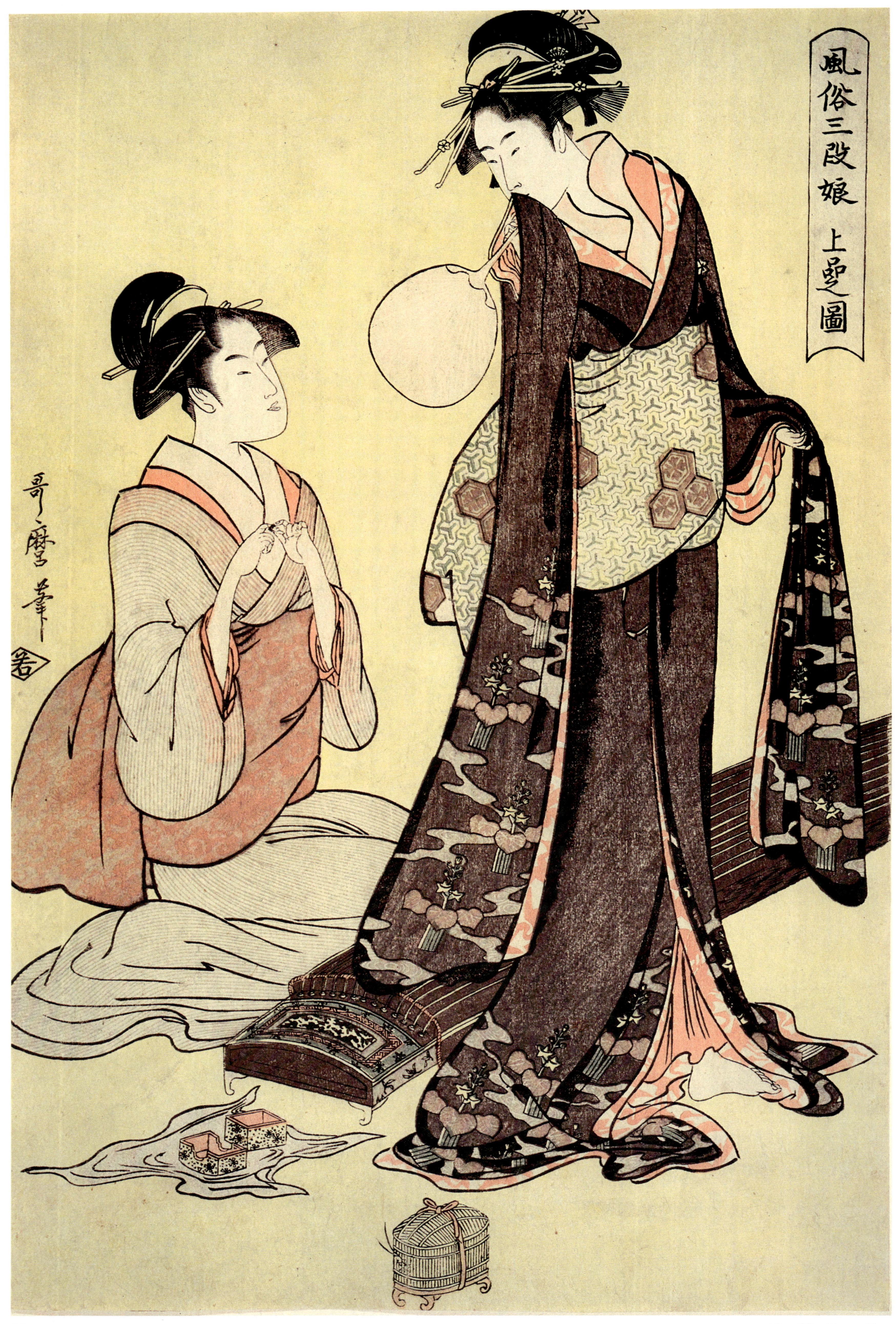

29.　*The Upper Class.*

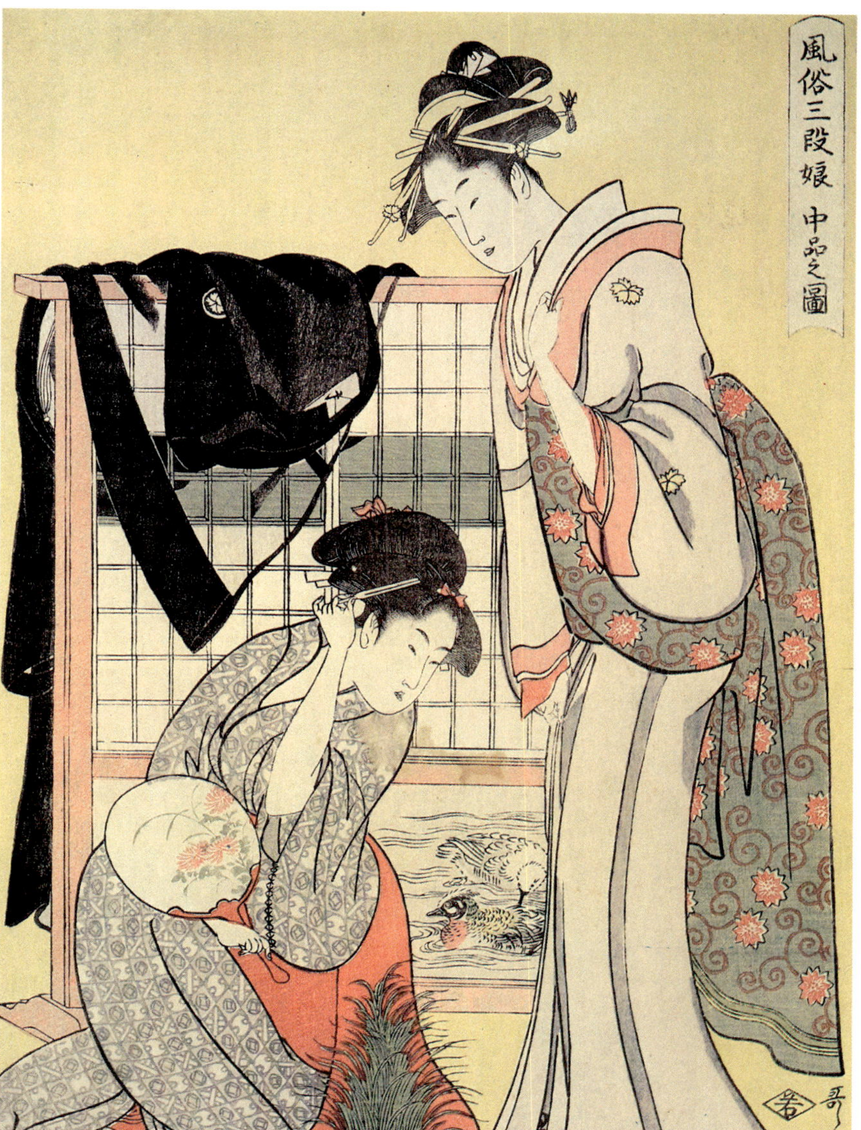

30. *The Middle Class.*

29–31. The series "Manners of Young Women of Three Classes."

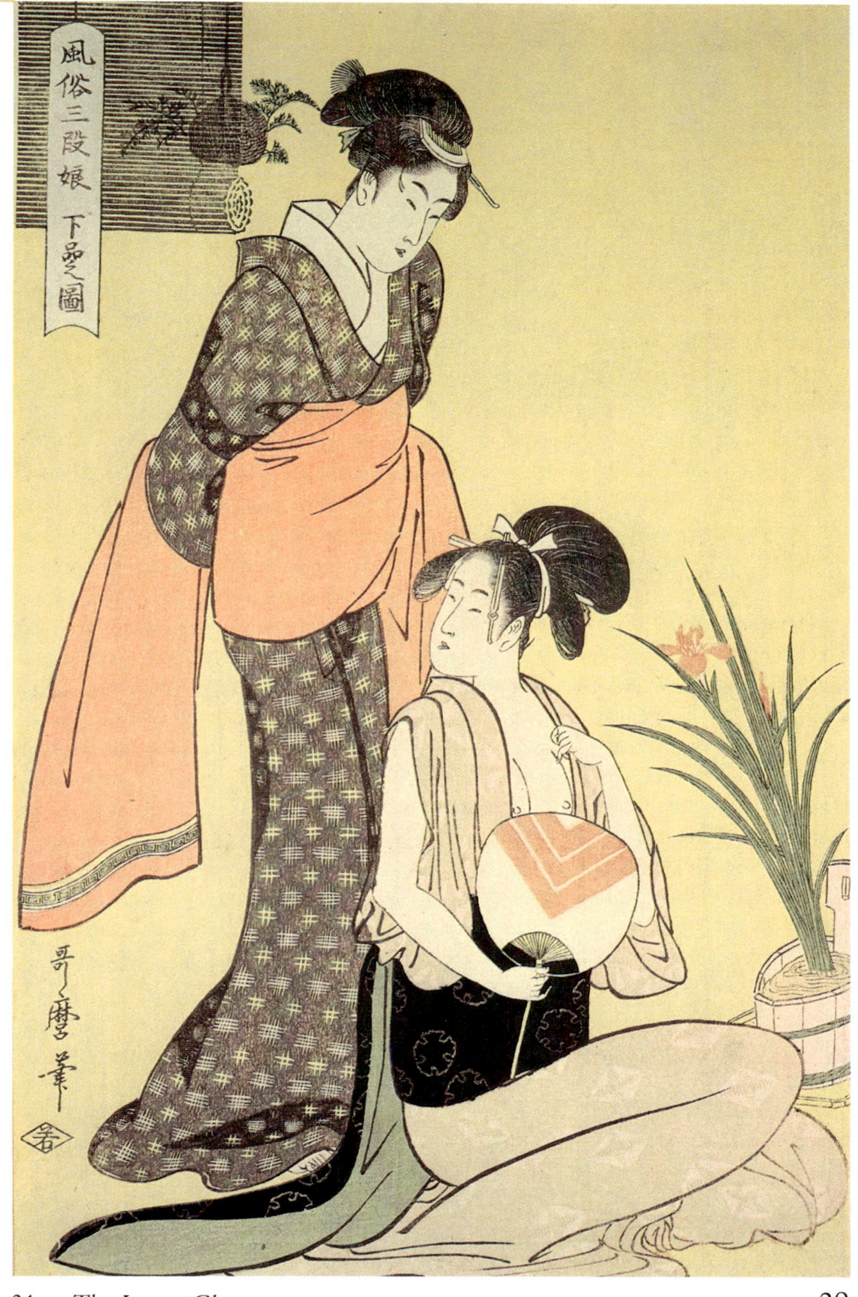

31. *The Lower Class.*

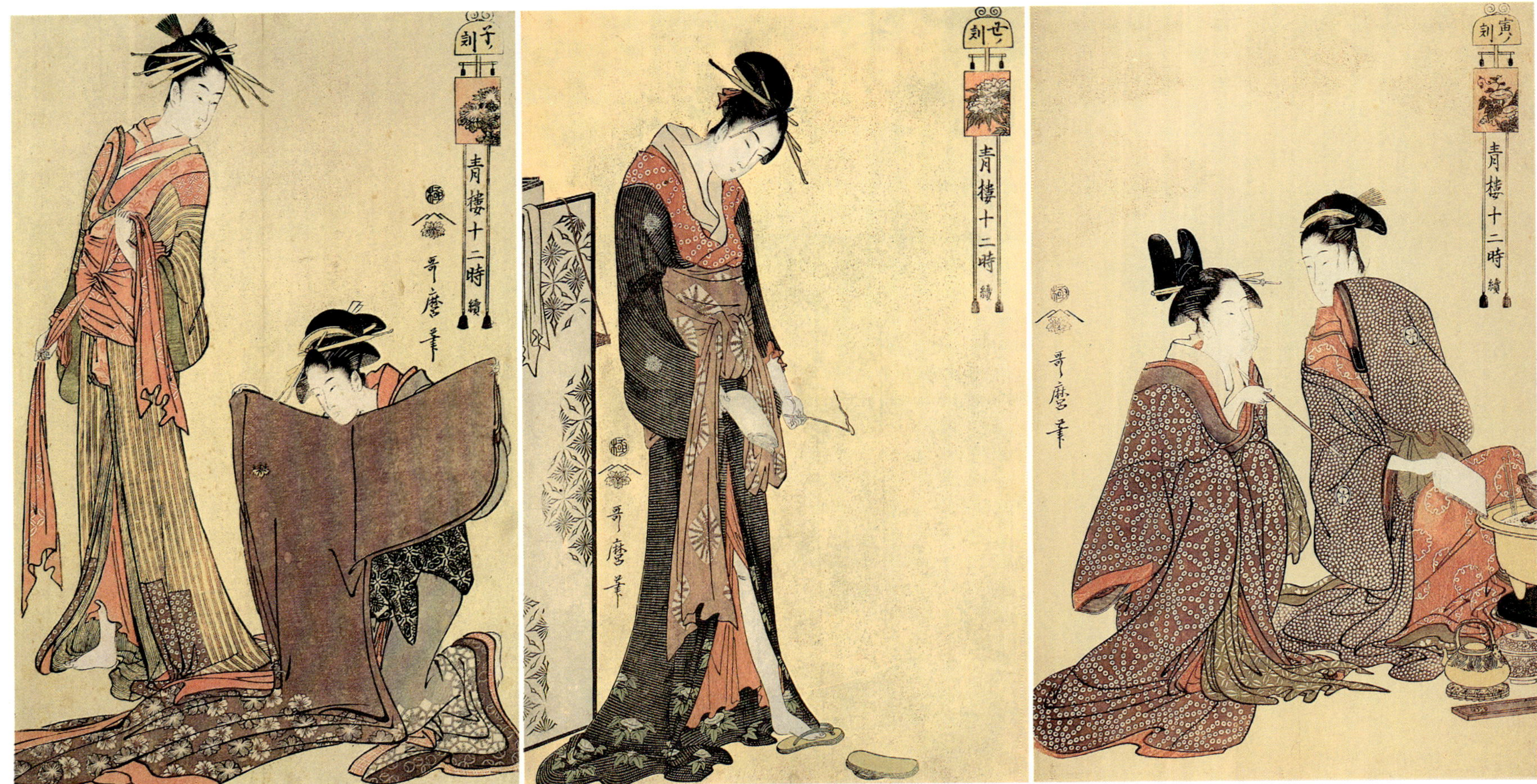

32. *The Hour of the Rat.*   33. *The Hour of the Ox.*   34. *The Hour of the Tiger.*

32–43.   The series "The Twelve Lunar Hours in the Pleasure Quarters."

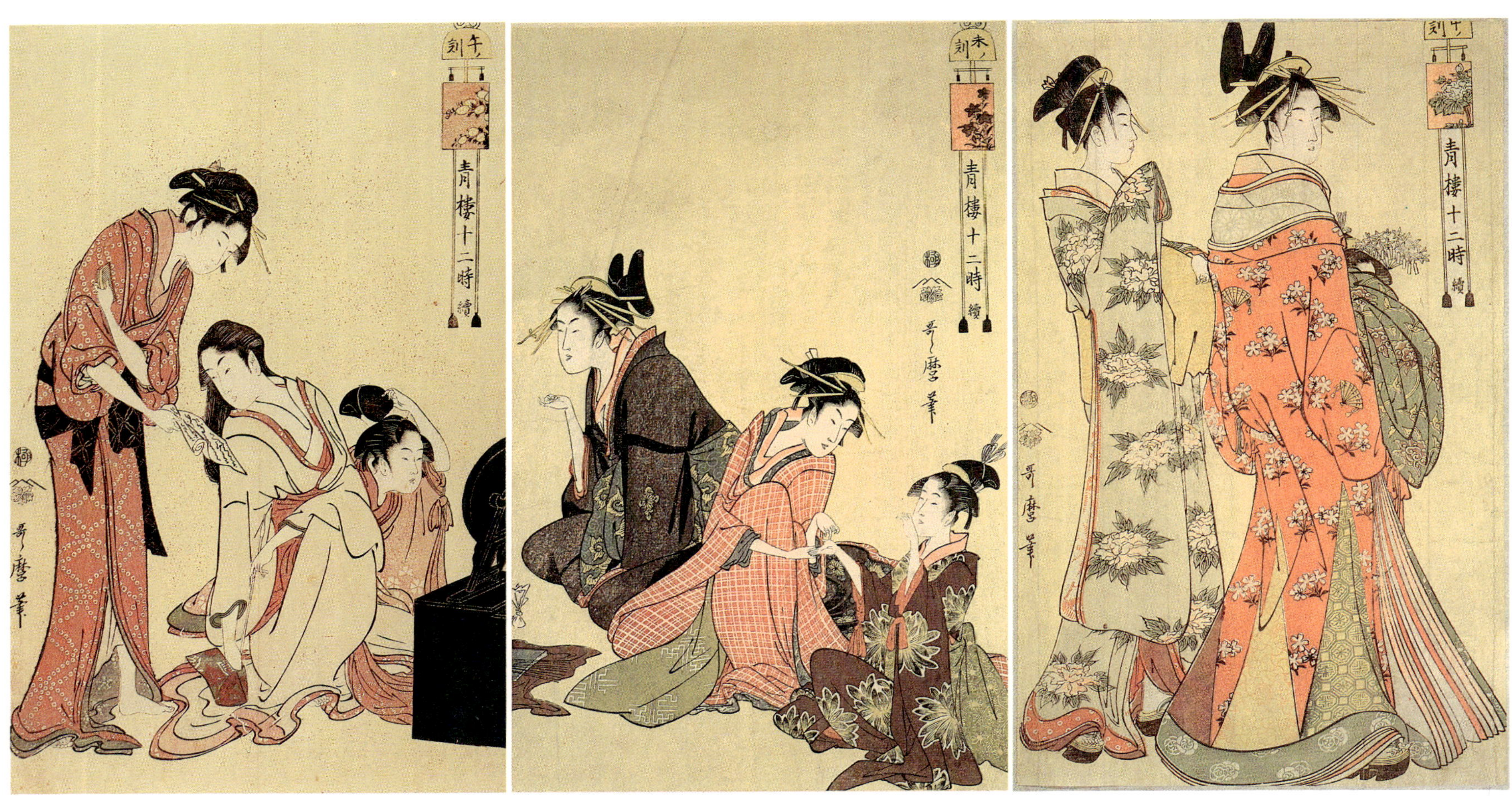

38. *The Hour of the Horse.*   39. *The Hour of the Ram.*   40. *The Hour of the Monkey.*

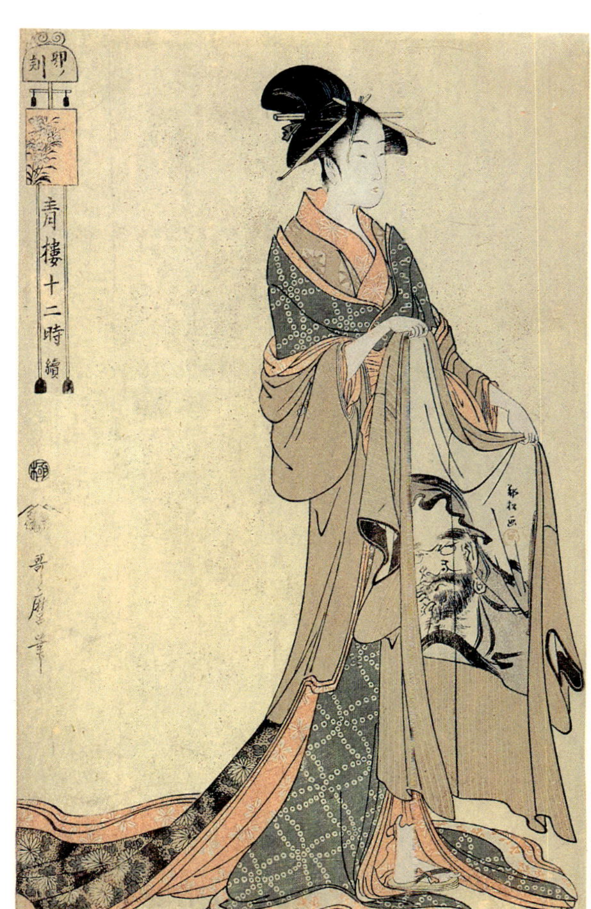
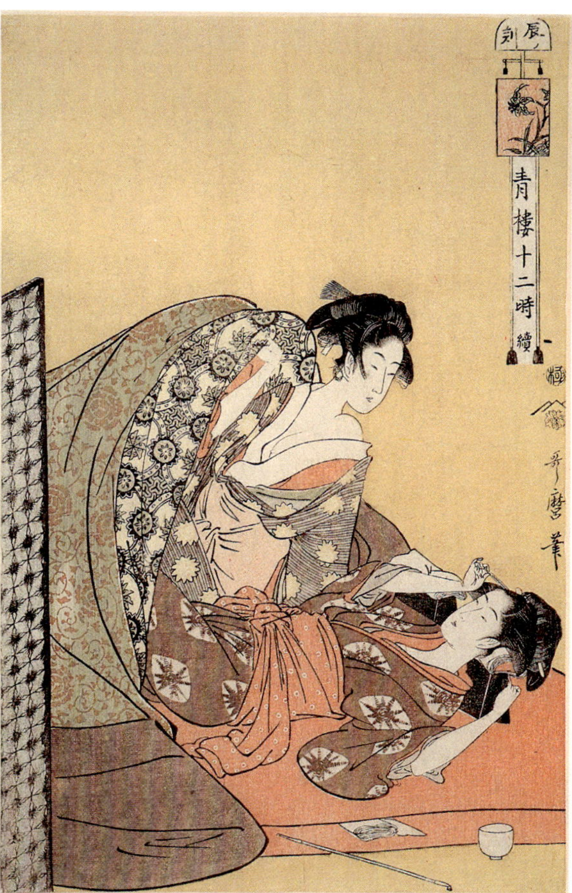
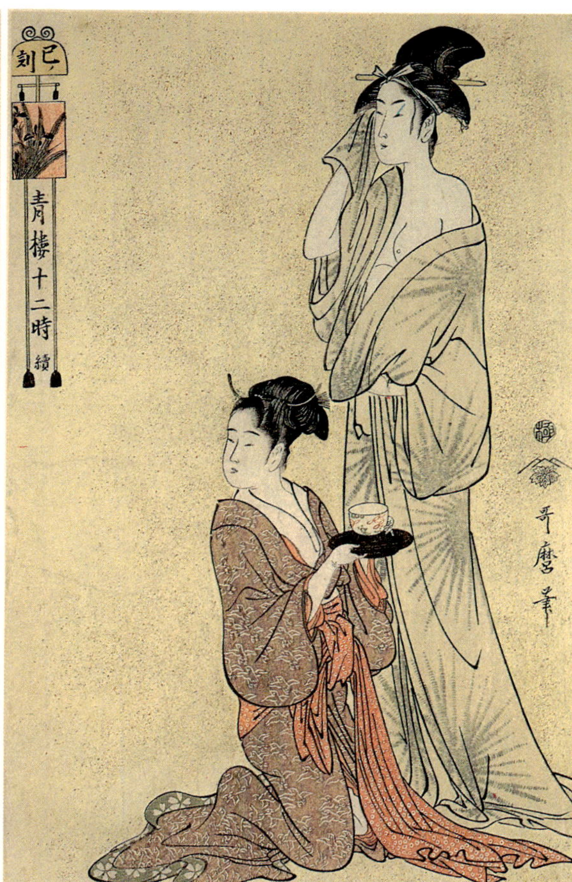

35. *The Hour of the Hare.*   36. *The Hour of the Dragon.*   37. *The Hour of the Snake.*

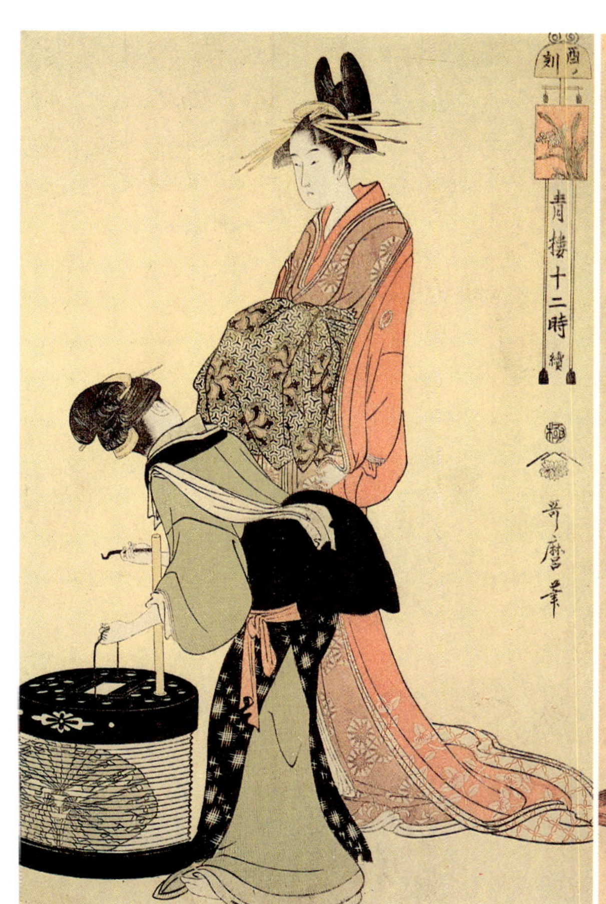
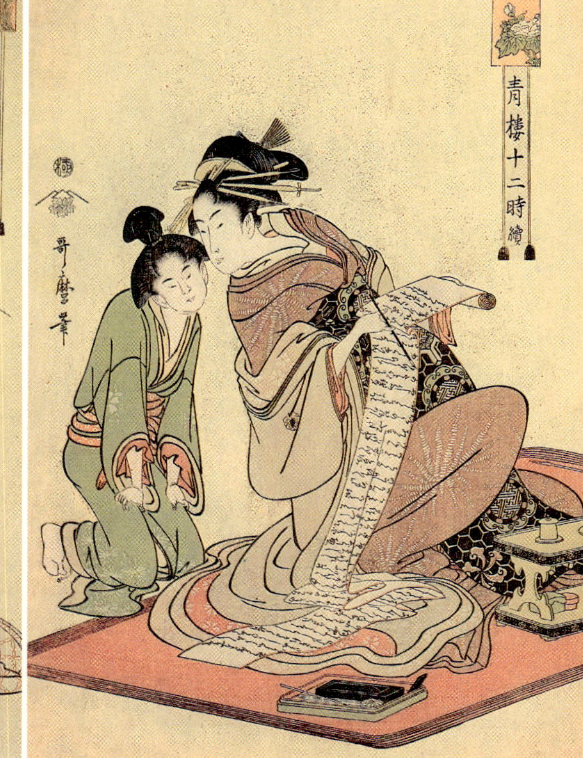
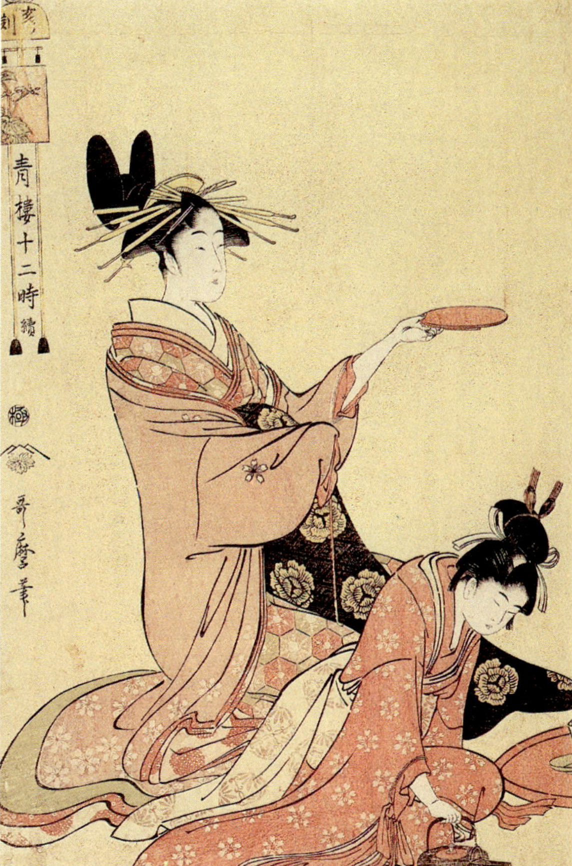

41. *The Hour of the Cock.*   42. *The Hour of the Dog.*   43. *The Hour of the Boar.*

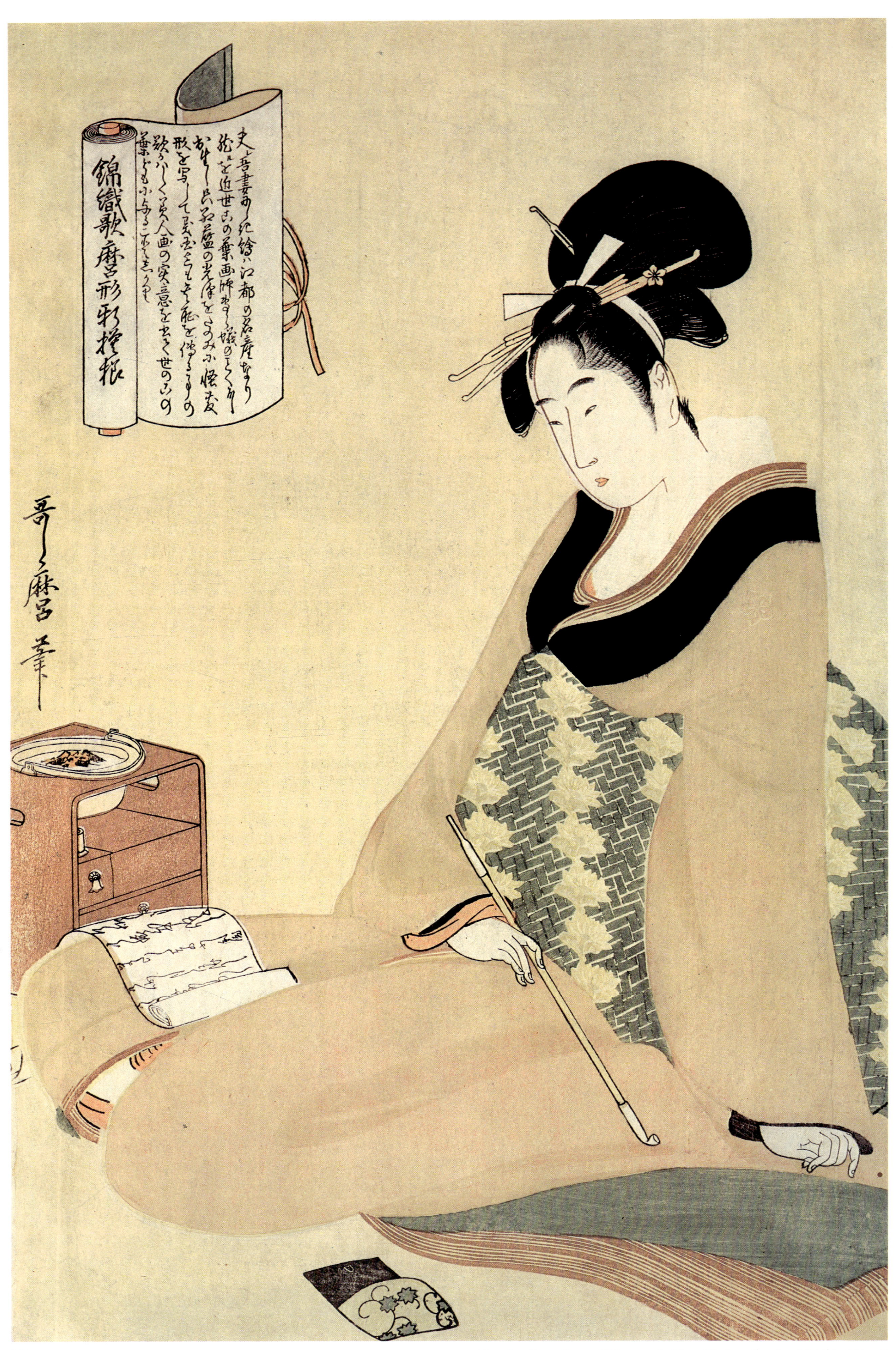

44. *Reading a Letter*: "Utamaro's New Designs for the *Nishiki-e* Print."

UTAMARO

There is little doubt that the *ukiyo-e* woodblock print is the most well known of Japan's traditional art forms among art lovers throughout the world. It was the discovery and subsequent popularity of the *ukiyo-e* print that kindled the wild enthusiasm for Japonisme in late nineteenth-century Europe. These lovely, polychrome prints also suggested a number of compositional techniques to the Impressionists, such artists as Manet, Monet, van Gogh, Gauguin, and Degas. One result of this vogue for *ukiyo-e* in the nineteenth century was that almost all of the outstanding prints surviving in Japan disappeared to reemerge in the West. Today, every museum in the West that takes an interest in Oriental art has a large collection of *ukiyo-e* prints—so large, in fact, that the representation of *ukiyo-e* often seems disproportionate to that of other genres of Japanese art.

In Japan, the birthplace of *ukiyo-e*, the value accorded them has traditionally been extremely low. Indeed, it is the sad truth that, until voices of high praise began to be heard from abroad, *ukiyo-e* prints were rarely taken seriously by collectors and critics, who prided themselves on their refined taste.

One reason for this attitude may, perhaps, be sought in the fact that *ukiyo-e* take as their medium the woodblock print more often than the original painting. In the traditional Japanese view of the pictorial arts, which was strongly influenced by Chinese attitudes, *ukiyo-e* were outside the pale of serious consideration simply because they were, in fact, woodblock prints. Moreover, the artists and publishers active in the genre of *ukiyo-e* sought their audience in a class that was by its very nature alienated from power and authority. They produced *ukiyo-e* for the townsmen (*chōnin*) class of the huge city of Edo, which, in the feudal society established by the Tokugawa shogunate, occupied the lowest strata of the social scale. Thus, *ukiyo-e* artists always concerned themselves with pictorial themes that emphasized the popular, the familiar, or the erotic. Indeed, the emphasis on erotic themes at times exceeded the limits of contemporary morality. This perceived frivolity in the choice of themes, as well as the facile quality of the medium of woodblock prints, made it difficult for art historians to react favorably to *ukiyo-e*.

It was inevitable, given this historical background and the essential nature of the genre, that *ukiyo-e* would receive a cool reception from Japan's intellectual elite. *Ukiyo-e* prints were "ready-made" commodities produced in large numbers for the masses, not for the solitary connoisseur. This meant that the popular themes dealt with in the prints had to be expressed in the most easily understood, the most accessible terms possible.

The necessity of appealing to a large audience thus placed basic limitations on the *ukiyo-e* artist. The freedom enjoyed by artists in other genres to indulge individual whims in theme and depiction, or to develop pretentious and vaguely suggestive modes of expression that hinted at rather than fully developed a theme, was intrinsically impossible in the genre of *ukiyo-e*. Yet, in my opinion, it was precisely this tireless effort to reach the widest possible audience that has made *ukiyo-e* universal in appeal, evoking a generally valid understanding and appreciation by people throughout the world, regardless of their cultural background.

Kitagawa Utamaro (1753–1806), active at the end of the eighteenth century, was the greatest master of *ukiyo-e* prints depicting beautiful women (*bijin-ga*). The setting for Utamaro's activity was Edo (modern Tokyo), which near the end of the eighteenth century was the center of a nation at peace and the capital of the Tokugawa shogun, who had declared a policy of national isolation. Utamaro searched every corner of this huge city, seeking out beautiful women of every conceivable type, differing in age, status, and circumstance. His keen observer's eye focused on their beauty, probing its depths, its nuances. Utamaro succeeded not only in capturing the outward beauty of these women, but also in depicting differences in personality, at times achieving a subtle, delicate representation of transient moods and fleeting psychological states. Utamaro's image of the beautiful woman, modest and limited in scope as it may seem by Western standards, achieved a high degree of perfection, and ultimately succeeds in expressing the reality of living people. His *ukiyo-e* prints are a sympathetic record of the lives of the lower classes of his time, and his prints of women possess the kind of universality that transcends historical and national boundaries. They demand a sincere aesthetic response—a response that cannot be explained as mere nostalgia for the exoticism of traditional Japan. Certainly this is true for the Westerner. It is no less true, however, for modern Japanese. For us, too, eighteenth-century Japan has become forever a distant foreign country.

Kitagawa Utamaro produced his greatest work during the Kansei era (1789–1801), and he was recognized even among his contemporaries as a master of *ukiyo-e* prints portraying beautiful women (*bijin-ga*). Indeed, Utamaro seems to have been alone among contemporary *ukiyo-e* artists in attaining a national reputation during his own lifetime. As is suggested by the fact that *ukiyo-e* were also called "Edo pictures," originally

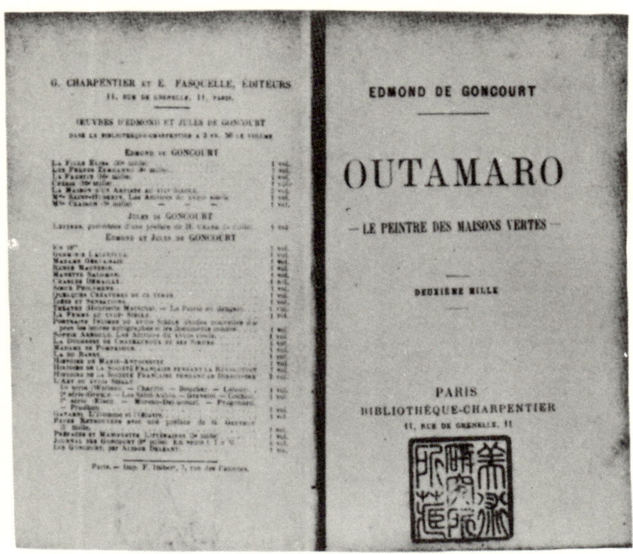

Fig. 1. Edmond de Goncourt's book *Utamaro: The Painter of the Pleasure Quarters*, 1891 edition.

they were a specialty of Edo, produced for the populace of the shogun's capital. It was by no means certain that they would be widely circulated throughout the country. Thus, Utagawa Toyokuni (1769–1825), who was active about the same time as Utamaro, seems to have been virtually unknown outside the city, although he commanded immense popularity in Edo for his prints of Kabuki actors (*yakusha-e*).

Despite Utamaro's unparalleled celebrity in his own world of popular culture, however, the art historian who attempts to trace his life and career immediately confronts the fact that there are practically no contemporary documents to aid him in his task. Strictly speaking, even the date of his birth is not absolutely certain, and although there are numerous theories concerning his birthplace and family background, none is generally recognized. Utamaro was an outstanding figure in the world of popular art and literature, but that world itself was at the bottom of the social scale. The low status of the *ukiyo-e* artist has meant that the details of Utamaro's life remain buried in obscurity. Sharaku has often been called the "enigmatic *ukiyo-e* master" because almost nothing is known of his life. At least in terms of riddles surrounding the biographies of outstanding *ukiyo-e* artists, however, he is certainly not alone.

The earliest extant record of *ukiyo-e* artists is *Ukiyo-e ruikō*. A kind of "who's who" of *ukiyo-e*, it was compiled by Ōta Nanpo during Utamaro's lifetime, probably around 1790. Ōta Nanpo (1749–1823), who was known by such literary pseudonyms as Yomo no Akara and Shokusanjin, was the central figure in the development of the popular literary genre of comic verse called *kyōka*, which was a major preoccupation of both professional writers and cultured dilettantes in the Tenmei era (1781–89).* Ōta Nanpo played a leading role in the lively, often erotic and hedonistic popular culture of the city, and was, of course, on intimate terms with Utamaro and other contemporary *ukiyo-e* artists. Indeed, Utamaro was a member of Ōta's *kyōka* circle, and there is little doubt that Ōta was familiar with the details of his life.

Ukiyo-e ruikō has thus become the basic source of material and the essential starting point for all research on *ukiyo-e*. After Ōta's original compilation, however, the text was copied and handed down by a great many people, and in the process underwent a number of revisions and enlargements. Thus, before we are able to ascertain what Ōta himself actually recorded concerning Utamaro, we have to establish a reliable text for *Ukiyo-e ruikō*. Here, we may now turn to a collection of miscellaneous contemporary documents recently introduced by Kitakōji Ken, *A Record of Things Just as I Heard Them* (*Kiku mama no ki*). This collection was compiled by Kimura Mokurō (1774–1856), another of Utamaro's contemporaries, and one volume in this collection, although it is titled *Research on Ukiyo-e* (*Ukiyo-e kōshō*), is thought to be very close to Ōta's original text. It contains the following account of Utamaro:

> Kitagawa Utamaro, personal name Yūsuke: Originally studied the style of the Kanō school as a disciple of Toriyama Sekien. Later he did paintings depicting the styles and manners of men and women. He lived temporarily with Tsutaya Jūzaburō, the picture book seller [*ezōshiya*]. He presently lives in Benkeibashi, Edo. Mainly, he produces *nishiki-e* [polychrome *ukiyo-e* prints].

Another reference to Utamaro appears in *An Outline of Ancient and Modern Yamato-e and Ukiyo-e* (*Kokin yamato-e ukiyo-e shikei*), an appendix to *Ukiyo-e ruikō* compiled by Sasaya Shinshichi Kuninori, who was also the first editor and commentator of *Ukiyo-e ruikō* after Ōta Nanpo.

> Kansei era [1789–1801]
> Kuemon-chō [Utamaro's residence]
> Utamaro
> A famous artist of pictures of women
> Unrivaled in this genre

What we know about Utamaro's life is essentially what we have been able to glean from such brief accounts. Utamaro's personal name was Yūsuke. He began his artistic career as a disciple of Toriyama Sekien, an artist of the Kanō school. Later, after venturing into the world of *ukiyo-e*, he won the friendship and patronage of Tsutaya Jūzaburō, one of the most influential publishers of the Edo period (1600–1867), and became famous as a master of prints depicting beautiful women (*bijin-ga*). Apparently none of the early commentators on *ukiyo-e* felt any interest in recording further details of Utamaro's personal life or his career. To the extent that we modern critics respond to Utamaro's artistic genius, however, we cannot help but feel the need to seek out the details of his career and to place him in the context of the remarkable Edo culture that he helped to create. Below, on the basis of the most recent research, I have attempted to provide a summary of

---

**Kyōka* literally means "mad *waka*," *waka* being the classical 31-syllable verse form. *Kyōka* were "mad" because humorous or satirical, often parodying *waka*, and because composed in vernacular Japanese. *Kyōka* were often collected in "picture books" (*ehon*), in which there were several pages of illustrations in color preceding the text. See the note to plate 3 at the back of the book for an example of a *kyōka*.

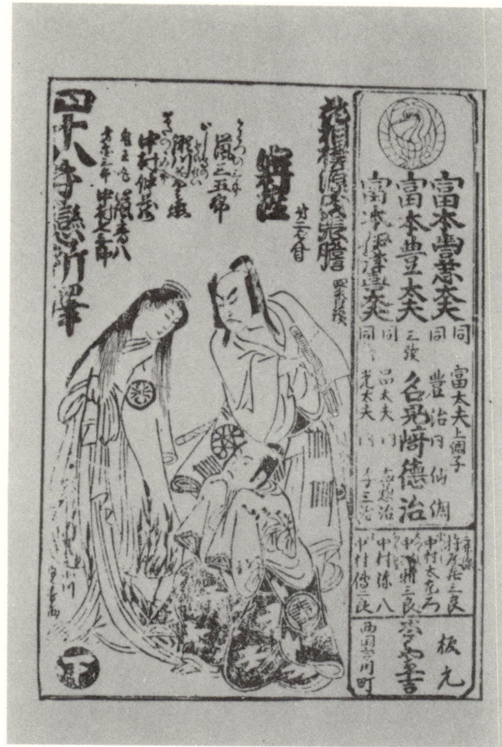

Fig. 2. The Kabuki play-book *Forty-eight Famous Love Scenes*; cover illustration by Utamaro, 1775.

Fig. 3. Utamaro's *Yoshizawa Iroha in the Role of Osato, Daughter of the Sushi House*; a Kabuki print, 1777.

what we know today about the development of Utamaro's art and the details of his life.

DISCIPLESHIP WITH SEKIEN

As stated above, there is some doubt concerning even the date of Utamaro's birth. However, based on generally recognized research indicating that he died in 1806 at the age of fifty-three (fifty-four by traditional Japanese count, in which a child is considered to be one year old at birth), Utamaro is thought to have been born in 1753. There is no generally accepted theory concerning the identities of his parents or the place of his birth, and we know nothing about the family's status or occupation. We do know that his family name was Kitagawa, and that as a child he was called Ichitarō. As an adult, he was called Yūsuke and later Yūki. The circumstances surrounding Utamaro's introduction to Toriyama Sekien are unclear, but he came under Sekien's tutelage while still a child and the relationship continued until Sekien's death in 1788.

In 1788 Utamaro published *A Collection of Crawling Creatures* (*Mushi erami*; figs. 9–11), an early work in a series of *kyōka ehon* (illustrated comic verse collections) that revolutionized the genre, as will be discussed below. In a postscript to this collection, Sekien provides tantalizing glimpses of Utamaro as a child, including the fact that he had been a keen observer of the world from an early age.

> Utamaro projects life itself onto his own heart; his technique is superb and his mastery of our style profound. My disciple's present volume, a collection depicting insects in nature, contains such paintings that were first painted in the artist's heart. Even as a child, Utamaro had a fine awareness of the world around him. For fun, he would try to catch fireflies, or capture crickets and grasshoppers that he would allow to move about freely on his outstretched palm as he observed them, completely engrossed.

This description provides a vivid image of Utamaro, or Ichitarō, in childhood. Precocious, devoted to art, he was already adept at depicting what he had observed with brush and ink.

Toriyama Sekien (1712–88) was Utamaro's only formal teacher. Tradition has it that Sekien had studied the Kanō style of painting as a disciple of Gyokuen (Kanō Toshinobu), who had succeeded his father as an official painter to the Tokugawa shogunate. It seems unlikely, however, that Utamaro would have been able to study with an artist of such lofty connections, and by the time Utamaro became his disciple Sekien

was living on the northern slope of Ueno Hill, his work aimed at the tastes of the merchants, artisans, and poor samurai who dominated Edo's townsmen culture. He excelled at depictions of the human form, and was especially known for paintings of goblins and other inhabitants of the supernatural world (*yōkai-ga*). Active mainly during the An'ei (1772–81) and Tenmei (1781–89) eras, he published a large number of "picture books" (*ehon*). His most famous work includes *An Album of Paintings by Sekien* (*Sekien gafu*), *A Collection of Toriyama's Paintings* (*Toriyamahiko*), *The Procession of One-hundred Goblins* (*Hyakki yakō*), and *Miscellaneous Gleanings from the Procession of One-hundred Goblins* (*Hyakki yakō shūi*). It is difficult to say that Sekien was an *ukiyo-e* artist if the term is rigidly defined. He is not known to have produced even one single-sheet polychrome print (*nishiki-e*), the genre in which an artist had to produce work to be recognized as a true master of *ukiyo-e*. These prints, because of the expense involved in producing them and because they were sold singly or in sets, were enormously prestigious, and even today many collectors regard *nishiki-e* as the only true *ukiyo-e*. Sekien did not produce in this genre, confining himself to the relatively simpler, and therefore less prestigious, genres of paintings for "picture books" and illustrations for popular literature. Nevertheless, he was intimately connected with the distinguished figures of the Edo publishing world and well known in literary circles as a talented *haiku* poet. More important perhaps, his disciples in art and *haiku* included such distinguished and highly individual talents in the fields of *ukiyo-e* and popular literature as Utamaro, Eishōsai Chōki, Koikawa Harumachi, and Shimizu Enjū. It may be said without exaggeration that Sekien is remembered today more for his contributions as a teacher, and for the achievements of his disciples, than for his own work. Utamaro was very fortunate indeed to have received guidance from such an outstanding teacher at the outset of his artistic studies, one who gave scope to the budding artist's natural talents.

UTAMARO'S DEBUT

In 1775, at the age of twenty-two, Utamaro made his debut as an *ukiyo-e* artist with a print for the cover of a Kabuki playbook entitled *Forty-eight Famous Love Scenes* (*Shijū hatte koi no showake*; fig. 2), which was distributed at the performance of the play at the famous Nakamura-za theater in November of the same year. Later, famous for his portrayals of beautiful women, he denied ever having done prints of Kabuki actors (*yakusha-e*), but it was only natural that the young Utamaro should have found his first opportunity to publish

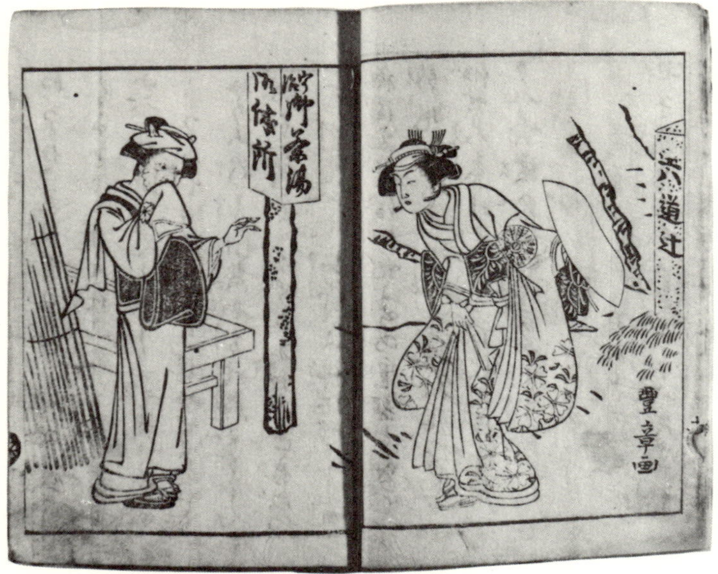

Fig. 4. Illustration by Utamaro for the book (*sharebon*) *Oki miyage*, 1779.

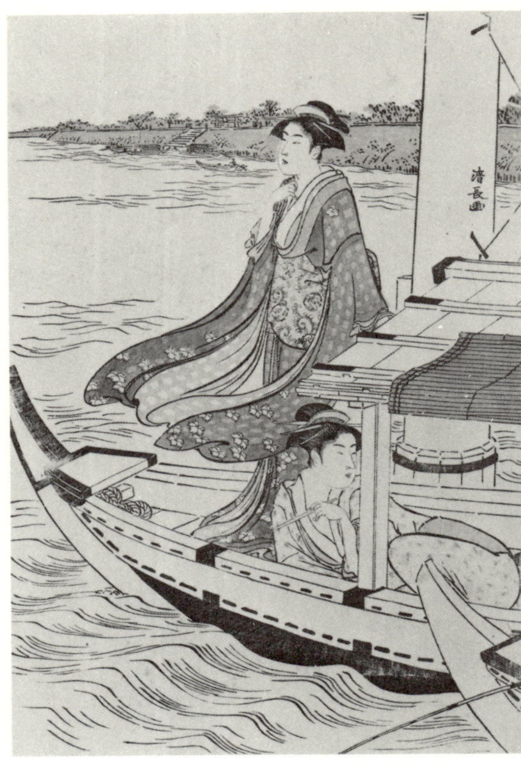

Fig. 5. One print of Torii Kiyonaga's triptych *Below the Bridge*, ca. 1784–85.

in this genre, in which huge demand and the need for hasty publication forced theaters to employ less well-established artists. There is some debate concerning the background of Utamaro's signature on this print, which was Kitagawa Toyoaki (or, according to some scholars, Toyoakira). The most commonly accepted theory for the origin of "Toyoaki," the first of Utamaro's artistic pseudonyms, is that Sekien granted him permission to use one of the Chinese characters of his own pseudonym, "Toyofusa." It was established practice in all Edo art and literary circles for a master to grant characters from his own pseudonym to favorite disciples.

The first true polychrome *ukiyo-e* prints had been developed just ten years earlier, in 1765, by Suzuki Harunobu and the group of *ukiyo-e* artists in his school. These new prints were called *nishiki-e*, or "brocade pictures," because the elaborate techniques of engraving and printing employed produced effects that were suggestive, at least to ambitious publishers, of the gorgeous *shokkō* brocades that were being imported from China during the period. With this achievement of revolutionary advances in technique, Harunobu had taken the art world by storm, and his influence was still strong among *ukiyo-e* artists of Utamaro's day. At the same time, however, such artists as Katsukawa Shunshō, a master of Kabuki actor prints, and Kitao Shigemasa, who specialized in prints of beautiful women, were beginning to produce work in a fresh, innovative style. Their work suggests a zesty determination to develop realistic styles, to break away from the dreamlike quality, the classical aestheticism of Harunobu's world. They sought inspiration in the daily lives of real people, and attempted to depict them in a more realistic fashion. This new style appeared quite early with the publication in 1776 of the three-volume "picture book" entitled *A Mirror of Lovely Images: Matching Beauties of the Yoshiwara* (*Seirō bijin awase sugata no kagami*), a joint effort by Shunshō and Shigemasa. They had been commissioned by Tsutaya Jūzaburō, the Edo publisher who was to become Utamaro's great patron. Impressed by the new styles they had developed, Tsutaya hoped that a work by these two young talents could compete with Suzuki Harunobu's "picture book" *Matching Beauties of the Yoshiwara* (*Seirō bijin awase*).

In the period after his debut, young Utamaro idolized these new masters, and devoted himself to learning their styles. Professionally, however, there were few signs during this period of training that Utamaro would emerge as the most celebrated artist of his time in the genre of *bijin-ga*. Through his twenties, Utamaro, still signing his work "Toyoaki," made his

living principally as an illustrator of popular literature (*gesaku*; fig. 4). Occasional commissions for single-sheet prints were for Utamaro, like any other young artist, in the genre of Kabuki actor pictures.

ARTIST ENCOUNTERS PUBLISHER

While Utamaro continued to scrape out a living as an obscure illustrator of popular literature, Torii Kiyonaga (1752–1815), only one year his senior, was already making his mark in the world of *ukiyo-e* (fig. 5). Still a new face, Kiyonaga had secured the patronage of Nishimura Eijudō, an established publisher, and was being lionized as a rising young star. It was against this background that Utamaro met Tsutaya Jūzaburō, and the encounter proved to be the turning point in his career. Tsutaya, a young publisher (*hanmoto*) just three years older than Utamaro himself, made his appearance just as Utamaro's skills were maturing and he was beginning to grope toward a stylistic breakthrough.

Tsutaya Jūzaburō, also known as Tsutajū, had ventured into the publishing world in 1774, at the early age of twenty-four. Two years later, in 1776, he had secured the cooperation of the larger, well-established publishing house of Yamazaki Kinbē in order to publish *A Mirror of Lovely Images: Matching Beauties of the Yoshiwara*, the gorgeous three-volume "picture book" that had been commissioned to Katsukawa Shunshō and Kitao Shigemasa. Regardless of a publisher's skill and daring in the development of new undertakings, however, it was impossible to win supremacy in the world of *ukiyo-e* publishing unless he could secure a virtual monopoly on the work of the most prominent artists. The publishing house of Nishimura Eijudō enjoyed such exclusive rights to the work of Torii Kiyonaga, whose *ukiyo-e* prints were winning great popularity. Kiyonaga's prints, which depicted groups of tall, willowy women in colorful settings that made the most of the bright open air, captured the gregarious, frank optimism of life during the Tenmei era (1781–89). One can well imagine Tsutaya's frustration in the face of Nishimura's conspicuous success. His most pressing task at this juncture was to discover someone to compete with Kiyonaga. Against this setting, the *ukiyo-e* artist and the publisher who were to reign supreme in the Edo publishing world had their first encounter. The timing was ideal for both.

In autumn of 1782, now twenty-nine (or thirty by the Japanese system), Utamaro hosted a banquet for the leading writers and artists of the day. Held at an exclusive restaurant near his home in the Shinobugaoka district of Ueno, the

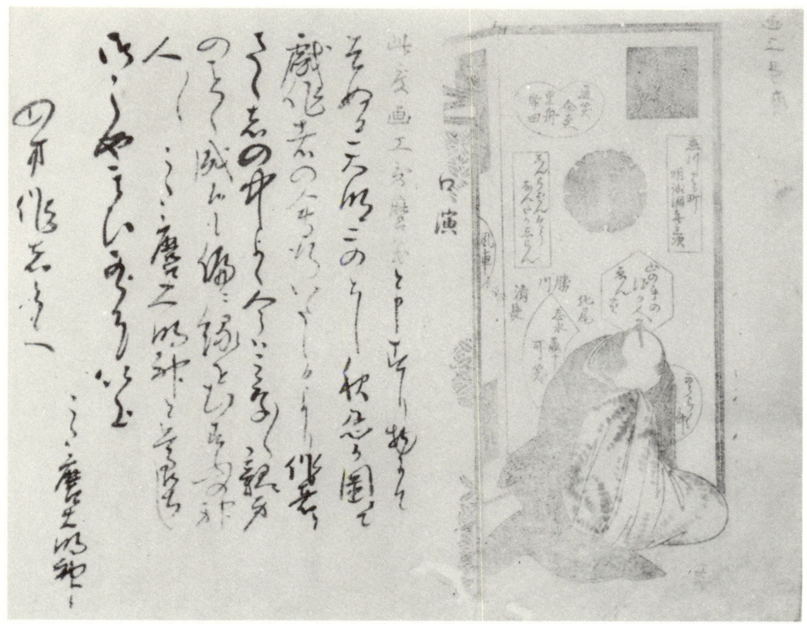

Fig. 6. A print by Utamaro appearing in Ōta Nanpo's *Shokusanjin's Collection of Drawings and Calligraphy*.

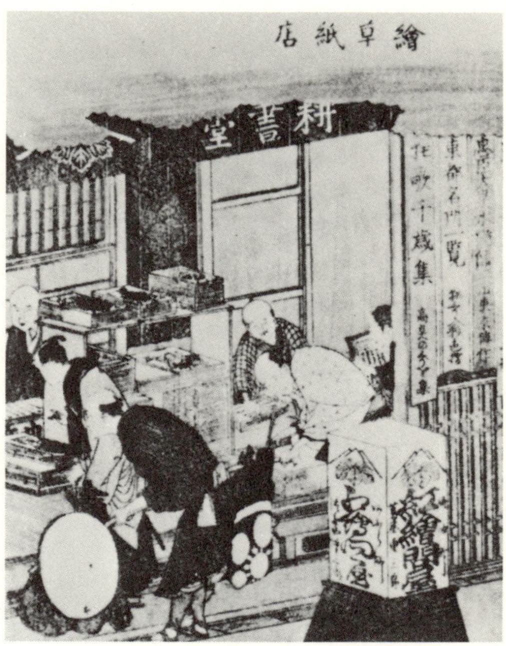

Fig. 7. Tsutaya's shop in Tōriabura-chō; from Hokusai's "picture book" *An Illustrated Tour through the Eastern Capital*, 1802.

banquet is thought to have been the occasion for the formal announcement of his new working name, Utamaro. As was common practice, Utamaro prepared a print for the occasion, which was distributed to his guests and has been preserved in Ōta Nanpo's *Shokusanjin's Collection of Drawings and Calligraphy* (*Shokusanjin hantori-chō*; fig. 6). In the foreground of the print is a self-portrait of Utamaro himself, bowing politely. Behind him is a screen displaying slips of paper bearing the names of his guests. Such screens, *harimaze byōbu*, were popular during the Edo period (1600–1867) for displaying collections of calligraphy or paintings. Alongside the names of prominent *kyōka* poets and writers, such as Ōta Nanpo, Akera Kankō, Koikawa Harumachi, and Hōseidō Kisanji, were the names of Kitao Shigemasa, Katsukawa Shunshō, and Torii Kiyonaga, the most prominent *ukiyo-e* artists of the day. It is difficult to believe that Utamaro, still a struggling young artist, could have staged such a gathering on his own. Rather, it seems much more likely that the banquet was the production of Tsutaya Jūzaburō, motivated by his appreciation of Utamaro's genius, as well as by his ambition to make his own mark by promoting the new artist's work.

Having secured the talents of this young, potentially brilliant artist, and having staged for him a lavish introduction to the leading figures in Edo's art and literary circles, Tsutaya immediately put him to work on paintings for *ukiyo-e* prints aimed at the New Year's market. The result of this work was *The Fantastic Travels of a Playboy in the Land of the Giants* (*Migi no tōri tashika ni uso shikkari gantori-chō*), published in 1783. He collaborated on this project, which was a "yellow-cover" book (*kibyōshi*), a genre of popular fiction in vogue at the time, with his friend Shimizu Enjū. Enjū, a rising young writer in the genre of "yellow-cover" books, worked under the name Namake no Bakahito Enjū, which means "Enjū, the Lazy Fool," and in a publisher's colophon Tsutaya claims that "both the author and the artist are making their debuts." Clearly, this project was one of Tsutaya's daring experiments. By assigning the two friends to the same project, he hoped that these young, energetic artists would spur each other on.

This work was apparently preceded by another joint effort by Utamaro and Enjū, *A Short History of the Sartorial Exploits of a Great Connoisseur of Inari Machi* (*Minari daitsūjin ryakuengi*), a "yellow-cover" book published in 1781. This work, also published by Tsutaya, has a preface signed "Utamaro, Dilettante of Shinobugaoka," which suggests that Utamaro had adopted his new working name before 1782. Shibui Kiyoshi, however, argues that the publication of *A Great Connoisseur of Inari Machi* must have been delayed. This argument, which has much to recommend it, is based on the facts that the banquet formally introducing Utamaro to the publishing world was not held until 1782 and that *The Fantastic Travels of a Playboy in the Land of the Giants*, bearing Tsutaya's note to the effect that the work was Utamaro's maiden effort, was not published until 1783. It is not certain that Shimizu Enjū brought Utamaro and Tsutaya together, but there is little doubt that 1782 was in fact the crucial year in which Utamaro began his lifelong friendship with Tsutaya and changed his working name to Utamaro. As a talent scout, Tsutaya was brilliant. Besides Utamaro, he launched the careers of such artists and writers as Santō Kyōden, Tōshūsai Sharaku, and Jippensha Ikku. His estimate of Utamaro's potential was proven to be sound, and he became the publisher for almost all of Utamaro's best work.

A PROBLEMATIC MARRIAGE

During the same important period that he began to make his mark in the art world, Utamaro seems to have married, rather late for a man of that day. Recently, Shibui Kiyoshi has suggested an interesting interpretation of the circumstances surrounding Utamaro's marriage. Shibui's deductions are quite ingenious, and I will summarize them below.

Already in his thirties, Utamaro apparently married the daughter of a *sake* dealer by the name of Okuda Heibē, whose trading house was across the street from the Great Gate of the Yoshiwara, one of Edo's great pleasure quarters. Shibui places the date of the marriage before the nineteenth day of the fourth lunar month of 1784, the date of the death of Kōzō, Heibē's son. Shibui's deduction is based on a statement by Utamaro, indicating that he was then married to Heibē's daughter, that appeared in a *kyōka* collection published by Tsutaya in commemoration of Kōzō's death, *Morohaku Sake to Soothe Your Departing Soul* (*Itami morohaku*). Shibui also suggests that, in all likelihood, Tsutaya himself arranged the marriage, hoping to ensure the happiness of this great artist and friend.

Tsutaya's publishing house had originally been located across the street from the Great Gate of the pleasure quarters, and even after 1783 when he moved his central operation to Tōriabura-chō in a different part of the city (fig. 7), Tsutaya maintained the shop as the headquarters for publishing *Yoshiwara saiken*, a guide to the pleasure quarters. It had also become a salon for gatherings of amateur *kyōka* poets. Indeed, Tsutaya contributed verses to *Morohaku Sake to Soothe Your Departing Soul*, as did his mother, and there is little doubt that his family, which lived only seven shops away from Heibē's

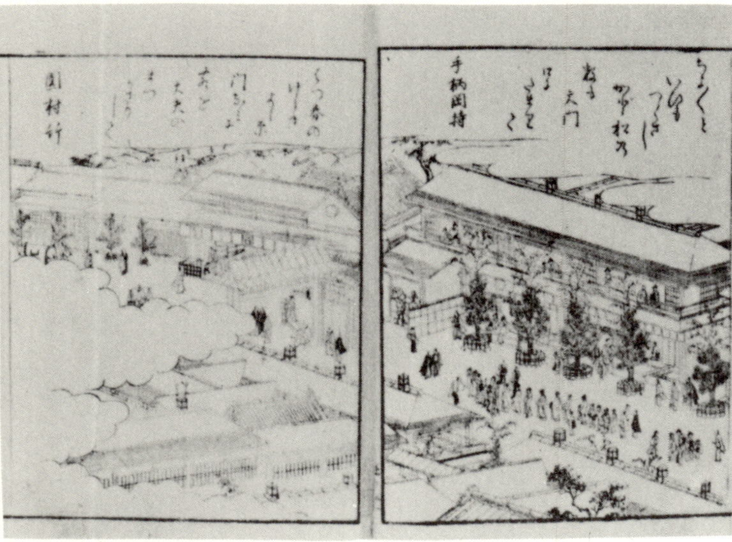

Fig. 8. *Famous Places in Edo*; a *kyōka ehon*
illustrated by Utamaro, 1786.

establishment, was on intimate terms with Heibē's. The prob-
lem confronting researchers now is whether Heibē's daughter
is the same woman who was interred at Senkōji temple with
the posthumous Buddhist name of Risei Shinnyō, and who is
known from temple records to have had some connection with
Utamaro. Senkōji temple, which was originally in Asakusa, is
the same temple at which Utamaro was buried.

In *A Record for Future Generations* (*Nochi no tame no ki*),
Takizawa (Kyokutei) Bakin, the most popular writer of the
period, wrote of Utamaro: "Utamaro has no wife and no
children. When he dies, he will become a lost, unmourned
soul." If Shibui's analysis is correct, Utamaro must have been
preceded in death by his wife, and either they had no children
or the children died prematurely. For all his success in the
world of art, it appears that Utamaro was ultimately to be
unhappy in his personal life. In the early years of the Tenmei
era (1781–89), however, he was working for Tsutaya and
anticipating a great leap forward. At the same time, he was
starting a new family, and it must have been a period of great
hope and anticipation.

THE FLOWERING OF UTAMARO'S ART

In 1786 Tsutaya published *Famous Places in Edo* (*Ehon Edo
suzume;* fig. 8), the first in a series of *kyōka ehon*, anthologies of
comic verse with pictures, featuring prints by Utamaro that
would revolutionize the genre. Utamaro devoted a great deal
of energy to the production of prints for *kyōka ehon* during
the five-year period from 1786 through 1790. With the excep-
tion of the last, *Landscapes and Comic Verse Featuring Yomogi
Island* (*Ehon Yomogi no Shima*), all were published by Tsutaya.

Earlier *kyōka ehon* had been smaller books without illustrations or with only simple monochrome illustrations. In the
period before the sumptuary edicts of the Kansei Reforms
(1787–93), however, *kyōka* poetry had reached the peak of its
popularity, and Tsutaya concentrated on producing gorgeous
kyōka collections featuring full-size *ōban* color prints by Utamaro. These large "picture books" exploited the skills of the
finest engravers and printers, and they were greeted with ac-
clamations from *kyōka* enthusiasts. At the same time, Utamaro's work in this genre had important implications for
ukiyo-e as well. In his prints for such *kyōka ehon* as *A Collection
of Crawling Creatures* (*Mushi erami;* figs. 9–11) and *A Multitude
of Birds* (*Momochidori;* figs. 12–13), Utamaro attempted to
bring the realism of *ukiyo-e*, which up to that time had been
characterized by a single-minded concentration on scenes from
the pleasure quarters, to such traditional landscape themes as

"flowers and birds" and "grass and crawling creatures." He
thus ventured into subject matter that had been the province of
classical *yamato-e* painting. Moreover, this early experience
with full-size color prints provided Utamaro with an invalu-
able opportunity to master the techniques of painting for
ukiyo-e prints, to learn to exploit the potential of the *ukiyo-e*
print as an artistic medium.

It was during this period also that Utamaro began to develop a distinctive style in the genre of *nishiki-e*, single-sheet
polychrome prints. No longer simply imitating the styles of
Kiyonaga and Kitao Shigemasa, Utamaro began to produce
prints of beautiful women (*bijin-ga*) in the bewitchingly
charming style that would characterize his masterpieces in that
genre. Outstanding prints thought to have been produced
during this early period include *The Ōmando Dance* (*Ōmando;*
pl. 2) from the series "*Geisha* at the Yoshiwara Niwaka
Festival" (*Seirō niwaka onnageisha no bu*), the triptych *Stylish
Amusements on an Excursion* (*Fūryū hana no iroka*), and the
diptych *Stylish Amusements of the Four Seasons* (*Shiki asobi hana
no iroka;* pl. 3). Although the influence of such predecessors as
Kiyonaga and Shigemasa may still be detected, the prints of
these early series are alive with Utamaro's determination to
bring new techniques to the *bijin-ga*, to develop a new style of
his own. If the prints are not yet up to the standards of his
greatest masterpieces in this genre, they are irresistible for their
energy. There is no publisher's seal on the prints of the three
series. However, in the scene depicted in the *Ōmando Dance* (pl.
2), a copy of *Yoshiwara saiken*, Tsutaya's guide to the pleasure
quarters, has been tossed carelessly onto the floor. Tsutaya's
publisher's seal has been represented on its cover, along with
the inscription, "Publisher, Tsutaya Jūzaburō." Given these
clues, and the probable dates of the prints, there seems to be
little doubt that Tsutaya was indeed the publisher. Moreover,
the remarkable beauty of the engraving and printing suggests
the care with which the engravers and printers were selected
and, therefore, the probability that a publisher of Tsutaya's
quality took a personal interest in ensuring that the artist's
conception of the prints was effectively realized. The prints
created through the collaboration of Utamaro and Tsutaya in
the genre of *kyōka ehon* and *bijin-ga* were greeted with cries of
admiration, and it was not long before the two men were
preeminent in the world of *ukiyo-e*.

A TEMPORARY SETBACK

The Kansei Reforms, sumptuary edicts formulated by Ma-
tsudaira Sadanobu, the powerful advisor to the Tokugawa

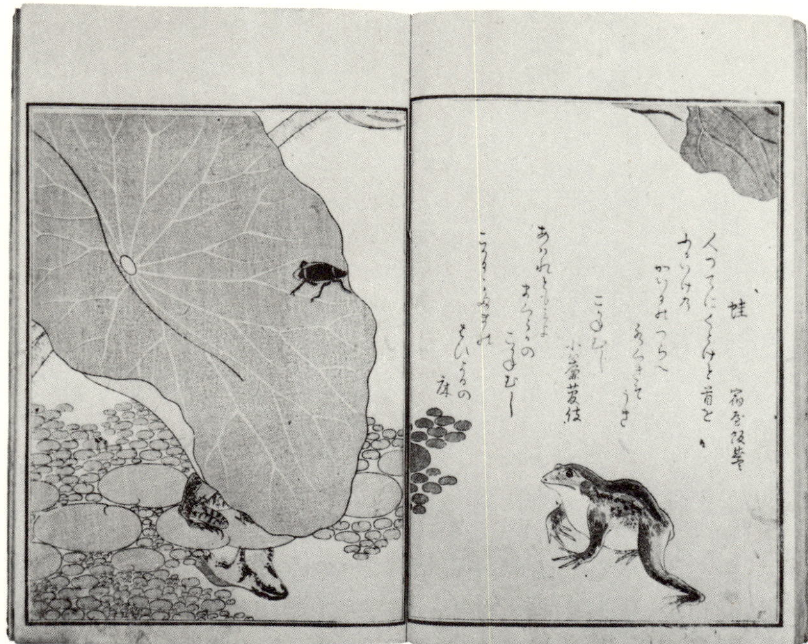

Fig. 9. *A Collection of Crawling Creatures*; a *kyōka ehon* illustrated by Utamaro, 1788.

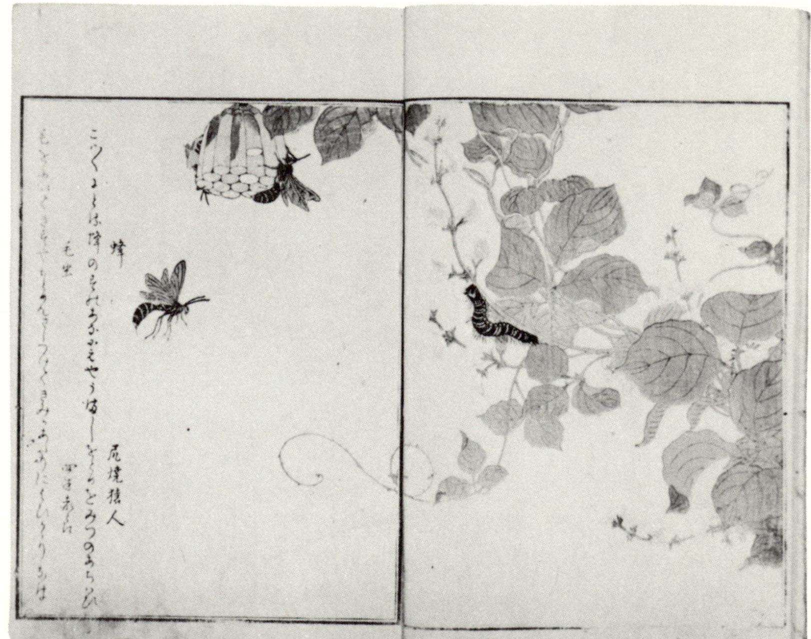

Fig. 10. *A Collection of Crawling Creatures*; a *kyōka ehon* illustrated by Utamaro, 1788.

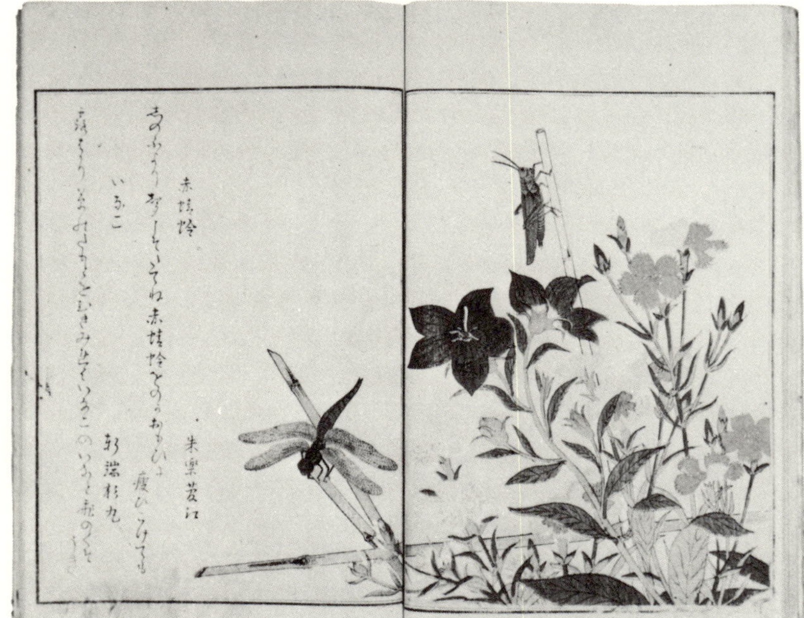

Fig. 11. *A Collection of Crawling Creatures*; a *kyōka ehon* illustrated by Utamaro, 1788.

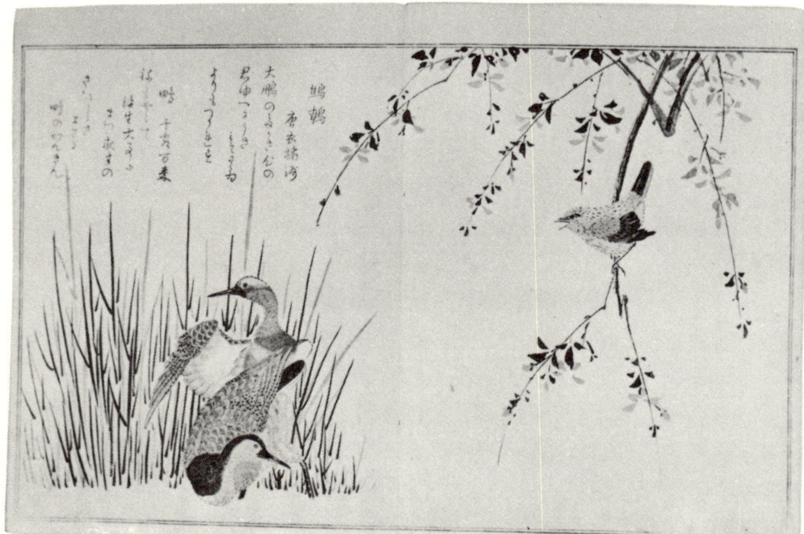

Fig. 12. *A Multitude of Birds*; a *kyōka ehon* illustrated by Utamaro, *ca.* 1790.

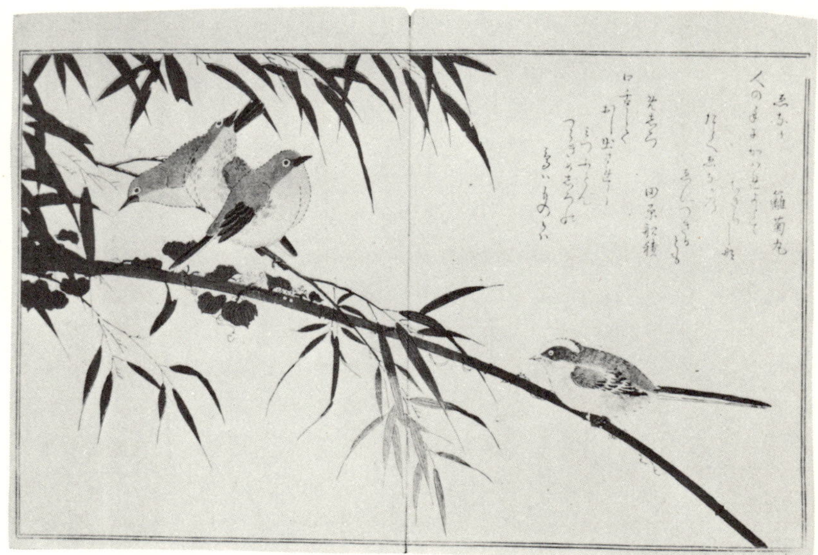

Fig. 13. *A Multitude of Birds*; a *kyōka ehon* illustrated by Utamaro, *ca.* 1790.

shogun, were carried out during the period from 1787 to 1793 in an effort to revitalize the samurai class. They were effective for only a short time, but the populace of Edo had grown so accustomed to ease and extravagance that the edicts succeeded in throwing Edo into a panic. The reforms were an especially serious blow to the publishing world. Censorship regulations were proclaimed twice in 1790, and were accompanied by the suppression of a number of works by popular writers, and punishment of the writers themselves. Koikawa Harumachi, who established the genre of "yellow-cover" books (*kibyōshi*) and developed its potential for parody and satire, had published a *kibyōshi* entitled *A Parrot's Discourse on the Disciplines of the Pen and the Sword* (*Ōmugaeshi bunbu nidō*) in 1789. The satire implicit in this humorous work did not escape the attention of indignant authorities of the shogunate, and Harumachi was summoned for questioning. Pleading illness, he did not appear, and died soon after the summons. One theory explaining Harumachi's untimely death holds that he committed suicide. Harumachi's real name was Kurahashi Noboru, and he was in Edo as a retainer of the rather small Ojima domain of Suruga. It is reasoned that he may have committed suicide fearing that trouble with the shogunate might implicate the Ojima *daimyō* himself. Whether the theory is valid or not, Harumachi's death stunned the Edo publishing world. He had been a disciple of Sekien's with Utamaro, and a well-known *ukiyo-e* artist. His censure was the first of a series of attacks on the publishing world by the shogunate.

Two years later, in 1791, Tsutaya himself was prosecuted for publishing three books by Santō Kyōden (Kitao Masanobu as an *ukiyo-e* artist). Kyōden spent fifty days in hand chains, but Tsutaya was sentenced even more severely. The shogunate confiscated half of his entire estate. Not content with this attack on the publishing world, the shogunate turned its attention to the *kyōka* circles. Ishikawa Masamochi, whose pen name was Yadoya no Meshimori, was banished from Edo during the same year. Ōta Nanpo, a leading figure in *kyōka* circles but also an important counselor to the shogunate, meekly submitted to these vicious attacks on the popular culture of Edo and never wrote *kyōka* or popular fiction again.

Santō Kyōden had perfected the genre of *sharebon*, realistic short stories depicting the life and manners of the pleasure quarters in a humorous, satirical vein. He had already published a good deal of work with Tsutaya and at the time of his arrest was the young lion among writers of popular literature. Thus, before his own arrest, Tsutaya had secured virtually exclusive rights to publish not only Utamaro's work, but also

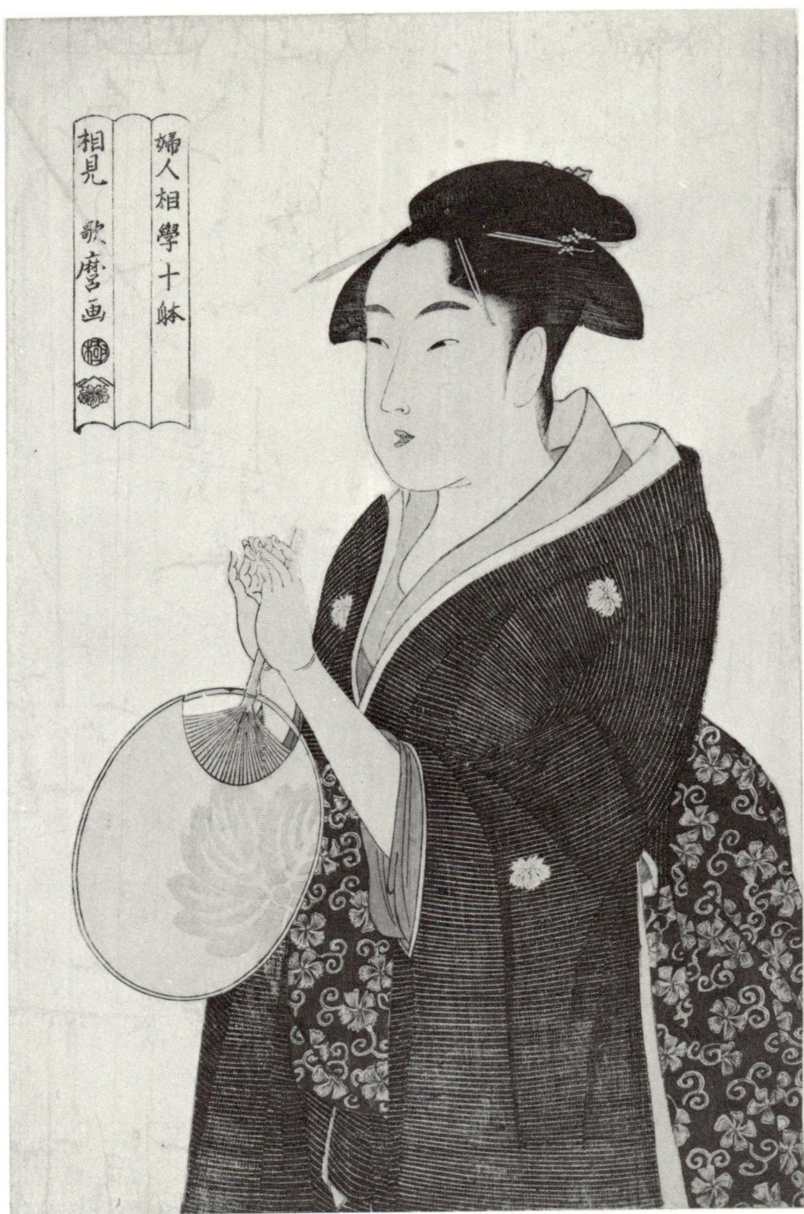

Fig. 14. Utamaro's *Woman with Fan*: "Ten Studies in Female Physiognomy," *ca.* 1792–93.

the work of this energetic writer. He was in an excellent position to sail with the wind when, suddenly, he became a target of the shogunate's attack on the publishing world. The Kansei Reforms must have seemed a bitter setback. However, Tsutaya was an extraordinary man. Even when it seemed that the shogunate had dealt him a blow from which he would never recover, he bided his time until the furor of the reforms had subsided and then launched into a new period of even more daring activity. The focus of this activity, and the project to which Tsutaya devoted his best efforts in planning and production, was a series of masterpieces by Utamaro in a new style of *ukiyo-e*, the magnificent *bijin ōkubi-e*, portraits of celebrated beauties that emphasize the subject's expression by depicting only the head and shoulders against a gorgeously executed background decorated with scattered mica dust.

MASTER OF THE BIJIN ŌKUBI-E

The techniques of the *ōkubi-e* (literally, "large-head pictures") had been developed already by the artists of the Katsukawa school, particularly in the work of Katsukawa Shunshō in his "large-head pictures of Kabuki actors" (*yakusha ōkubi-e*). As a literal rendering of the word *ōkubi-e* suggests, the essential departure from other *ukiyo-e* styles is that the *ōkubi-e* brings the facial expressions of its subjects into sharper focus by depicting only the upper half or the upper two-thirds of the body. Indeed, Shunshō's disciple, Shunkō, developed an even more daring technique called "large-face pictures" (*ōkao-e*), in which only the subject's head was depicted.

Utamaro himself had become increasingly dissatisfied with existing styles in the *bijin-ga* genre, which produced an endless succession of stylized, ideal beauties completely lacking facial expression or individuality. Irresistibly attracted by the ex-

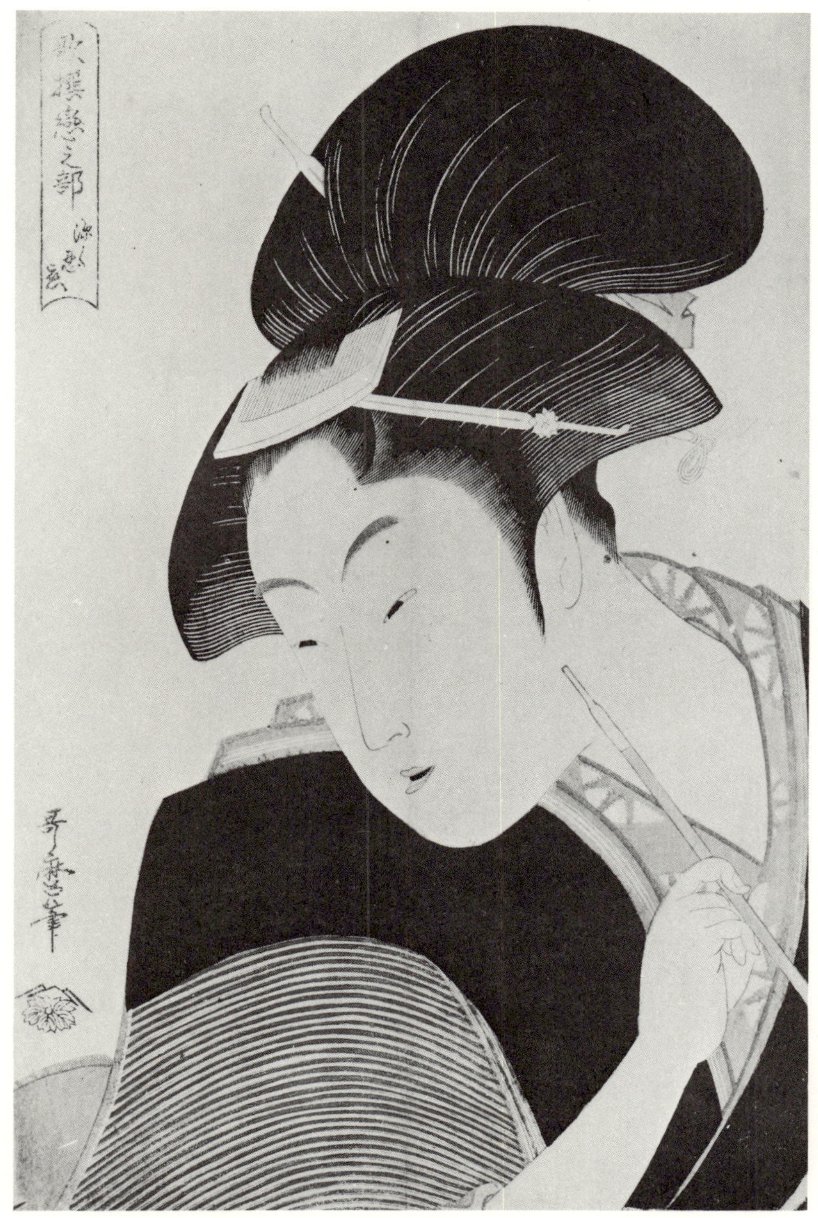

Fig. 15. Utamaro's *Love Deeply Concealed*: "Great Love Themes of Classical Poetry," *ca.* 1793.

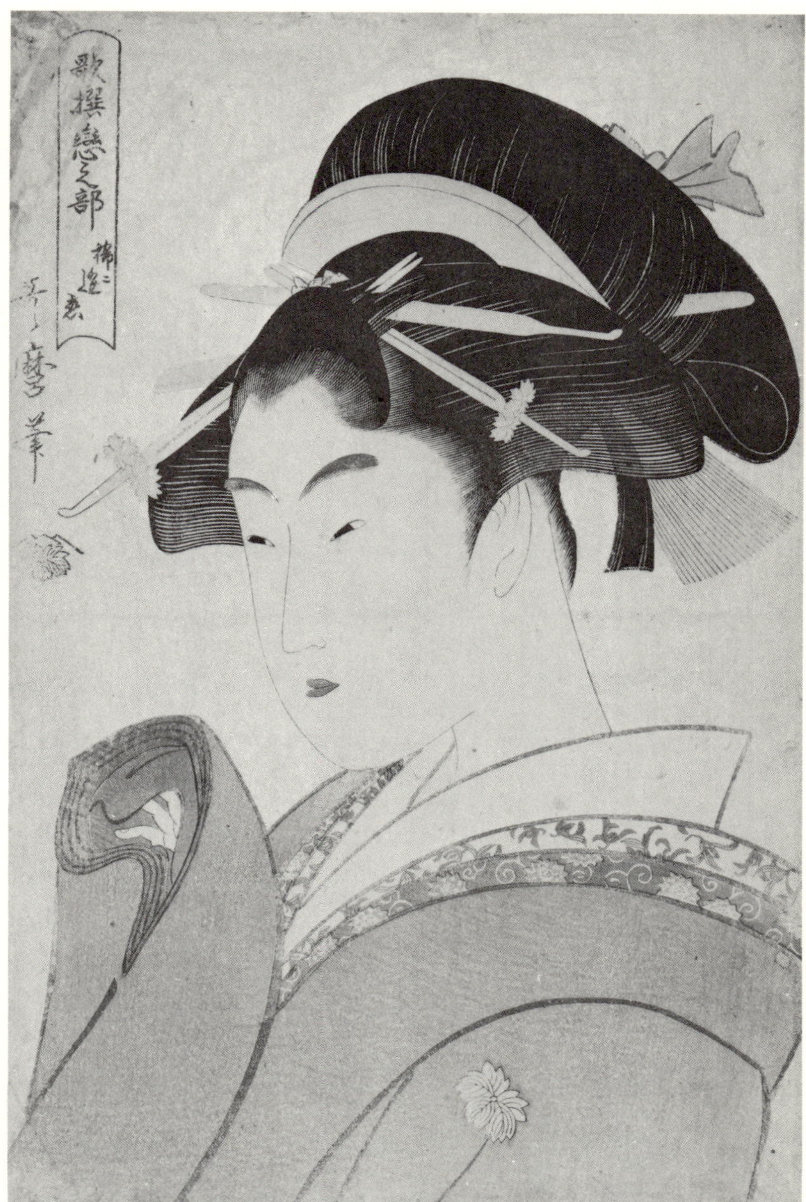

Fig. 16. Utamaro's *Rarely Met Love*: "Great Love Themes of Classical Poetry," *ca.* 1793.

pressive power and heightened realism of the styles employed in the Katsukawa school's "large-head pictures of Kabuki actors," Utamaro began to exploit these new techniques in his *bijin-ga*. His first work in the new style, published around 1790–91, was a series entitled "Contemporary Edo Dancers Arrayed for the Yoshiwara Niwaka Festival" (*Tōsei odoriko zoroe*; pl. 1). The prints of this series are characterized by simple, straightforward composition and restraint in the complexity of engraving and selection of colors. The vestiges of Kiyonaga's influence that may be detected in Utamaro's earlier work (see plates 2 and 3) have been swept away, and the publication of this series amounted to a formal announcement that Utamaro had established a new style of his own. Having established himself in this genre, and with the success of his revolutionary *kyōka ehon*, it is understandable that Utamaro began to use a seal that reads, "With These Works I Establish an Artistic House in My Own Right." This seal appears on prints produced for two *kyōka ehon* published in 1789, *Melodious Allegories Illustrated* (*Ehon tatoe no fushi*) and *Parting Gifts of the Ebb Tide* (*Shiohi no tsuto*). It was thus that Tsutaya made a brilliant comeback in the period following the Kansei Reforms, becoming more successful than ever before with Utamaro's new *bijin ōkubi-e*.

Utamaro reached the peak of his artistic creativity, and achieved his greatest mastery of the *bijin ōkubi-e*, in two series published in the period from 1792 to 1793, "Great Love Themes of Classical Poetry" (*Kasen koi no bu*; pls. 17–18, figs. 15–16) and "Ten Studies in Female Physiognomy" (*Fujin sōgaku juttai*; pls. 4–5, half-title page, fig. 14), the latter first published as "Female Facial Types of Ten Classes" (*Fujo ninsō juppon*). In the prints of these series, Utamaro confronted the most difficult challenges in portraying human figures. He

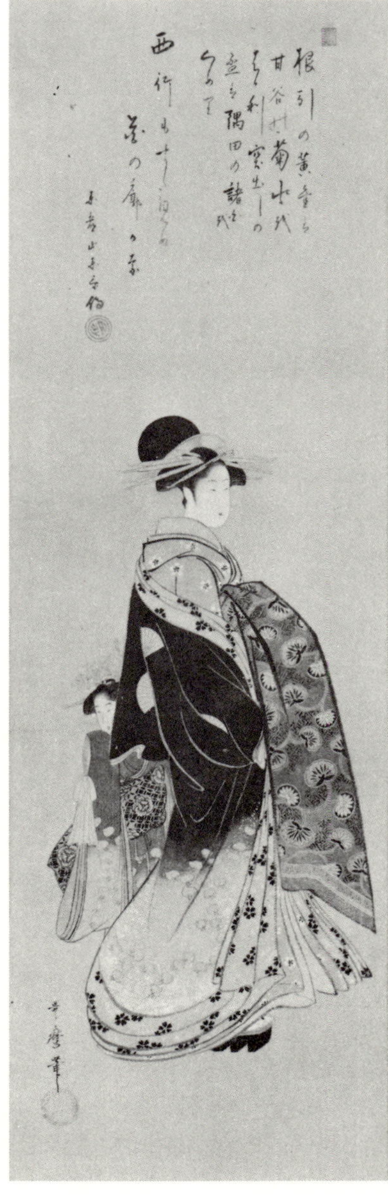

Fig. 17. Utamaro's *Courtesan with Child Attendant*; a painting with inscription by Santō Kyōden, 1790s.

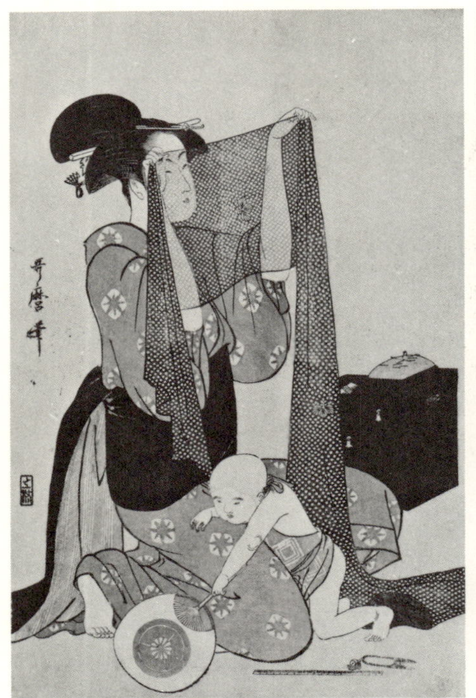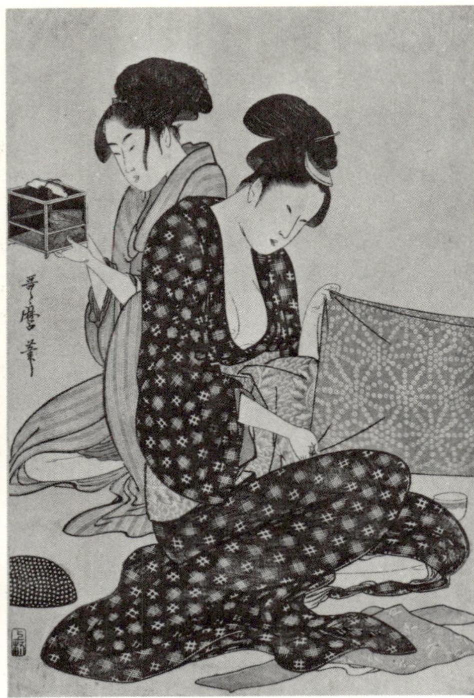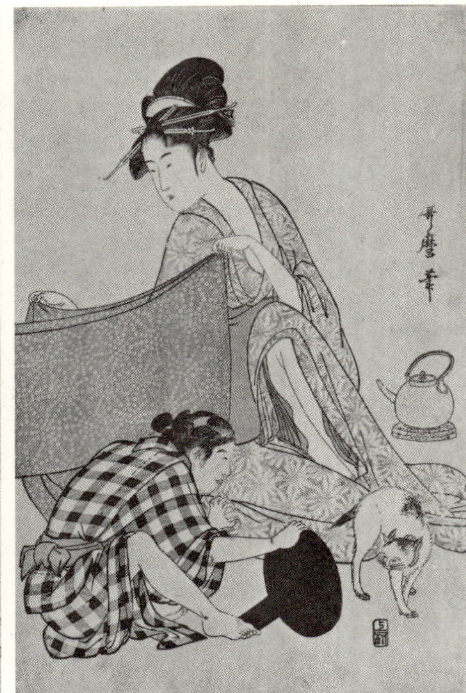

Fig. 18. Utamaro's triptych *Needlework, ca.* 1795–96.

attempted to express the subjective, individual traits of his subjects in terms of such qualities as character and personality, and sought daring techniques that would enable him to capture even fleeting emotional and mental states. In the prints of the series "Great Love Themes of Classical Poetry," Utamaro captured the subtle nuances of passion in the expressions of women of different ages and classes as their emotions wavered between rapture and despair. The series "Ten Studies in Female Physiognomy" depicts women of every class and social background that Utamaro had had an opportunity to observe. As attempts to capture differences in the characters of these women, the prints of the series are characterized by careful delineation of facial expressions and gestures expressive of the manners and ethos of his subject's social milieu. Besides the two titles of the series, many of the prints bear a signature reading, "Studies in Physiognomic Judgment of Character by Utamaro." Indeed, Utamaro was an unparalled observer, a physiognomist of beautiful women. In the *bijin ōkubi-e* Utamaro had discovered his métier, and his popularity increased by leaps and bounds as he began to produce prints of the celebrated beauties of Edo, clearly identifying them by name.

In 1794 Tsutaya Jūzaburō introduced the enigmatic Tō-shūsai Sharaku. Although Sharaku's career lasted only ten months, from the fifth lunar month of 1794 to the second month of 1795, he is known to have published over 140 prints during that short period (fig. 19). His brilliant "large-head portraits of Kabuki actors" (*yakusha nigao ōkubi-e*) were a unique achievement, and in 1794, apparently in emulation, Utamaro published a series of *bijin-ga* entitled "A Collection of Portraits of Reigning Beauties" (*Tōji zensei nigao zoroe*). After Sharaku abruptly disappeared from the scene, Utamaro substituted the word "beauties" (*bijin*) for the word "portrait" (*nigao*) in the title, and the series was published under the new title, "A Collection of Reigning Beauties" (*Tōji zensei bijin zoroe*; pls. 13–16). The earlier title, however, clearly suggests Utamaro's determination to vie with the brilliant new artist and the degree to which Utamaro felt Sharaku's influence. Utamaro's series was quite successful, featuring as it did the most popular of the courtesans of the highest rank (*tayū*) in the Yoshiwara pleasure quarters. Such celebrated *tayū* as Hanaōgi (pl. 13) and Takigawa (pl. 14) of the Ōgiya, as well as Hanazuma of the Hyōgoya (pl. 16), were at the height of their popularity. During the same period, Utamaro also produced single prints in the genre of *bijin-ga*, featuring such celebrated beauties as the *geisha* Tomimoto Toyohina and the teahouse girls Okita (pl. 23) of the Naniwaya and Ohisa of

the Takashimaya. Indeed, it is unlikely that even one of the celebrated beauties of the day failed to catch Utamaro's attention and to appear in his prints. In any of these prints, it is possible to overlook Utamaro's attention to the individuality of real, living women, and to view the portrayals as mere repetitive stereotypes of Utamaro's own image of ideal beauty. In each of the prints, however, slight peculiarities of posture or facial expression suggest the unique beauty of each of Utamaro's models.

Indeed, Utamaro observed the multitudinous variations in feminine beauty with untiring enthusiasm, and constantly sought new techniques for expressing them more effectively. In order to capture the soft warmth of a woman's skin, he experimented with new backgrounds and compositional techniques. To heighten the effects of flesh tones, he employed the techniques of *kirazuri* and *kitsubushi*. *Kirazuri*, a favorite technique of Utamaro's, was a method of printing the background in two stages, first applying a light color to the high quality paper, and then a light film of glue onto which mica dust (*kira*) was sprinkled, or applying glue into which the mica dust had already been mixed (see plates 4, 18). *Kitsubushi* was a simpler background technique employed to enhance flesh tones as well as the colors of garments. This printing technique simply produced light-yellow backgrounds of various shades of brightness (see plates 14, 27, 31).

Utamaro also exploited a printer's technique known as *karazuri*, in which the printer spread the print over a carved woodblock that had not been prepared with colors and pressed it firmly onto the relief carving. This technique produced both concave and convex lines on the print's surface, giving it a three-dimensional effect, and was often employed by *ukiyo-e* artists to suggest the folds of garments or the texture of feathers in prints depicting birds. In Utamaro's *bijin-ga* the technique is exploited not only in this conventional fashion, but also in the outlines of his subject's face, or the swell of her breasts. This new application of the technique of *karazuri* is particularly effective in the prints of the series "A Sundial of Maidens" (*Musume hidokei*; pls. 8–12); unfortunately the results of *karazuri* are not readily perceptible in reproduction. In the same series, Utamaro omitted the outlines of his subject's faces completely, relying on the contrast of soft flesh-tones against a bright yellow background (*kitsubushi*) to achieve a striking effect. Utamaro's brilliant originality is nowhere more in evidence than in a series entitled "Utamaro's New Designs for the *Nishiki-e* Print" (*Nishiki-ori Utamaro-gata shinmoyō*; pl. 44), where he used new techniques of line and color in a way

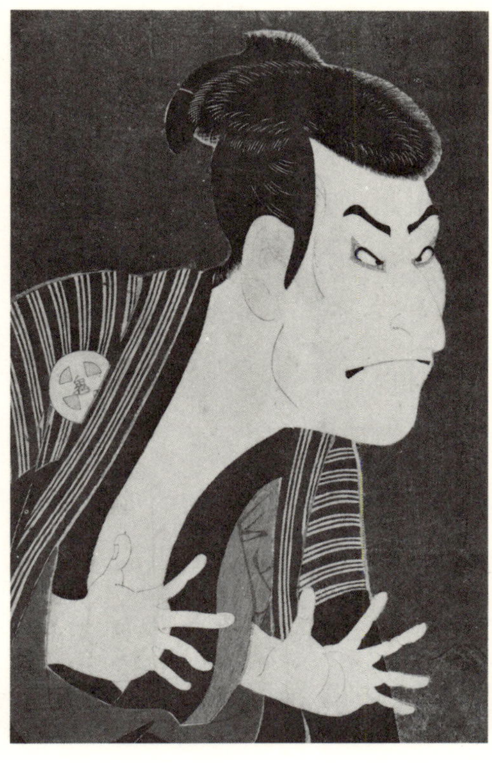
Fig. 19. Tōshūsai Sharaku's *Ōtani Oniji in the Role of Yakko Edobē*, 1794.

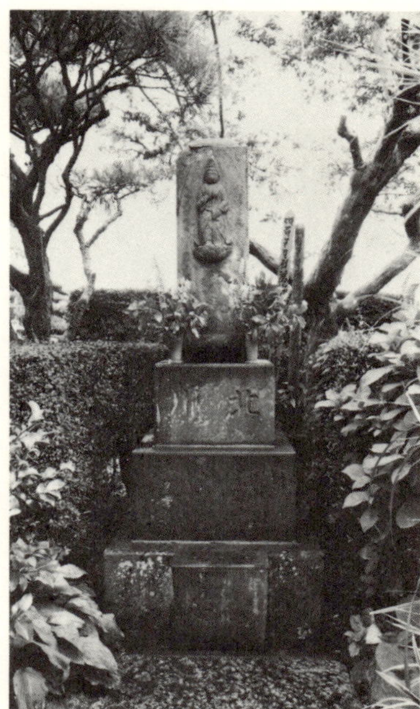
Fig. 20. Utamaro's grave at Senkōji temple in Setagaya Ward, Tokyo.

that was unprecedented in traditional Oriental painting. The outlines of the face are done in lines of vermilion, and the texture and quality of the subject's garments are suggested by subtle shading that also conveys the soft warmth of the flesh the garments conceal.

Utamaro's *bijin-ga*, based as they are on the artist's own careful observations of feminine psychology, constituted a sharp criticism of existing approaches to the genre, which had produced a succession of stereotyped, ideal images of feminine beauty. In "Utamaro's New Designs for the *Nishiki-e* Print," he consciously undertook the task of demonstrating the true essence of the *bijin-ga* to the "inferior artists as numerous and insignificant as the leaves of trees." One perceives in this statement Utamaro's sense of pride and self-confidence as the unrivaled master of the *bijin-ga*.

DECLINE, PUNISHMENT, AND DEATH

Utamaro's popularity was at its peak, and commissions were pouring in, not only from Tsutaya but also from other publishers eager to offer their patronage, when Utamaro was dealt a tragic blow. On the sixth day of the fifth lunar month of 1797, Tsutaya Jūzaburō, a consistent source of friendship, support, and creative stimulation, died at the age of forty-seven, bitterly mourned by his friends.

Utamaro's despair is evident in the decline of his subsequent work. With the loss of his life-long friend and patron, Utamaro's work quickly lost the classical elegance of the *bijin ōkubi-e* he had done for Tsutaya. Perhaps as a reaction to the refinement of these earlier prints, Utamaro began to produce *bijin-ga* in which an attitude of decadence and self-abandonment is evident even in the expressions of his models. It is undeniable, however, that this decadence in Utamaro's work was accompanied by a similar trend in the work of other artists. Indeed, one should not overlook the fact that Utamaro's style in his declining years foreshadowed the styles of such artists of the late Edo period as Kunisada, Kuniyoshi, and Eisen. By a strange irony of fate, Utamaro's personal tragedy overlapped the trend toward decadence and disintegration in Edo's townsmen culture during the period just before the collapse of the Tokugawa shogunate.

Isolated, perhaps alienated, with neither a wife nor children to care for him, Utamaro continued to pour out a stream of work in response to constant requests from publishers eager to exploit his name and his fading talent. He produced an occasional masterpiece, but excessive output resulted in a number of lamentable failures that needlessly damaged his

reputation. Among the better works of his last years, "The Eyeglasses of a Watchful Parent" (*Kyōkun oya no megane*; pls. 26−28) and "A Tenfold Study in Female Physiognomy" (*Fujin sōgaku juttai*, in which the character for "ten" is different from that in the more famous "Ten Studies in Female Physiognomy") are particularly worthy of attention. Even in these prints, however, we do not find the depth of subjectivity found in the reserved realism of "Great Love Themes of Classical Poetry" (pls. 17−18, figs. 15−16) and "Ten Studies in Female Physiognomy" (pls. 4−5, half-title page, fig. 14). Perhaps because he had developed his powers of observation to the point that he saw subtle distinctions in feminine emotional states that could not be expressed within the genre of the *bijin ōkubi-e*, Utamaro was finally forced to employ a technique in which his own artistic work expressed only the outward features, and the subjective nuances were filled in with written explanations on the print.

In 1804 Utamaro published a *nishiki-e* that was based on the well-known *Record of Hideyoshi* (*Taikōki*), which had been banned as a subject for popular art and literature. He was imprisoned for three days, and spent fifty more days in hand chains. The townsmen of Edo, who were constantly under the thumbs of the shogunate's samurai retainers, were almost unanimously sympathetic with Toyotomi Hideyoshi and his family. Utamaro's punishment was essentially the result of the shogunate's displeasure at the tendency of publishers of popular fiction and art to exploit Hideyoshi's popularity by producing literary and art works based on themes of his glory and subsequent downfall at the hands of the wily Tokugawa Ieyasu, to be found in *A Record of Hideyoshi*. In spite of his punishment by the shogunate, Utamaro, who was possessed of a sturdy vitality, continued to produce a large quantity of work in response to constant requests from the fans of his *bijin-ga*. Unfortunately, these last works are largely repetitious stereotypes, bearing hardly any trace of the brilliance that characterized his best work. Two years after his punishment by the shogunate, Utamaro fell ill and died, ending his colorful career at the age of fifty-three. He was buried at Senkōji temple in Asakusa (presently located in the Setagaya Ward of Tokyo) with the Buddhist posthumous name of Shūen Ryōkō Shinshi. With no grandchildren to attend the grave, it soon fell into disrepair. It was rebuilt in 1917 by people who loved Utamaro and his work (fig. 20). It is still impossible for me to recall his brilliant career without feeling deep emotion.

Notes on the Color Plates

<table>
<tr><td colspan="3" align="center">STANDARD PRINT SIZES</td></tr>
<tr><td>double ōban</td><td>60 cm.</td><td>× 32 cm.</td></tr>
<tr><td>ōban</td><td>39 cm.</td><td>× 26 cm.</td></tr>
<tr><td>chūban</td><td>28 cm.</td><td>× 20 cm.</td></tr>
<tr><td>hosoban</td><td>30 cm.</td><td>× 15 cm.</td></tr>
<tr><td>hashira-e</td><td>70 cm.</td><td>× 12 cm.</td></tr>
<tr><td colspan="3">Note: These sizes vary slightly according to how the paper was cut.</td></tr>
</table>

1.   *The Yoshiwara Sparrow Dance*: from the series "Contemporary Edo Dancers Arrayed for the Yoshiwara Niwaka Festival" (*Tōsei odoriko zoroe: Yoshiwara suzume*). *Ōban* size. Published by Tsutaya Jūzaburō, *ca.* 1790–91. Tokyo National Museum.

Utamaro created the new genre of *bijin ōkubi-e*, a genre that emphasized the facial features and expressions of his subjects rather than full-length figures, during the Kansei era (1789–1801). The prints in this new style cast the upper half of the figure against a background of pale mica dust, a technique called *kirazuri*. This is one of five prints in a series that is thought to be Utamaro's earliest work in *bijin ōkubi-e*. Each of the prints depicts a dancer of the Yoshiwara pleasure quarters in the characteristic costume of one of the dance comedies performed during the Niwaka festival. The prints in this series, aside from that illustrated, are *The Heron Maiden Dance* (*Sagi musume*), *The Lion Maiden Dance* (*Shakkyō*), *The Sanbasō Dance* (*Sanbasō*), and *The Dōjōji Temple Dance* (*Dōjōji*). The "Yoshiwara Sparrow Dance" is replete with nuances and historical allusions combining a thinly veiled account of conditions in the pleasure quarters with the famous love story of Minamoto no Yoshiie and Taka no Sei, a favorite theme of Kabuki as well as of traditional dance. Utamaro's use of subdued colors against a light background heightens the effect of the print's daring composition.

2.   *The Ōmando Dance*: from the series "Geisha at the Yoshiwara Niwaka Festival" (*Seirō niwaka onnageisha no bu: Ōmando*). *Ōban* size. Published by Tsutaya Jūzaburō, *ca.* 1783–84. Tokyo National Museum.

Held during the eighth lunar month each year, the Niwaka festival was perhaps the most splendid of the many festivals that took place in the pleasure quarters. Donning their most gorgeous attire, or resplendent in the costumes of the dance comedies to be performed each day, male and female *geisha* formed a procession through the central avenue of the Yoshiwara, stopping to perform at teahouses along the way.

As explained in the text, the prints of this series bear no publisher's seals. However, besides the fact that the prints were done during the Tenmei era (1781–89), in which Utamaro's relationship with Tsutaya was very close, the fact that in the present print a copy of Tsutaya's publication *Yoshiwara saiken*, a guidebook to Yoshiwara, has been tossed onto the floor supports the deduction that this series was indeed a project of Tsutaya's. It is in this series that Utamaro, who had achieved great skill in realistic depiction under the influence of Kiyonaga, began to develop his characteristic, individual style. Surely this was possible because of the support and understanding of Tsutaya Jūzaburō.

3.   *Stylish Amusements of the Four Seasons* (*Shiki asobi hana no iroka*). *Ōban* diptych. Publisher unknown, *ca.* 1783–84. British Museum.

This diptych depicts a group of young Edoites about to embark on a boat ride on the Sumida River. In the print on the right, a young samurai leans against the roof of the excursion boat as he fans himself and wipes the sweat from his chest. Two examples of *kyōka*, one by Yomo no Akara (Ōta Nanpo) and the other by Akera Kankō, decorate his fan. That by Ōta reads as follows:

Haru no yo no	A spring evening,*
Koko hitotoki mo	Here, for even an hour
Senkin ni	A thousand in gold
Kaemashi mono o	It might cost you.
Hana ga sanmon	But a flower is only a few pennies.

The samurai's companion is a beautiful young maiden. Or, is she perhaps a *geisha*? The woman enjoying the coolly refreshing scene through the diaphanous fabric of the male figure's *haori*, judging from the rather subdued pattern of her kimono, seems to be a little older than her two companions. On the left, two women, each wearing something to protect her face from the sun, and a young boy are walking toward the boat along a wooden landing pier. This diptych is an example of Utamaro's relatively early work in the genre of polychrome *ukiyo-e* prints (*nishiki-e*), and the influence of Torii Kiyonaga is still quite pronounced.

*Note by the translator: Here, a clever pun has been made on the word *haru*, which in the Edo period (1600–1867) referred to the erotic pleasures that could be enjoyed in the pleasure quarters as well as to its usual meaning, "spring." Thus, though the flower (*hana*) is as transient as a spring evening, and therefore just as precious, it is a fraction of the cost of a few moments of fleeting sensual pleasure. This poem also employs the technique of *honkadori*, in which the inspiration from a classical *waka* poem becomes that of the new *kyōka*. A spring evening is often associated in classical poetry with a fleeting dream, which may or may not be associated with courtly love.

4.   *The Hedonist*: from the series "Ten Studies in Female Physiognomy" (*Fujin sōgaku juttai: Uwaki no sō*). *Ōban* size. Published by Tsutaya Jūzaburō, *ca.* 1792–93. Tokyo National Museum.

While the word *uwaki* suggests wantonness or promiscuity in modern Japanese, it did not always have that meaning for Utamaro and his contemporaries. Rather, it often referred to a rather flighty, showy character who was apt to dash from one fad to another in pursuit of the most up-to-date styles. Utamaro's effective exploitation of a white mica dust background (*shirokira*) sets off the figure, who is wearing the light garment (*yukata*) donned after a bath, and heightens the effect of subtle colors that wonderfully suggest the texture of a young woman's skin just after a hot bath. In the woman's rather flirtatiously half-open mouth, and the seductive expression of her eyes, Utamaro has captured the essence of a showy, hedonistic young woman of the period. The print offers ample evidence to support Utamaro's claim that he was a physiognomist of feminine types.

The original title of the series, "Female Facial Types of Ten Classes" (*Fujo ninsō juppon*), was changed to the present title before the series was completed.

5.   *A Woman Playing a Poppin*: from the series "Ten Studies in Female Physiognomy" (*Fujin sōgaku juttai: Poppin o fuku onna*). *Ōban* size. Published by Tsutaya Jūzaburō, *ca.* 1792–93. Honolulu Academy of Arts (James A. Michener Collection).

This fresh, carefree beauty was probably the daughter of a prosperous merchant family. This impression is suggested by the bold design of her *furisode*, a garment worn by young unmarried women, in which stylized cherry blossoms are scattered gaily over a bright red checked pattern. She is playing with a *poppin*, a simple glass musical toy that enjoyed great popularity during the Kansei era (1789–1801). Utamaro has marvelously captured her just when she seems about to achieve a more mature, voluptuous beauty but has yet to lose the innocence and unworldliness of childhood.

6. *Painting the Lips* (*Beni-tsuke*). *Ōban* size. Published by Uemura Yohē, *ca.* 1796–97. British Museum.
Kneeling before her toilet, the woman depicted here has just blackened her teeth and is now applying red color (*beni*) to her lips. Judging from the fact that she has blackened her teeth but has not shaved her eyebrows, she might very well be a courtesan. With a mirror held before her inclined body, the woman's pose somehow achieves a fragile balance, suggesting the precariousness of her lot in life. Utamaro has captured the listlessness and the sadness of the scene with extraordinary skill, and these emotions pervade the entire print.

7. *The Widow of Hinodeya*: from the series "Six Famous Beauties Challenge the Magnificence of the Six Poetic Geniuses" (*Kōmei bijin rokkasen: Hinodeya no goke*). *Ōban* size. Published by Ōmiya Gonkurō, *ca.* 1796. Tokyo National Museum.
Utamaro adored the fresh beauty of a woman who had just stepped out of the bath and made it a favorite theme of his prints depicting beautiful women. The widow of Hinodeya was one of the most celebrated beauties of Edo when the print was published. That it is indeed she who is depicted here with shaved eyebrows must be deduced from the "riddle picture" (*hanji-e*) in the upper left-hand corner of the print. The morning sun suggests Hinodeya (literally, "the rising sun shop"), while the *go* board and the clippings of hair (*ke*) together suggest *goke*, or "widow."

The technique of hinting at the identities of the artist's models in such riddle pictures was an ingenious device designed to circumvent a shogunal edict of 1796 (Kansei 8) banning the practice of recording the names of models on the prints themselves. At the same time, of course, the riddle pictures must have enhanced the enjoyment of customers, who were given a new opportunity to test their wits.

8–12. "A Sundial of Maidens" (*Musume hidokei*), a series of five prints. *Ōban* size. Published by Murataya Jirobē, *ca.* 1795–96. Tokyo National Museum.
Although the time period denoted by the Japanese words *toki* or *koku*, or an "hour" in the lunar system, was not precisely two hours in duration, the day was divided into twelve units of roughly two hours each represented by the twelve horary symbols of the lunar calendar. In the series of genre prints entitled "A Sundial of Maidens," Utamaro depicts the daily lives of young women of the townsmen class during each of the "hours" from the Hour of the Dragon (*tatsu no koku*, or 8:00 A.M.) to the Hour of the Monkey (*saru no koku*, 4:00 P.M.). Besides the present series, Utamaro produced another series of prints during the same period, "The Twelve Lunar Hours in the Pleasure Quarters" (*Seirō jūni toki*; pls. 32–43), which depicts the lives of courtesans during each of the twelve "hours" that made up a full day's lunar cycle. One may detect a common element in both series—the artist's determination to capture and depict every aspect of the manners and customs of women he observed in the city of Edo.

In the present series, Utamaro has used an unconventional technique in the omission of outlines for exposed flesh. The swell of breasts and the outlines of noses are suggested by the technique of embossing (*karazuri*), and the models' mouths are only hinted at by splashes of red color (*beni*). Even more daring is Utamaro's treatment of the figures' faces, in which outlines are omitted completely, and the contours of the faces are suggested by effective contrast with the pale yellow backgrounds. This daring experimentation with new techniques succeeds in capturing the fresh beauty of these daughters of the townsmen class without sacrificing the gentle softness of skin textures, and produced work that suggests an image of feminine beauty never before possible in the genre of *ukiyo-e*.

Plate 12. *The Hour of the Dragon* (*Tatsu no koku*; 8:00 A.M.): These two young women have just gotten up, and are admiring some potted morning glories after going out to the garden to wash their faces and brush their teeth.

Plate 8. *The Hour of the Snake* (*Mi no koku*; 10:00 A.M.): In this print, one young lady has just finished the morning housework, and still has her sleeves tucked up as she wipes her hands. Her companion is checking the lines of her freshly arranged coiffure in a hand mirror.

Plate 9. *The Hour of the Horse* (*Uma no koku*; 12:00 noon): The young woman standing on the left is holding a change of clothes under her arm as she wipes water from her ear. The seated figure holds, clenched in her teeth, a small bag filled with bran called a *nukabukuro*, which was used in the bath for scrubbing and stimulating the skin. This print illustrates the custom during this period for young women to take their baths during the Hour of the Horse. An inscription on the print notes, "In ancient times, when women took their baths during the Hour of the Monkey [4:00 P.M.], this scene would have been seen later in the day."

Plate 10. *The Hour of the Ram* (*Hitsuji no koku*; 2:00 P.M.): The attitude assumed by this young woman, leaning lightly against a screen as she smokes, suggests the atmosphere of leisurely tranquility and quiet in a townsman's home during the hours of the early afternoon.

Plate 11. *The Hour of the Monkey* (*Saru no koku*; 4:00 P.M.): This print depicts a young woman in full dress, about to go out for an excursion accompanied by an attendant. Her bright, cheerful expression suggests that perhaps she is on her way to the theater.

13–16. *Hanaōgi of the Ōgiya*; *Takigawa of the Ōgiya*; *Komurasaki of the Tamaya*; *Hanazuma of the Hyōgoya*: from the series "A Collection of Reigning Beauties" (*Tōji zensei bijin zoroe: Ōgiya-uchi Hana*; *Takigawa*; *Tamaya-uchi Komurasaki*; *Hyōgoya-uchi Hanazuma*). *Ōban* size. Published by Wakasaya Yoichi, *ca.* 1794. Tokyo National Museum.
In 1794, Tōshūsai Sharaku, the brilliant artist whose enigmatic career seems to have ended almost as soon as it began, secured the patronage of Tsutaya Jūzaburō and electrified the *ukiyo-e* world with his portraits of Kabuki actors (*yakusha nigao-e*), which were printed in gorgeous editions with mica dust (*kirazuri*) backgrounds. It seems that Utamaro, who by now was well established as the preeminent master of the *bijin-ga*, received a good deal of stimulus from the sudden appearance of this phenomenal artist, who, like himself, had caught the keen critical eye of Tsutaya Jūzaburō. Utamaro almost immediately published a series of *bijin-ga* titled "A Collection of Portraits of Reigning Beauties" (*Tōji zensei nigao zoroe*) that represents a rather clear confession of his competitive feelings toward the new artist. The strong deformation of the figures and daring composition of the prints, in which the figures seem almost too large for the space, as well as the exaggerated movements of, for instance, the figures' hands, may be seen as clear evidence of Sharaku's influence. After Sharaku's departure from the world of *ukiyo-e*, Utamaro, recovering his normal pace, eliminated the word "portrait" (*nigao*) from the series title, replacing it with "beauties" (*bijin*) to give us the title of the series as it is represented on these illustrations.

Four prints from the series, which has ten in all, are reproduced here, each portraying one of the famous courtesans of the equally famous *geisha* houses in the Yoshiwara: Hanaōgi and Takigawa of the Ōgiya, Komurasaki of the Tamaya, and Hanazuma of the Hyōgoya, all of whom were popular during the 1790s.

17–18. *Revealed Love*; *Contemplative Love*: from the series "Great Love Themes of Classical Poetry" (*Kasen koi no bu: Arawaruru koi*; *Mono omou koi*). *Ōban* size. Published by Tsutaya Jūzaburō, *ca.* 1793. Museum of Fine Arts, Boston (Spaulding Collection).
A woman in love reveals her feelings in a transformed expression that is open to even the most casual observer. In classical Japanese poetry, this aspect of feminine love was expressed as a love that "revealed itself in the slightest expression even when the woman does her best to conceal her feelings." The expression, indeed every movement, of the model in *Revealed Love* suggests her happiness as she recalls fleeting moments of love. The use of a fresh, almost transparent blue against a background of mica dust on a pink field (*benikira*) is a beautiful example of Utamaro's ingenuity in the use of backgrounds; and the skillful transformations of the traditional styles of depiction of the face and hands, as well as the model's hair and drapery, are innovations unique to Utamaro's prints in this period.

If I were asked to choose one of Utamaro's prints as his greatest masterpiece, I would select *Contemplative Love* without hesitation. The print is unrivaled among Japanese paintings in the power with which Utamaro has expressed the depth and intensity of his subject's thoughtfulness. Moreover, he has captured a state of mind that is quite different from the contemplation depicted in such Western works as Rodin's "The Thinker." It is characterized by a uniquely Oriental emotional quality that pervades traditional Japanese culture. In Japan, this attitude was called *nasake* or *mono no aware*, often translated as "a refined sense of the sadness of things."

The woman depicted in *Contemplative Love* has shaved her eyebrows, suggesting that she is the young wife of a prosperous merchant. Her expressionless face heightens the effect of her pose, as she listlessly supports the weight of her elaborate coiffure on a delicate hand, giving herself up to thoughts of an impossible love. Perhaps she is recalling a maidenly love that ended with her marriage, or suffering from contemplations of dread and shame because of an ongoing illicit affair.

19–20. *Flower-patterned Cottons at Shirokiya*; *Bold Patterns Now on Sale at Kameya*: from the series "Modern Beauties in Summer Kimono" (*Natsu ishō tōsei bijin*: *Shirokiya shiire no kafu-muki*; *Kameya shiire no ōgata-muki*). *Ōban* size. Published by Izumiya Ichibē, *ca.* 1805. Tokyo National Museum.
These prints are from a series that introduced the new summer fabrics offered by the famous kimono shops of Edo, which besides Kameya and Shirokiya included Echigoya, Matsuzakaya, and Daimaru. In each print, along with the title, is a representation of the cloth banner (*noren*) that hung across the entrance of the shops. Kameya's *noren* features an idealized representation of a turtle (*kame*), which was the shop's trademark. In *Bold Patterns Now on Sale at Kameya*, Utamaro has taken great care to capture the detail of the fabric, in which a bold rope pattern has been achieved by leaving areas of cloth undyed. The woman portrayed here is ideal as a model for kimono, demonstrating the unconscious grace required to keep the lines of her kimono perfect even while she plays with a rowdy child.

Shirokiya opened in the stylish Nihonbashi district of Edo in 1662, and by 1805 was one of the most famous kimono dealers in the city. The flower-patterned cottons (*kafu-muki*) depicted here were a cotton calico fabric decorated with grass and flower designs, usually referred to as *in-kafu* fabrics, or Indian-style cottons. The model is wearing the kimono against her naked skin. It was always one of *ukiyo-e*'s functions to keep stylish Edoites well informed of the latest fashions. Here that function seems to overlap with the explicit advertisement of specific products of famous dealers. The use of colors in these prints is fresh and lucid, and they represent Utamaro's best work in his last fading years.

21. *A Scene on the Bridge and Below It* (*Hashi no ue shita*). *Ōban* size. Published by Ōmiya Gonkurō, *ca.* 1797–98. Tokyo National Museum.
The area along the banks of the Sumida River, which flowed through the eastern section of Edo where many townsmen lived, became the setting for the lively urban culture of the city. Ryōgoku Bridge was the largest of a number of bridges spanning the river, and the six *ōban* prints of this ambitious composition depict the people of Edo enjoying the river's cool evening breezes after a hot summer's day.

On the river beneath the bridge, a group of women in the center of the composition enjoy their *sake* in the roofed cabin of a boat. The women in the unshaded boat have opened their parasol to avoid the hot summer sun. Utamaro, though renowned as a painter of beautiful women, has nevertheless depicted the two boatmen as young, handsome gallants, one reclining atop the roof of the boats, the other standing with pole in hand.

On the bridge above, Utamaro has portrayed a group of tall, beautiful women, their parasols open as they come and go across the bridge, or lean on the railing to take in the scene on the river below. In the extreme upper right, behind the standing woman holding a round fan, can be glimpsed the paraphernalia of a water seller. These peddlers took advantage of the fact that fresh, clean water was scarce in this section of the city, which stood on land reclaimed from the ocean, and brought cool, clear water from distant fresh-water springs. This water, which was slightly sweetened, was especially welcome during the hot days of summer.

The six prints that make up the composition could, of course, be enjoyed singly or together. Arranged with the three scenes on the bridge horizontally above, and the remaining three below, they produce a large, well-designed composition. Indeed, the ingenious conception of the individual prints, and the total composition, is the most striking feature of the work.

22. *Beauties in the Kitchen* (*Daidokoro bijin*). *Ōban* diptych. Published by Uemura Yohē, *ca.* 1795–96. Tokyo National Museum.
This diptych depicts a kitchen scene in the home of a townsman family. In the center of the scene, a large pot for boiling water and a smaller one in which a stew is simmering have been placed in the large hearth, while in the foreground two buckets of water are resting atop a large water barrel. On the right, one young woman is blowing on the coals through a bamboo pipe, and a young girl screws up her face against the smoke as she tries to dip out some hot water. On the left there is a woman peeling an eggplant for the stew, while an older woman dries a lacquer bowl she has just finished washing. The older woman is carrying a small child on her back, and in this print we are able to catch a glimpse of the typical relationship between women and their small children in the Edo period (1600–1867).

As is clear from this work, *ukiyo-e* did not confine themselves to portraits of courtesans or Kabuki actors, or to depictions of the gorgeous manners and customs of the pleasure quarters. Occasionally they produced genre paintings that provide a realistic view of the lives of ordinary Edo townsmen. In Utamaro's case, this seems to have been more a matter of responding to the demands of his publisher, and he also produced a triptych entitled *Needlework* (*Harishigoto*; fig. 18) for Uemura. This work is one of his masterpieces in a distinctive style of genre painting.

23. *Okita, the Teahouse Girl at the Naniwaya* (*Naniwaya Okita*). *Hosoban* size, printed on both sides. Publisher unknown, *ca.* 1793–94. Okazaki Heijirō.
Okita was a waitress at a teahouse (*mizujaya*) called Naniwaya in Asakusa, one of the liveliest districts in Edo. Teahouses like the Naniwaya served hot tea, and provided a stylish atmosphere for a rest during an excursion to one of the temples or famous sight-seeing spots in the district. Okita was neither a courtesan nor a *geisha*, but a daughter of the townsmen class itself, and she was known for her grace and good humor as well as for her beauty. Along with Takashima Ohisa, another teahouse girl (*mizujaya musume*) whose well-known teahouse, Senbeiya, was located in the Ryōgoku district, Okita was one of the famous beauties of the 1790s.

Okita was fifteen years old in 1793, and it is thought that this painting was done at just about that time. She is depicted in a graceful pose as she balances a cup of fine green tea on a serving tray in her left hand and carries a box of smoking utensils in her right, preparing to serve a customer. A special technical feature of the print is that Utamaro has captured Okita's figure from the front on one side of the print and from the rear on the other side, precisely within the same silhouette. Utamaro produced a similar print depicting Okita's rival, Takashima Ohisa, from the front and rear, as she strikes a delicate pose in which she is gently waving a fan. There is a publisher's seal on these prints, but it has not yet been satisfactorily identified.

24–25. *Oiran*; *Teppō*: from the series "Five Dark Shades of Ink in the Northern District" (*Hokkoku goshiki-zumi*: *Oiran*; *Teppō*). *Ōban* size. Published by Isemago, *ca.* 1794–95. Tokyo National Museum and Ōta Memorial Museum of Art.
Located in the northern suburbs of Edo, the Yoshiwara was popularly referred to as the Northern District (or, literally, North Country). One of the difficulties in understanding the customs of the Edo pleasure quarters is that the courtesans were carefully ranked according to their beauty and talents, as well as by the position and wealth of their patrons. This series of five prints is unique in including the lowest-ranking courtesans, who were little more than prostitutes.

Oiran occupied the highest rank among the women depicted in the series and, therefore, the *oiran* in plate 24 is depicted in a pose that suggests her refinement. She has just washed her hair and, before putting it up, checks the tip of her writing brush as she prepares to write a seductive note to an unattentive patron. Her expression as she ponders over her letter seems to suggest the artifice of an accomplished actress in the world of the pleasure quarters rather than the passion of a woman in love.

Of the five courtesans depicted in this series, *geigi* ranked next in beauty and accomplishments to *oiran*. After *geigi*, the conditions of the courtesan's life rapidly become worse with the *kiri no musume*, *kashi*, and *teppō*, who occupied shabby houses along the banks of the canal that ran through the first and second districts of Kyō-machi in the Yoshiwara pleasure quarters.

The origin of the designation *teppō* for the lowest rank of prostitutes gives us an insight into the townsmen culture of that time. *Teppō* was a slang expression for the Japanese variety of puffer fish called *fugu*, which was, and still is, a delicacy among gourmets. Certain of the *fugu*'s organs contained a deadly poison, however, and the gourmet ran the risk of being "shot down," as if by a musket (*teppo*), even when eating a well-prepared fish. Likewise, it was common knowledge that a man who spent time with a lowly *teppo* prostitute ran the risk of contracting venereal disease. The parallels between these two risky pleasures resulted in one of the countless witticisms that characterized the ethos of the townsmen culture. The depiction of this lowly prostitute (pl. 25), her large breasts carelessly exposed and a piece of toilet paper between her teeth, captures all too vividly the sordidness of a woman's life at the bottom of society.

26–28. *The Drunken Courtesan*; *The Lazybones*; *The Hussy*: from the series "The Eyeglasses of a Watchful Parent" (*Kyōkun oya no megane: Namayoi; Gūtarabē; Bakuren*). Ōban size. Published by Tsuruya Kinsuke, *ca.* 1803.
By the early years of the Kansei era (1789–1801), Utamaro had perfected his *ōkubi bijin-ga*, his depictions of only the upper half of the subject's body, and had achieved portrayals of feminine beauty unparalleled in their expression of the unique qualities of women of different ages, classes, and personalities, as well as fleeting mental states. By the time the ten prints in this series were produced, however, Utamaro seems to have pursued his untiring observation of women beyond the expressive limits of painting, and especially of woodblock printing, and it was during this period that he began increasingly to rely on wordy written explanations of his subject's personality and mental state. Despite this indication of Utamaro's frustration at his failure to expand the expressive power of his medium, the prints of this series may be regarded as masterpieces of Utamaro's later years.
In *The Drunken Courtesan* (pl. 26), Utamaro expounds the impropriety of allowing women to drink. The written passage that fills the upper portion of the print records the nonsensical monologue of the hopelessly drunken courtesan, who is holding her cup upside down and is unable to focus her eyes. She has twisted up her mouth and seems to be berating someone but, as the writing attests, she can no longer make anyone understand what she is saying. Despite the intrusive explanation, Utamaro's depiction of a woman helplessly intoxicated retains a good deal of expressive power.
Similarly, in *The Lazybones* (pl. 27), Utamaro has captured a slovenly young woman who is brushing her teeth in her night clothes, having just arisen from bed. Her disheveled coiffure, the loose strands of hair at the nape of her neck, as well as her careless posture and lack of modesty, combine to suggest almost cruelly the character of a lazy woman, neglectful of her person.
In *The Hussy* (pl. 28), Utamaro offers an admonishment for the woman who tends to be a hussy—uncultured, wanton, and careless of others. This woman is quaffing *sake* in an attitude of complete abandon, as she tips the Western-style goblet exposing her right arm almost to her shoulder. Her kimono is open at the neck, and she is holding a whole boiled crab in her left hand. Utamaro's depiction vividly captures the aspect of a wanton, who, in despair of life, has forsaken the reserved modesty demanded of a young Japanese woman who aspires to feminine charm.

29–31. *The Upper Class*; *The Middle Class*; *The Lower Class*: the series "Manners of Young Women of Three Classes" (*Fūzoku sandan musume: Jōbon no zu; Chūbon no zu; Gebon no zu*). Ōban size. Published by Wakasaya Yoichi, *ca.* 1795–96. Tokyo National Museum (pls. 30–31).
The three prints of this series divide the daughters of the townsmen class into upper, middle, and lower orders, depicting their daily lives and manners during the hot summer months, and were designed to be viewed separately or as a triptych.
The two women in *The Upper Class* (pl. 29) might very well be a young woman and her mother. The young woman is holding a round fan and wearing a light silk kimono with long sleeves in the *furisode* style, suggesting that she has not reached the age of adulthood. The older woman, about to play the *koto*, is slipping on finger picks. The box resting on its loosened cloth cover held the finger picks, and the small cage in the foreground is for insects, whose crying voices were considered to be very pleasant in traditional Japan. Appropriately enough for a print depicting the "upper class," they are apparently about to begin a *koto* lesson.
In the print titled *The Middle Class* (pl. 30), two young women are admiring some water rushes that are being carefully cultivated in a beautiful shallow vase. They have taken off their light silk jackets,

which are hanging on the rack behind them, and are clearly at their ease. Their graceful poses and modest expressions suggest the refinement aspired to by women of this class.
In *The Lower Class* (pl. 31), the rather unpretentious life-style of two young women of the lower class is portrayed. One of them has stood up to loosen her *obi*, while the other has opened her kimono to fan herself. The water rushes arranged artlessly in a wooden pail normally used for carrying water seem an appropriate highlight for the relaxed, decidedly pert figures of the two girls, who are at once likable and easy to identify with. The simple composition is highly successful in evoking the pleasure of enjoying a cool evening breeze after a hot summer's day in Edo.

32–43. *The Hour of the Rat* (*Ne no koku*); *The Hour of the Ox* (*Ushi no koku*); *The Hour of the Tiger* (*Tora no koku*); *The Hour of the Hare* (*U no koku*); *The Hour of the Dragon* (*Tatsu no koku*); *The Hour of the Snake* (*Mi no koku*); *The Hour of the Horse* (*Uma no koku*); *The Hour of the Ram* (*Hitsuji no koku*); *The Hour of the Monkey* (*Saru no koku*); *The Hour of the Cock* (*Tori no koku*); *The Hour of the Dog* (*Inu no koku*); *The Hour of the Boar* (*I no koku*): the series "The Twelve Lunar Hours in the Pleasure Quarters" (*Seirō jūni toki*). Ōban size. Published by Tsutaya Jūzaburō, *ca.* 1795–96. Tokyo National Museum (pls. 32–37, 39–41, 43).
As in the series titled "A Sundial of Maidens" (pls. 8–12), this series is arranged according to the twelve horary signs of the lunar calendar. In the present series, Utamaro depicted the aspects of the pleasure quarters and the lives of the courtesans during each of the twelve lunar time periods (of approximately two hours each) between the Hour of the Rat, 12:00 midnight, and the Hour of the Boar, 10:00 P.M., offering glimpses of the pleasure quarters at times when it was closed to customers as well as more familiar scenes. His portrayal of the courtesans as tall, willowy beauties reflects the influence of Chōbunsai Eishi, who had abandoned his career as a counselor to the shogunate to become an *ukiyo-e* artist. This depiction, together with the elegance and grace of the figures' movements and postures, expresses an aspect of the courtesans that is unstained by the essential ugliness and sadness of their profession.

44. *Reading a Letter*: from the series "Utamaro's New Designs for the *Nishiki-e* Print" (*Nishiki-ori Utamaro-gata shinmoyō: Fumiyomi*). Ōban size. Published by Tsuruya Kinsuke, *ca.* 1801–4.
By the beginning of the Kyōwa era (1801–4), Utamaro enjoyed immense popularity in Edo as the unrivaled master of prints of beautiful women (*bijin-ga*), and it was natural that a succession of countless lesser artists attempted to produce imitations of his work. Angered by the appearance of these epigones, Utamaro gave vent to his feelings in a famous colophon that he skillfully worked into the title of this print. In this statement of his intention to produce a series of models representing his inimitable style, one senses an awareness of his own position that borders on arrogance.

> The Azuma *nishiki-e* is one of the famous products of Edo. Recently, however, inferior artists as numerous and insignificant as the leaves of the trees have appeared one after the other. They are really quite like a horde of ants. Relying merely on the lustrous beauty of our red and blue dyes, these imitators produce hideous prints. Lately, these poor imitations are finding their way to places outside Edo, and this can only bring shame to our city. Thus, it is with sadness that I have decided to produce these prints as examples of the true essence of the Edo *bijin-ga* for these pitiful creatures to follow.

The prints of this series do, in fact, represent Utamaro's most daring experiment with unprecedented innovations of his own creation. The outlines of faces are done in vermilion lines, and in his treatment of kimono Utamaro has abandoned the lines produced by brush strokes in traditional Oriental painting, employing delicate techniques of shading to suggest the quality of the material. These innovations were highly successful in capturing the expression of a woman lost in thoughts of love, as well as in suggesting the gentle refinement of her bearing and dress.

Bibliography

Akiyama, Terukazu. *Japanese Painting*. New York: Rizzoli International Publications, 1978.

Chibbett, David. *The History of Japanese Printing and Book Illustration*. Tokyo and New York: Kodansha International, 1977.

Hillier, J. *Japanese Color Prints*. New York: Dutton, 1972.

———. *The Japanese Print: A New Approach*. Rutland, Vt. and Tokyo: Tuttle, 1975.

Keene, Donald. *World Within Walls*. New York: Harper and Row, 1976.

Kikuchi, Sadao. *Utamaro*. Elmsford, N.Y.: Japan Publications, 1976.

Kobayashi, Tadashi. *Ukiyo-e*. Tokyo and New York: Kodansha International, 1982.

Lane, Richard. *Erotica Japonica: Masterworks of Shunga Painting*. Elmsford, N.Y.: Japan Publications, 1978.

———. *Images from the Floating World: The Japanese Print*. New York: Putnam, 1978. .

Lee, Sherman E. *Japanese Decorative Style*. New York: Harper and Row, 1972.

———. *A History of Far Eastern Art*. Rev. ed. Englewood Cliffs, N.J.: Prentice-Hall, 1974.

Michener, James. *The Floating World*. New York: Random House, 1954.

———. *Japanese Prints: From the Early Masters to the Modern*. Rutland, Vt. and Tokyo: Tuttle, 1963.

Narazaki, Muneshige. *The Japanese Print: Its Evolution and Essence*. Tokyo and New York: Kodansha International, 1966.

———. *Kiyonaga*. Masterworks of Ukiyo-e. Tokyo and New York: Kodansha International, 1969.

———, and Kikuchi, Sadao. *Utamaro*. Masterworks of Ukiyo-e. Tokyo and New York: Kodansha International, 1969.

Noma, Seiroku. *The Arts of Japan*. 2 vols. Standard ed. Tokyo and New York: Kodansha International, 1978.

Paine, R.T., and Soper, Alexander. *The Art and Architecture of Japan*. Rev. ed. New York: Penguin, 1975.

Society for the Study of Japonisme, ed. *Japonisme in Art: An International Symposium*. Tokyo and New York: Committee for the Year 2001 and Kodansha International, 1980.

Suzuki, Jūzō. *Sharaku*. Masterworks of Ukiyo-e. Tokyo and New York: Kodansha International, 1969.

———, and Oka, Isaburō. *The Decadents*. Masterworks of Ukiyo-e. Tokyo and New York: Kodansha International, 1969.

Swann, Peter. *A Concise History of Japanese Art*. Rev. ed. of *An Introduction to the Arts of Japan*, 1958. Tokyo and New York: Kodansha International, 1979.

Takahashi, Seiichiro. *Traditional Woodblock Prints of Japan*. Tokyo and New York: Weatherhill, 1972.

Warner, Langdon. *The Enduring Art of Japan*. New York: Grove Press, 1958.

Italian Text

1. *La danza del passero di Yoshiwara*: dalla serie "Danzatori contemporanei di Edo acconciati per la Festa di Niwaka a Yoshiwara" (*Tōsei odoriko zoroe: Yoshiwara suzume*). Formato *ōban*. Edita da Tsutaya Jūzaburō, 1790–91. Tokyo, Museo Nazionale.
Utamaro creò il nuovo genere di *bijin ōkubi-e*, genere che, durante l'epoca di Kansei (1789–1801) accentua i lineamenti del volto e le espressioni dei personaggi, piuttosto che le figure intere. Le stampe in questo nuovo stile pongono contro uno sfondo di polvere di mica chiara la figura a mezzo busto, tecnica chiamata *Kirazuri*. Questa è una delle cinque stampe di una serie che si ritiene essere la prima opera di Utamaro del genere *bijin ōkubi-e*. Ciascuna opera rappresenta una danzatrice dei quartieri di piacere di Yoshiwara nel costume caratteristico di una delle commedie rappresentate durante il festival di Niwaka. Le stampe che fanno parte di questa serie, oltre a quella qui riprodotta, sono *La danza della vergine airone (Sagi musume)*, *La danza della vergine leone (Shakkyō)*, *La danza di Sanbasō (Sanbasō) e la danza del Tempio Dōjōji (Dōjōji)*. La "Danza del passero di Yoshiwara" è ricca di sfumature e allusioni storiche che uniscono, a una versione delicatamente velata delle condizioni nei quartieri di piacere, la famosa storia d'amore di Minamoto no Yoshiie e di Taka no Sei, un tema prediletto sia dal Kabuki sia dalla danza tradizionale. L'uso particolare in Utamaro, di colori smorzati contro uno sfondo luminoso accentua nella stampa l'effetto della composizione ardita.

2. *La danza Ōmando*: dalla serie "Geisha al festival di Niwaka a Yoshiwara" (*Seirō niwaka onna geisha no bu: Ōmando*). Formato *ōban*. Edita da Tsutaya Jūzaburō, 1783–84. Tokyo, Museo Nazionale.
Il festival di Niwaka, che si svolgeva durante l'ottavo mese lunare di ogni anno, era forse il più bello dei tanti festival che avevano luogo nei quartieri di piacere. Adornati con gli abiti più sfarzosi o risplendenti nei costumi delle commedie danzate che si rappresentavano ogni giorno, accompagnatori e *geisha* formavano un corteo che percorreva il viale centrale della Yoshiwara fermandosi per fare spettacolo alle case da té lungo la via.
Come viene precisato nel testo, le stampe che fanno parte di questa serie non portano alcun sigillo dell'editore. Tuttavia, oltre al fatto che appartengono all'epoca Tenmei (1781–89), quando l'amicizia di Utamaro con Tsutaya era molto stretta, il fatto che nella stampa qui riprodotta una copia della pubblicazione di Tsutaya *Yoshiwara saiken*, una guida a Yoshiwara, appare buttata sul pavimento, corrobora la deduzione che questa serie fosse appunto un progetto di Tsutaya. Proprio qui Utamaro, che già sotto l'influenza di Kiyonaga aveva raggiunto una mirabile capacità di rappresentazione realistica, cominciò a sviluppare il proprio stile caratteristico e, senza alcun dubbio, questo fu possibile grazie alla comprensione e partecipazione di Tsutaya Jūzaburō.

3. *Eleganti divertimenti delle quattro stagioni (Shiki asobi hana no iroka)* Dittico *ōban*. Editore ignoto, 1783–84 circa. British Museum.
Il dittico ritrae un gruppo di giovani abitanti di Edo mentre si imbarcano per una gita sul fiume Sumida. Nella stampa a destra, un giovane samurai si appoggia al tetto dell'imbarcazione mentre si fa aria col ventaglio e asciuga il sudore del petto. Due esempi di *kyōka*, uno di Yomo no Akara (Ōta Nanpo) e l'altro di Akera Kankō, decorano il suo ventaglio. Quello di Ōta dice:

Haru no yo no	Una notte di primavera
Koko hitotoki mo	Qui, anche solo per un'ora
Senkin ni	un migliaio, in oro
Kaemashi mono o	può costarti
Hana ga sanmon	ma un fiore solo pochi centesimi.

La dama del samurai è una giovane e bella fanciulla; o, forse una *geisha?* La donna che gode della scena calma, rinfrescante, attraverso il tessuto trasparente dell'*haori* della figura maschile, a giudicare dalla fantasia abbastanza smorzata del kimono sembra essere più vecchia dei suoi compagni. Sulla sinistra, due donne, entrambe con indosso qualcosa che protegge i volti dal sole, e un ragazzo giovane camminano verso la barca lungo un pontile in legno. Questo dittico è un esempio dell'opera di Utamaro fra i primi o quasi nel genere delle stampe *ukiyo-e* policrome (*nishiki-e*) e qui l'influenza di Torii Kiyonaga è ancora molto pronunciata.
Nota del traduttore: Qui la parola *haru* contiene un sottile gioco di parole; nel periodo di Edo (1600–1867) essa si riferiva ai piaceri erotici di cui si poteva godere nei quartieri di piacere e, allo stesso tempo, aveva il significato usuale di "primavera". Quindi, benché il fiore (*hana*) abbia durata tanto breve quanto quella di una notte di primavera, e quindi sia allo stesso modo prezioso, esso costa infinitamente meno di pochi minuti d'amore fuggevole. Questa poesia usa inoltre la tecnica di *honkadori* dove l'ispirazione di una *waka* classica diviene quella di una nuova *kyōka*. Una notte di primavera, nella poesia classica, viene sovente associata a un sogno fuggevole che, a sua volta, può o meno venir associato a un raffinato amore di corte.

4. *L'edonista*: dalla serie "Dieci studi di fisionomia femminile" (*Fujin sōgaku juttai: Uwaki no sō*). Formato *ōban*. Edita da Tsutaya Jūzaburō, 1792–93 circa. Tokyo, Museo Nazionale.
Mentre nel moderno Giappone il termine *uwaki* suggerisce dissolutezza e promiscuità, per Utamaro e i suoi contemporanei non sempre aveva lo stesso significato. Se mai, è riferito sovente a caratteri piuttosto volubili e vistosi capaci di passare da un entusiasmo all'altro sempre alla ricerca degli stili più in voga. L'uso che Utamaro fa del fondo di polvere di mica bianca (*shirokira*) è estremamente efficace, stagliando la figura che porta l'indumento chiaro (*yukata*) indossato dopo il bagno e accentuando l'effetto dei colori tenui che mirabilmente suggeriscono la finezza dell'incarnato di una giovane donna subito dopo un bagno caldo. Nella bocca della donna, socchiusa e sensuale, e nell'espressione seducente degli occhi Utamaro ha colto l'essenza della giovane donna vanitosa e amante dei piaceri di quel periodo. Per questo la stampa offre argomenti evidenti alla pretesa di Utamaro di definirsi fisionomista di tipi femminili.
Il titolo originale "Tipi di volti femminili di dieci classi" (*Fujo ninsō juppon*) fu cambiato nel titolo attuale prima che la serie venisse completata.

5. *Donna che gioca con un Poppin*: dalla serie "Dieci studi di fisionomia femminile" (*Fujin sōgaku juttai: Poppin o fuku onna*) Formato *ōban*. Edita da Tsutaya Jūzaburō, 1792–93. Honolulu Academy of Art.
Questa bellezza fresca, spensierata era probabilmente la figlia di un ricco mercante. L'impressione è suggerita dal disegno marcato del suo *furisode*, un indumento indossato da giovani donne non maritate, dove fiori di ciliegio stilizzati si distribuiscono vivacemente su una fantasia a scacchi rosso brillanti. Sta giocando con un *poppin*, un semplice gioco musicale in vetro che ebbe grande popolarità all'epoca Kansei (1789–1801). Utamaro ha colto in modo magistrale la giovane mentre sembra sul punto di aprirsi a una bellezza più matura e sensuale, ma ancora non ha perduto l'innocenza e l'immaterialità della fanciullezza.

6. *Dipingendo le labbra (Beni-tsuke)*. Formato *ōban*. Edita da Uemura Yohei, 1796–97.
Inginocchiata davanti alla toeletta, la donna qui ritratta si è appena anneriti i denti e sta per colorare di rosso (*beni*) le labbra. A giudicare dal fatto che i suoi denti sono anneriti ma le sopracciglia non sono

rasate, può verosimilmente trattarsi di una cortigiana. Collo specchio davanti al corpo inclinato, la posa della donna raggiunge in qualche modo un equilibrio fragile che suggerisce la precarietà di tutto ciò che la vita le offre in questo momento. Utamaro ha colto la svogliatezza e la tristezza della scena con straordinaria maestria, e questi sentimenti pervadono tutta la stampa.

7. *La vedova di Hinodeya:* dalla serie "Sei famose beltà sfidano la magnificenza dei Sei Geni Poetici" (*Kōmei bijin rokkasen: Hinodeya no goke*). Formato *ōban.* Edita da Ōmiya Gonkurō, 1796. Tokyo, Museo Nazionale.
Utamaro amava la fresca bellezza della donna appena uscita dal bagno e ne ha fatto uno dei temi favoriti delle sue rappresentazioni di bellezza femminile. La vedova di Hinodeya era una delle più celebrate bellezze di Edo quando la stampa fu edita. Che senza dubbio qui sia ritratta lei, con le sopracciglia rasate, deve dedursi dall'"immagine indovinello" (*hanji-e*) nell'angolo in alto a sinistra della stampa. Il sole del mattino allude a Hinodeya (letteralmente "il negozio del sole nascente") mentre il *go* abbandonato e la rasatura dei capelli (*ke*) insieme suggeriscono *goke,* cioè vedova.
La tecnica di fare allusione all'identità della modella dell'artista con queste immagini-indovinello era uno stratagemma ingegnoso per aggirare un editto shogunale del 1796 (Kansei 8) che bandiva l'uso di indicare sulle stampe i nomi delle modelle. Allo stesso tempo, naturalmente, le immagini-indovinello devono aver aumentato il divertimento dei clienti, che avevano così una nuova opportunità di saggiare il proprio intuito.

8–12. "Una meridiana di fanciulle" (*Musume hidokei*), serie di cinque stampe. Formato *ōban.* Edita da Murataya Jirobē, 1795–96 circa. Tokyo, Museo Nazionale.
Benché il periodo di tempo indicato dai termini giapponesi *toki* o *koku,* cioè "ora" nel sistema lunare, non durasse esattamente due ore, il giorno era suddiviso in dodici unità approssimativamente di due ore ciascuna, rappresentate dai dodici simboli orari del calendario lunare. Nella serie di stampe di genere intitolata "Una meridiana di fanciulle", Utamaro descrive la vita quotidiana di giovani donne della classe cittadina in ciascuna "ora", da quella del "Dragone" (*tatsu no koku,* le 8) a quella della "Scimmia" (*saru no koku,* le 16). Accanto a questa serie, Utamaro, nello stesso periodo, ne produsse un'altra: "Le dodici ore lunari nei quartieri di piacere" (*Seirō jūni toki;* tavole 32–43) che ritrae la vita delle cortigiane durante ciascuna delle dodici "ore" che compongono il ciclo completo del giorno lunare. In entrambe le serie si può ritrovare un elemento comune, la determinazione dell'artista a cogliere e descrivere ogni aspetto degli usi e dei costumi femminili da lui osservati nella città di Edo.
Nella serie qui riprodotta, Utamaro usa una tecnica non convenzionale che consiste nell'omettere i contorni delle parti in vista della figura e del volto. Il volume dei seni e il profilo del naso sono suggeriti attraverso la tecnica del risalto (*karazuri*) e le bocche delle modelle sono accennate soltanto con macchie di colore rosso (*beni*). Ancora più ardito è il modo di Utamaro di trattare i volti dei suoi personaggi, dove i profili sono completamente scomparsi e i contorni sono suggeriti dall'efficace contrasto con lo sfondo giallo pallido. La sperimentazione audace di nuove tecniche permette di cogliere efficacemente la fresca bellezza di queste figlie della classe cittadina senza sacrificare la morbidezza dell'incarnato e un'immagine di bellezza femminile fin'allora impossibile nel genere degli *ukiyo-e.*
Tavola 12. *L'Ora del Dragone* (*Tatsu no koku;* le 8): Le due giovani donne che vi compaiono si sono appena levate e, dopo essere uscite in giardino per lavarsi viso e denti, stanno ammirando alcune "glorie del mattino" (convolvoli) raccolte in un vaso.
Tavola 8. *L'Ora del Serpente* (*Mi no koku;* le 10): In questa stampa una giovane dama ha appena terminato i lavori domestici del mattino e le sue maniche sono ancora rimboccate mentre si asciuga le mani. La sua compagna controlla nello specchio a mano la linea della propria pettinatura appena acconciata.
Tavola 9. *L'Ora del Cavallo* (*Uma no koku;* mezzogiorno, le 12): La giovane donna in piedi sulla sinistra, stringe sotto il braccio un cambio d'abiti mentre si asciuga l'acqua dall'orecchio. La donna seduta tiene, serrandola saldamente fra i denti, una piccola borsa colma di crusca chiamata *nukabukuro,* che veniva usata nel bagno per strofinare e tonificare la pelle. Questa stampa descrive l'uso delle donne, in voga in questo periodo, di prendere il bagno durante l'Ora del Cavallo. Un'iscrizione sulla stampa annota: "In tempi antichi, quando le donne prendevano il bagno durante l'Ora della Scimmia (le 16), questa scena si sarebbe vista più tardi nella giornata."

Tavola 10. *L'Ora dell'Ariete* (*Hitsuji no koku;* le 14): L'atteggiamento assunto da questa giovane donna, che fuma appoggiata delicatamente contro un paravento, suggerisce l'atmosfera di tranquillità lenta e di pace della casa cittadina durante le ore del primo pomeriggio.
Tavola 11. *L'Ora della Scimmia* (*Saru no koku;* le 16): Questa stampa ritrae una giovane donna, completamente abbigliata, in procinto di uscire, accompagnata da un servitore. La sua espressione vivace e allegra lascia supporre che stia forse per recarsi a teatro.

13–16. *Hanaōgi della Ōgiya; Takigawa della Ōgiya; Komurasaki della Tamaya; Hanazuma della Hyōgoya:* dalla serie "Collezione di beltà d'oggi all'apice della fama" (*Tōji zensei bijin zoroe: Ōgiya-uchi Hana; Takigawa Tamaya-uchi Komurasaki; Hyōgoya uchi Hanazuma*). Formato *ōban.* Edita da Wakasaya Yoichi, 1794. Tokyo, Museo Nazionale.
Nel 1794, Tōshūsai Sharaku, il brillante artista la cui enigmatica carriera sembra avere avuto fine quasi subito dopo essere cominciata, ottenne la protezione dell'editore Tsutaya Jūzaburō e elettrizzò il mondo dell'*ukiyo-e* con i suoi ritratti di attori del *Kabuki* (*Yakusha nigao-e*) che venivano stampati in edizioni sfolgoranti con sfondi di polvere di mica (*kirazuri*). Sembra che Utamaro, che già si era imposto come il miglior maestro dei *bijin-ga,* abbia ricevuto un forte stimolo dall'apparire improvviso di questo prodigioso artista, come lui stesso, aveva colpito l'acuto occhio critico di Tsutaya Jūzaburō. Utamaro quasi subito pubblicò una serie di *bijin-ga* intitolata "Collezione di ritratti di beltà all'apice della fama" (*Tōji zensei nigao-zoroe*) dove si rivelano abbastanza chiaramente i suoi sentimenti di competitività verso il nuovo artista. La forte distorsione delle figure e la composizione audace delle stampe, dove le figure sembrano quasi troppo grandi rispetto allo spazio, come pure l'esagerazione dei movimenti, ad esempio quella delle mani dei personaggi, possono essere visti come chiara evidenza dell'influenza di Sharaku. Dopo la scomparsa di Sharaku dal mondo degli *ukiyo-e* Utamaro, ritrovato il ritmo di sempre, eliminò il termine "ritratto" (*nigao*) dal titolo della serie, sostituendolo con "beltà" (*bijin*) lasciandoci il titolo della serie come è presentato in queste illustrazioni.
Sono qui riprodotte quattro stampe della serie che si compone di dieci: ciascuna rappresenta una nota cortigiana delle altrettanto note case di *geisha* della Yoshiwara: Hanaōgi e Takigawa della Ōgiya, Komurasaki della Tamaya e Hanazuma della Hyōgoya, tutte famose durante gli anni 1790.

17–18. *Amore svelato; Amore contemplativo:* dalla serie "Grandi temi d'amore della poesia classica" (*Kasen koi no bu: Arawaruru koi; Mono omou koi*). Formato *ōban.* Edita da Tsutaya Jūzaburō, 1793 circa. Museum of Fine Arts, Boston (Collezione Spaulding)
Una donna innamorata rivela i propri sentimenti attraverso un'espressione mutata che si palesa anche all'osservatore più distratto. Nella poesia giapponese classica questo aspetto dell'amore femminile veniva espresso come amore che "rivela se stesso nell'espressione più sottile anche quando la donna fa di tutto per nascondere i propri sentimenti". L'espressione, ma ancor più ogni movimento della modella suggeriscono in *Amore svelato* la sua felicità mentre richiama fugaci attimi d'amore. L'uso di un tono di blu fresco, quasi trasparente, contro lo sfondo di polvere di mica in campo rosa (*benikira*) è uno stupendo esempio dell'ingegno di Utamaro nell'uso degli sfondi, e l'abilissima trasformazione dei modi tradizionali di ritrarre il volto e le mani come pure i capelli della modella e i drappeggi sono innovazioni uniche nelle stampe di Utamaro di questo periodo.
Se mi fosse chiesto di scegliere una fra tutte le stampe di Utamaro come il suo maggior capolavoro, sceglierei senza esitazione *Amore contemplativo.* La stampa non ha paragone in tutta la pittura giapponese per la forza con cui Utamaro ha espresso la profondità e l'intensità del raccoglimento del suo personaggio. Inoltre egli ha colto uno stato d'animo che è del tutto differente dalla contemplazione espressa in opere occidentali quali "Il pensatore" di Rodin; esso è caratterizzato da una qualità di emozione esclusivamente orientale che permea tutta la cultura giapponese tradizionale. In Giappone questo atteggiamento veniva chiamato *nasake* o *mono no aware* spesso tradotto con "il senso raffinato della tristezza delle cose".
La donna ritratta in *Amore contemplativo* porta le sopracciglia rasate e questo suggerisce che si tratta della giovane sposa di un ricco mercante. Il volto privo di espressione accentua l'effetto della posa, mentre svogliatamente sostiene con la mano delicata il peso dell'acconciatura composita, abbandonandosi al pensiero d'un amore impossibile. Forse sta ricordando un amore di gioventù finito col matrimonio, o sta soffrendo di timore e vergogna per il protrarsi di una relazione illecita.

19–20. *Audaci fantasie da poco in vendita da Kameya; Cotoni a fantasie floreali da Shirokiya:* dalla serie "Bellezze moderne in kimono estivi" (*Natsu ishō tōsei bijin: Kameya shiire no ōgata-muki; Shirokiya shiire no kafu-muki*). Formato *ōban*. Edita da Isumiya Ichibē, 1805 circa. Tokyo, Museo Nazionale.

Queste stampe fanno parte di una serie che presentava i nuovi tessuti estivi offerti dai più noti negozi di kimono di Edo che, oltre a Kameya e Shirokiya comprendevano Echigoya, Matsuzakaya e Daimaru. In ogni stampa è rappresentata,. accanto al titolo, l'insegna (*noren*) appesa sull'entrata dei negozi. La *noren* di Kameya rappresenta una tartaruga stilizzata (*kame*), che era anche il marchio di fabbrica del negozio. In *Audaci fantasie da poco in vendita da Kameya* Utamaro pone particolare cura nella descrizione dei dettagli del tessuto dove l'originale fantasia di una fune è stata ottenuta lasciando senza tintura zone di tessuto. La donna qui ritratta è una modella ideale per kimono, dimostrando la naturale grazia che si richiede perché le linee del kimono siano perfette anche mentre gioca con un bimbo vivace.

Shirokiya cominciò a Nihonbashi, l'elegante distretto di Edo, nel 1662 e nel 1805 era uno dei più famosi negozi di kimono di tutta la città. I cotoni a fantasia floreale (*kafu-muki*) qui descritti erano tessuti di cotone stampato, decorati con disegni di erbe e di fiori che solitamente si definivano *in-kafu*, cioè cotoni di stile indiano. La modella indossa il kimono sulla pelle nuda. Una delle funzioni delle *ukiyo-e* è sempre stata quella di tenere al corrente gli eleganti abitanti di Edo, degli ultimi indirizzi della moda. Qui questa funzione sembra sovrapporsi all'esplicito annuncio di capi specifici offerti da negozi di grido. L'uso dei colori è in queste stampe fresco e brillante costituendo la migliore produzione di Utamaro nei suoi ultimi anni ormai sbiaditi.

21. *Scena sopra e sotto il ponte (Hashi no ue shita).* Formato *ōban*. Edita da Ōmiya Gonkurō, 1797–98 circa. Tokyo, Museo Nazionale.

L'area lungo le sponde del fiume Sumida, che scorreva attraverso la zona orientale di Edo dove erano concentrate le abitazioni di molti cittadini, diventò il centro della cultura vivace cittadina. Il ponte Ryōgoku era il più grande dei vari ponti che si stendevano attraverso il fiume e le sei stampe *ōban* di quest'ambiziosa composizione rappresentano la gente di Edo mentre gode gli aliti della fresca brezza serale del fiume, dopo una calda giornata d'estate. Sul fiume, sotto il ponte, un gruppo di donne al centro della composizione, assapora il *sake* nella coperta d'una imbarcazione. Le donne sulla barca priva di riparo hanno i parasoli per proteggersi dal caldo sole estivo. Utamaro, benché rinomato come pittore di bellezze femminili ha tuttavia ritratto i barcaioli come due giovani bellissimi, l'uno adagiato in cima al tetto della barca, l'altro in piedi mentre regge il timone.

Sul ponte Utamaro ha ritratto un gruppo di alte, bellissime dame con i parasoli aperti mentre vanno su e giù o si affacciano al parapetto per osservare la scena sul fiume sottostante. Nella parte più alta a destra, dietro la donna in piedi con il ventaglio rotondo si possono scorgere le attrezzature d'un acquaiolo. Questi piccoli venditori traevano vantaggio dal fatto che in questa zona della città, che si ergeva su una terra strappata all'oceano, l'acqua fresca e pulita era scarsa, e ne portavano di chiara e fredda da lontane sorgenti. Quest'acqua, che veniva leggermente addolcita, era particolarmente gradita durante le afose giornate d'estate. Ciascuna delle sei stampe che formano l'intera composizione, com'è naturale può essere apprezzata singolarmente o insieme con le altre. Le tre scene che si svolgono sopra il ponte e le tre sotto, accostate le une sopra le altre, si uniscono a comporre una visione ampia e ben disegnata. Proprio la concezione ingegnosa delle singole stampe e la composizione nella sua unità rappresentano gli elementi che più colpiscono dell'intera opera.

22. *Beltà in cucina (Daidokoro bijin).* Dittico *ōban*. Edito da Uemura Yohē, 1795–96 circa. Tokyo, Museo Nazionale.

Il dittico qui riprodotto descrive una scena nella cucina di una famiglia di cittadini. Al centro della scena, una grande pentola per far bollire l'acqua e una più piccola dove sobbolle un intingolo sono state poste sull'ampio focolare, mentre in primo piano due secchie d'acqua stanno appoggiate su una grande botte d'acqua. A destra, una giovane donna sta soffiando sui carboni con una canna di bambù e una fanciulla distoglie il volto dal vapore mentre cerca di attingere acqua calda. A sinistra, una donna sta pelando una melanzana per l'intingolo, mentre una più vecchia asciuga una ciotola laccata che ha appena finito di lavare. La donna più anziana porta un bimbo adagiato sulla schiena: questa stampa ci offre così la possibilità di dare un'occhiata al particolare mondo dei rapporti fra donne e i loro figli piccoli nel periodo di Edo (1600–1867).

Come compare chiaramente da quest'opera gli *ukiyo-e* non si limitano a ritrarre cortigiane o attori del *Kabuki* o a descrivere i fantasmagorici usi dei quartieri di piacere. A volte si realizzavano pitture di genere che permettevano uno sguardo realistico sulla vita usuale dei cittadini di Edo. Nel caso di Utamaro, questo sembra essere stato piuttosto un modo di assecondare i desideri del suo editore: per Uemura egli realizzò infatti anche il trittico intitolato *Ricamo* (*Harishigoto;* tavola 17). Quest'opera è uno dei suoi capolavori in uno stile particolare della pittura di genere.

23. *Okita, la ragazza della casa de tè a Naniwaya (Naniwaya Okita).* Formato *hosoban*, stampata su entrambe le facce. Editore ignoto, 1793–94 circa. Okazaki Heijirō.

Okita era una cameriera presso la casa da tè (*mizu cheya*) Naniwaya a Asakusa, uno dei più brillanti distretti di Edo. Le case da té, come Naniwaya, servivano tè caldo e offrivano un'elegante atmosfera di riposo durante l'escursione a uno dei templi o durante la visita ai monumenti del distretto. Okita non era né una cortigiana né una *geisha*, ma essa stessa figlia della classe cittadina ed era conosciuta per la grazia e il buonumore come per la bellezza. Insieme con Takashima Ohisa, un'altra ragazza che lavorava nella famosa casa da tè Senbaiya nel distretto di Ryōgoku, Okita era una delle bellezze più celebri dell'era Kansei (1789–1801).

Nel 1793 Okita aveva quindici anni e si pensa che questo dipinto appartenga proprio a quell'anno. Ella à rappresentata in una posa ricca di grazia mentre colla mano sinistra regge in equilibrio su un vassoio una tazza di raffinato tè verde e colla destra porta un servizio da fumo, apprestandosi a servire un cliente. Una caratteristica tecnica particolare della stampa è che Utamaro ha ripreso Okita di fronte da una parte della stampa e da dietro sul verso, esattamente all'interno della stessa silhouette. Utamaro eseguì una stampa analoga che ritrae la rivale di Okita, Takashima Ohisa, di fronte e di spalle in una posa gentile mentre sta facendo ondeggiare delicatamente un ventaglio. Queste stampe sono marcate con il sigillo di un editore che però non è stato ancora identificato con certezza.

24–25. *Oiran; Teppō:* dalla serie "Cinque sfumature scure di inchiostro nel distretto del Nord" (*Hokkoku goshiki-zumi: Oiran; Teppō*). Formato *ōban*. Edita da Isemago 1794–95 circa.

Situato nei sobborghi a nord di Edo, il quartiere di Yoshiwara era comunemente noto come il Distretto del Nord (o, letteralmente, Borgo del Nord). Uno degli aspetti che rendono di difficile comprensione i costumi dei quartieri di piacere di Edo è che le cortigiane erano accuratamente classificate sia per bellezza e talento sia per posizione e ricchezza dei protettori. Questa serie di cinque stampe è la sola a includere le cortigiane di più basso rango, che erano poco più che prostitute.

Tra le donne dipinte in questa serie, le *oiran* occupavano il rango più elevato e, perciò, quella della tavola 24 è ritratta in una posa che rivela la sua raffinatezza. Si è appena lavata i capelli e, prima di raccoglierli, controlla la punta del pennello mentre si prepara a scrivere un biglietto di richiamo a un protettore disattento. La sua espressione, mentre riflette sulla lettera, sembra rivelare più l'artificio di un abile attore nel mondo dei quartieri di piacere che non la passione di una donna innamorata.

Delle cinque cortigiane rappresentate nella serie, le *geigi* vengono subito dopo le *oiran* per bellezza e talento. Dopo le *geigi*, le condizioni di vita delle cortigiane peggiorano notevolmente con le *kiri no musume*, le *kashi* e le *teppō*, che occupavano abitazioni malconce lungo gli argini del canale che percorre il primo e il secondo distretto di Kyō-machi nei quartieri di piacere del Yoshiwara.

L'origine del termine *teppō* per designare il rango più basso delle prostitute ci permette una sguardo nella cultura cittadina del tempo. *Teppō* è un'espressione colloquiale che si riferisce a una varietà giapponese di pesce chiamata *fugu:* questo era, ed è ancora una delicatezza per i buongustai. Tuttavia, certi organi del *fugu* contengono un veleno mortale, e il buongustaio, quando mangia uno di questi pesci, anche se accuratamente preparato, va incontro al rischio di essere "colpito" come da un moschetto (*teppō*). Allo stesso modo, era luogo comune che passando del tempo in compagnia delle modeste prostitute *teppō*, un uomo corresse il rischio di contrarre una malattia venerea. Il parallelo tra questi due rischiosi piaceri nasce da una delle innumerevoli battute di spirito che caratterizzano il costume della cultura cittadina. Il ritratto di questa modesta prostituta (tavola 25) col grande seno trasandatamente messo in mostra e un pezzo di salvietta di carta tra i denti, coglie fin troppo vividamente lo squallore della vita delle donne di infimo rango.

26–28. *La Cortigiana ebbra; I fannulloni; La sfacciata:* dalla serie "Gli occhiali di un genitore attento" (*Kyōkun oya no megane; Gutarabē; Namayoi; Bakuren*). Formato *ōban.* Edita da Tsuruya Kinsuke, 1803 circa.
Nei primi anni dell'epoca Kansei (1789–1801), Utamaro perfezionò il suo *okibi bijin-ga,* cioè la rappresentazione della sola metà superiore della figura della modella, e compose ritratti di beltà femminili senza paragone nell'esprimere le caratteristiche peculiari di donne d'età, classe e temperamento diversi, come pure i fuggevoli stati d'animo. All'epoca in cui furono riprodotte le dieci stampe di questa serie perciò Utamaro sembra aver spinto la sua infaticabile osservazione della donna oltre i limiti espressivi della pittura, e in particolare della stampa con matrici lignee e proprio in questo periodo Utamaro cominciò ad affidare sempre più allo scritto la spiegazione della personalità e dello stato d'animo del suo personaggio. Nonostante questo indichi la frustrazione di Utamaro per l'impotenza a espandere le possibilità espressive del suo mezzo, le stampe di questa serie possono essere considerate fra i capolavori degli ultimi anni dell'artista.

Ne *La Cortigiana ebbra* (tavola 26), Utamaro mostra quanto sia sconveniente lasciar bere le donne. Il brano scritto che riempie la parte alta della stampa riporta il monologo privo di senso della cortigiana irrimediabilmente dedita all'alcool che tiene in mano la tazza rovesciata, incapace di mettere a fuoco lo sguardo. La sua bocca è distorta quasi stesse sgridando qualcuno ma, come il monologo dimostra, più nessuno può capire quello che sta dicendo. Nonostante la spiegazione inopportuna, l'immagine che Utamaro offre di una donna intossicata senza speranza è carica di notevole forza espressiva.

Allo stesso modo ne *I fannulloni* (tavola 27) Utamaro ha colto la trascuratezza di una giovane donna appena levatasi dal letto mentre, ancora in abbigliamento da notte, si lava i denti. L'acconciatura scarmigliata, ciocche di capelli disciolte alla nuca, come pure la posa trascurata e la mancanza di riserbo si fondono suggerendo in modo alquanto crudo il carattere di una donna indolente priva di cura per la propria persona.

Ne *La sfacciata* (Tavola 28) Utamaro esprime un ammonimento per la donna che tende a essere impertinente, incolta, frivola e incapace di attenzione per gli altri. La donna qui rappresentata sta tracannando del *sake* in atteggiamento di completa rilassatezza e regge la coppa in stile occidentale mostrando il braccio destro fin quasi alla spalla. Il suo kimono lascia scoperto il collo, e la mano sinistra tiene un intero granchio bollito. Il ritratto di Utamaro coglie con lucidità l'aspetto di una libertina che, disperata della vita, ha dimenticato il riserbo e la modestia richieste a una giovane giapponese che aspiri al fascino femminile.

29–31. *La classe alta; La classe media; La classe inferiore:* dalla serie "Atteggiamenti di giovani donne di tre classi" (*Fūzoku sandan musume: Jōbon no zu; Chūbon no zu; Gebon no zu*). Formato *ōban.* Edita da Wakasaya Yoichi, 1795–96 circa. Tokyo, Museo Nazionale.
Le tre stampe di questa serie dividono le ragazze della classe dei cittadini in alto, medio e basso ceto, rappresentando la loro vita quotidiana e gli atteggiamenti nei mesi della calda estate; sono state disegnate per essere guardate sia separatamente sia come trittico.

Le due donne de *La classe alta* (tavola 29) possono senz'altro essere una giovane e sua madre. La giovane regge un ventaglio tondo e indossa un kimono di seta chiara con lunghe maniche stile *furisode:* questo lascia intendere che non ha ancora raggiunto l'età adulta. La donna più matura sta suonando il *koto* e arpeggia coi plettri. L'astuccio appoggiato sul tessuto per ricoprire lo strumento contiene i plettri e la piccola gabbia in primo piano è per insetti le cui voci lamentose erano ritenute estremamente piacevoli nel Giaponne tradizionale. Come conviene a una stampa che rappresenta "la classe alta" stanno, sembra, per iniziare una lezione di *koto.*

Nella stampa intitolata *La classe media* (tavola 30), due giovani donne stanno ammirando alcuni giunchi coltivati con estrema cura in un bel vaso poco profondo. Hanno tolto le giacche di seta chiara che stanno appese sulla grata dietro di loro e sono chiaramente a loro agio. Le pose graziose e le espressioni riservate suggeriscono la raffinatezza che emana da donne di questo ceto.

Ne *La classe inferiore* (tavola 31) è rappresentato lo stile di vita piuttosto privo di pretese di due giovani donne del ceto inferiore. Una di esse si è alzata in piedi per sciogliere l'*obi,* mentre l'altra ha aperto il kimono per farsi aria col ventaglio. I giunchi accomodati senz'arte in una secchia di legno di quelle normalmente usate per trasportare l'acqua sembrano un'allusione appropriata alle figure rilassate e decisamente insolenti delle due ragazze, che subito gli si possono assimilare agevolmente. La composizione semplice è particolarmente efficace nell'evocare il piacevole godimento della brezza serale dopo una calda giornata d'estate a Edo.

32–43. *L'Ora del Topo (Ne no koku); L'ora del Bue (Ushi no koku); L'ora della Tigre (Tora no koku); L'ora della Lepre (U no koku); L'ora del Dragone (Tatsu no koku); L'ora del Serpente (Mi no koku); L'ora del Cavallo (Uma no koku); L'ora dell'Ariete (Hitsuji no koku); L'ora della Scimmia (Saru no koku); L'ora del Gallo (Tori no koku); L'ora del Cane (Inu no koku); L'ora dell'Orso (I no koku):* dalla serie "Dodici ore lunari nei quartieri di piacere" (*Seirō jūni toki*). Formato *ōban.* Edita da Tsutaya Jūzaburō, 1795–96 circa. Tokyo, Museo Nazionale.
Come la serie intitolata "Una meridiana di fanciulle" (tavole 8–12) questa si articola secondo i dodici simboli orari del calendario lunare. Qui Utamaro ha dipinto gli aspetti dei quartieri di piacere e la vita delle cortigiane durante ciascuno dei dodici periodi del giorno lunare di due ore ciascuno, approssimativamente tra l'ora del Topo, le 24 mezzanotte, e l'ora dell'Orso, le 22, offrendo sia squarci dei quartieri di piacere in vari momenti, quando erano chiusi ai clienti, sia scene più familiari. I suoi ritratti di cortigiane, come bellezze alte e flessuose riflette l'influenza di Chōbunsai Eishi che aveva abbandonato la carriera di consigliere dello shogunato per diventare artista di *ukiyo-e.* Questa panoramica insieme con l'eleganza e la grazia dei movimenti e delle pose delle figure ritrae un aspetto delle cortigiane per nulla intaccato dall'essenziale squallidità e tristezza della loro professione.

44. *Leggendo una lettera:* dalla serie "Nuovi disegni di Utamaro per la stampa *Nishiki-e*" (*Nishiki-ori Utamaro-gata shinmoyō: Fumiyomi*). Formato *ōban.* Edita da Tsuruya Kinsuke, 1801–4 circa.
All'inizio dell'era Kyōwa (1801–4), Utamaro godette a Edo di immensa fama come maestro senza rivali nelle stampe di bellezze femminili (*bijin ga*), ed è naturale che uno stuolo di artisti minori cercasse di imitare le sue opere. Irritato per l'apparire di questi epigoni, Utamaro diede sfogo ai suoi sentimenti in un celebre colophon che insinuò abilmente nel titolo di questa stampa. In questa proclamazione dell'intento di realizzare una serie di modelli che rappresentassero il suo stile inimitabile, si percepisce una consapevolezza della sua posizione che sfiora l'arroganza.

La *nishiki-e* di Azuma è una delle famose produzioni di Edo. Recentemente, tuttavia, artisti di inferiore talento, tanto numerosi e insignificanti quanto le foglie degli alberi, sono apparsi uno dopo l'altro. Essi rassomigliano a un'orda di formiche. Facendo affidamento solo sulla bellezza lucente dei nostri rossi e blu, questi imitatori producono stampe orrende. Poi queste disgraziate imitazioni cercano una sistemazione fuori Edo, e ciò può arrecare solo vergogna alla nostra città. Perciò, è con tristezza che ho deciso di realizzare queste stampe con esempi dell'essenza autentica del *bijin-ga* in modo che vengano seguiti da questi penosi individui.

Le stampe di questa serie rappresentano infatti il più audace esperimento di Utamaro, con innovazioni senza precedenti di sua invenzione. I contorni delle figure sono dati con linee vermiglie e nel modo di trattare i kimono Utamaro abbandona le linee eseguite con tratti di pennello, cari alla pittura orientale tradizionale, per usare delicate tecniche di ombreggiatura che evochino la qualità della materia. Queste innovazioni permisero di cogliere con estrema sensibilità l'espressione di una donna perduta in pensieri d'amore come pure di suggerire la raffinatezza squisita del portamento e dell'abito.

French Text

1. *La danse des passereaux d'Yoshiwara*: appartenant à la série "Danseurs d'Edo contemporains parés pour le festival de Niwaka à Yoshiwara" (*Tōsei odoriko zoroe: Yoshiwara suzume*). Format *Ōban*. Publiée par Tsutaya Jūzaburō, vers 1790–91. Musée national de Tokyo.
Durant la période Kansei (1789–1801), Outamaro créa un nouveau genre, le genre *bijin ōkubi-e*, qui mettait en valeur les traits et les expressions du visage de ses sujets plutôt que de dépeindre des personnages en pied. Les estampes de ce nouveau style présentent le torse du personnage sur un arrière-plan de poussière de mica de teintes pâles, technique appelée *Kirazuri*. Cette estampe, qui fait partie d'une série de cinq estampes, est probablement la première oeuvre d'Outamaro dans le genre *bijin ōkubi-e*. Chaque estampe représente une danseuse des quartiers réservés d'Yoshiwara dans le costume caractéristique d'une des comédies dansées du festival de Niwaka. Les autres estampes de cette série sont *La danse nuptiale du héron* (*Sagi musume*), *La danse nuptiale du lion* (*Shakkyō*), *La danse Sanbasō* (*Sanbasō*), *La danse du temple Dōjōji* (*Dōjōji*). La "Danse des passereaux d'Yoshiwara" est pleine de nuances et d'allusions historiques qui combinent un témoinage franc des conditions qui existaient dans les quartiers réservés et la célèbre histoire d'amour de Minamoto no Yoshiie et de Tara no Sei, thème favori du Kabuki et des danses traditionnelles. L'emploi par Outamaro de couleurs douces sur un arrière-plan clair souligne l'effet de la composition audacieuse de l'estampe.

2. *La danse Ōmando*: appartenant à la série "*Geisha* au festival de Niwaka à Yoshiwara." (*Seirō niwaka onna geisha no bu: Ōmando*). Format *Ōban*. Publiée par Tsutaya Jūzaburō, vers 1783–84. Musée national de Tokyo.
Le festival de Niwaka, qui avait lieu le huitième mois solaire de chaque année, était sans doute le plus splendide des nombreux festivals tenus dans les quartiers réservés. Vêtus de leurs plus beaux atours ou des magnifiques costumes des comédies dansées quotidiennement, les *geisha* et leurs partenaires formaient un défilé à travers l'avenue centrale d'Yoshiwara, s'arrêtant en chemin pour jouer dans les maisons de thé.
Comme le texte l'explique, les estampes de cette série ne portent pas les cachets de l'éditeur. Cependant, du fait qu'elles furent réalisées durant la période Tenmei (1781–89), durant laquelle les rapports entre Outamaro et Tsutaya étaient très étroits, et que de plus, dans la gravure actuelle, un exemplaire de la publication de Tsutaya's *Yoshiwara saiken*, guide de Yoshiwara, a été jeté par terre, soutient la déduction que cette série était bien un projet de Tsutaya. C'est dans cette série qu'Outamaro, qui avait acquis une grande habileté dans la représentation réaliste sous l'influence de Kiyonaga, commença à développer son style particulier, très caractéristique. Le soutien et la compréhension de Tsutaya Jūzabuzō y sont certainement pour beaucoup.

3. *Divertissements élégants des quatre saisons* (*Shiki asobi hana no iroka*). Diptyque *Ōban*. Editeur inconnu, vers 1783–84. British Museum.
Ce diptyque représente un groupe de jeunes gens d'Edo prêts à embarquer pour une promenade en bateau sur le fleuve Sumida. Sur l'estampe de droite, un jeune samuraï appuyé sur le toit du bateau de promenade s'évente et essuie la sueur de sa poitrine. Deux exemples de *kyōka*, l'un de Yomo no Akara (Ōta Nanpo) et l'autre d'Akera Kankō décorent son éventail. Celui d'Ōta dit:

Haru no yo no	Une soirée de printemps
Koko hitotoki mo	Ici, en seulement une heure
Senkin ni	Vous pouvez dépenser
Kaemashi mono o	Mille pièces d'or
Hana ga sanmon	Mais une fleur ne coûte que
	quelques sous

La compagne du samouraï est une jolie jeune fille. Ou peut-être une *geisha*? La dame qui prend plaisir à regarder la scène pleine de fraîcheur qui l'entoure à travers le tissu diaphane de l'*haori* du personnage masculin, semble, d'après son kimono plutôt sobre, un peu plus âgée que les deux autres personnages. A gauche, deux femmes, chacune portant quelque chose pour protéger son visage du soleil, et un jeune homme marchent vers le bateau le long d'une jetée en bois. Ce dyptique est une exemple de l'oeuvre relativement précoce d'Outamaro dans le genre des estampes polychromes *ukiyo-e* (*nishiki-e*) et l'influence de Torii Kiyonaga est encore très évidente.

Note du traducteur: un amusant jeu de mots a été fait ici sur le mot *haru*, qui dans la période Edo (1600–1867) signifiait les plaisirs érotiques des quartiers réservés, tout en conservant son sens ordinaire "printemps." Ainsi, quoique la fleur (*hana*) soit aussi éphémère qu'une soirée de printemps et donc tout aussi précieuse, elle ne coûte qu'une fraction du coût de quelques moments de plaisir sensuel passager. Ce poème emploie également la technqiue de *hon-kadori*, selon laquelle l'inspiration d'un poème *waka* classique devient celui d'un nouveau *kyōka*. Une soirée de printemps est souvent associée dans la poésie classique à un rêve flottant, qui peut ou n'être pas associé à l'amour courtois élégant.

4. *L'hédoniste*: appartenant à la série "Dix études de la physionomie féminine." (*Fujin sōgaku juttai: Uwaki no sō*). Format *Ōban*. Publiée par Tsutaya Jūzaburō, vers 1792–93. Musée national de Tokyo.
Quoique le terme *uwaki* suggère libertinage ou promiscuité en japonais moderne, il n'avait pas toujours cette signification pour Outamaro et ses contemporains. Il était plutôt applicable à une personne au caractère quelque peu changeant et affecté, susceptible de passer d'une marotte à une autre, à la recherche des modes dernier cri. L'exploitation efficace par Outamaro d'un arrière-plan en poussière de mica blanc (*shirokira*) met en valeur le sujet, qui porte le vêtement léger (*yukata*) mis après le bain et souligne l'effet des couleurs subtiles qui suggèrent merveilleusement la texture de la peau d'une jeune femme qui sort d'un bain chaud. Par la facon dont il rend la bouche entre-ouverte plutôt taquine et l'expression séduisante des yeux de cette femme, Outamaro a capturé l'essence d'une jeune femme hédoniste et affectée de cette période. Cette estampe prouve très bien qu'Outamaro avait raison d'affirmer qu'il était un bon physionomiste des types féminins.
Le titre original de la série "*Types faciaux féminins de dix classes*" (*Fujo ninsō juppon*) fut changé avant l'achèvement de la série.

5. *Femme jouant avec un poppin*: appartenant à la série "Dix études de la physionomie féminine" (*Fujin sōgaku juttai: Poppin o fuku onna*). Format *Ōban*. Publiée par Tsutaya Jūzaburō, vers 1792–93. Académie d'art d'Honolulu.
Cette fraîche et insouciante beauté était probablement la fille d'une famille de marchands prospères. Cette impression est suggérée par la conception audacieuse de son *furisode*, vêtement porté par les jeunes femmes non mariées, qui comporte des fleurs de cerisier gaiement éparpillées sur un fond de carreaux rouge vif. Elle joue avec un *poppin*, simple jouet musical en verre extrêmement populaire durant la période *Kansei* (1789–1801). Outamaro a capturé de façon merveilleuse le moment précis où elle semble atteindre une beauté voluptueuse plus mûre mais où elle n'a pas encore perdu l'innocence et la candeur de l'enfance.

6. *Peinture des lèvres* (*Beni-tsuke*). Format *Ōban*. Publiée par Uemura Yohe, vers 1796–97.
Agenouillée devant son coffre de toilette, la femme représentée par cette estampe vient de se noircir les dents et applique maintenant du rouge (*beni*) sur ses lèvres. Si on juge par le fait qu'elle s'est noirci les dents

mais qu'elle ne s'est pas rasé les sourcils, il s'agit sans doute d'une courtisane. La pose de cette femme, qui se penche vers un miroir qu'elle tient à la main, atteint d'une certaine façon un équilibre fragile, qui suggère le caractère précaire de son lot dans l'existence. Outamaro a capturé le caractère apathique et triste de cette scène avec un talent extraordinaire et l'estampe tout entière est pénétrée de ces émotions.

7. *La veuve d'Hinodeya*: appartenant à la série "Six beautés célèbres jettent un défi à la magnificence des six génies poétiques" (*Kōmei bijin rokkasen: Hinodeya no goke*). Format *Ōban*. Publiée par Omiya Gonkurō, vers 1796. Musée national de Tokyo.
Outamaro adorait la beauté pleine de fraîcheur d'une femme qui vient de sortir du bain et en a fait un thème favori de ses estampes qui représentent des belles femmes. La veuve d'Hinodeya était l'une des beautés les célèbres d'Edo lorsque cette gravure fut publiée. Que c'est vraiment elle qui est représentée ici avec des sourcils rasés doit être déduit de "l'image devinette" (*hanji-e*) qui se trouve dans le coin gauche supérieur de la gravure. Le soleil du matin suggère Hinodeya (littéralement "l'échoppe du soleil levant") et la plaque de *go* et les boucles de cheveux coupés (*ke*) mis côte-à-côte suggèrent *goke* ou "veuve."

La technique consistant à indiquer l'identité des modèles de l'artiste par allusions discrètes contenues dans de telles images devinettes est une idée ingénieuse conçue pour tourner un édit shogounal de 1796 (Kansei 8) qui interdisait la pratique d'indiquer les noms des modèles sur les gravures mêmes. Il est évident que les images devinettes devaient par la même occasion augmenter le plaisir des clients à qui il était donné une nouvelle opportunité de mettre la vivacité de leur esprit à l'épreuve.

8–12. *"Un cadran solaire de jeunes filles"* (*Musume hidokei*), série de cinq gravures. Format *Ōban*. Publiée par Murataya Jirobē, vers 1795–96. Musée national de Tokyo.
Quoique la période de temps appelée par les mots japonais *toki* ou *koku*, ou "une heure" dans le système solaire, était d'environ deux heures, la journée était divisée en douze de ces unités, chaque unité étant représentée par un des douze symboles horaires du calendrier lunaire. Dans la série de gravures de genre appelée "Un cadran solaire de jeunes filles," Outamaro dépeint la vie quotidienne de jeunes femmes appartenant à la classe bourgeoise durant chacune des "heures, de l'heure du Dragon (*tatsu no koku*, ou 8 heures du matin) à l'heure du Singe (*sazu no koku*, 4 heures du soir). En plus de cette série, Outamaro produisit, durant la même période, une autre série de gravures "Les douze heures lunaires dans les quartiers du plaisir" (*Seirō jūni toki*; Planches 32–43), qui dépeint la vie des courtisanes durant chacune des douze "heures" qui constituent un cycle lunaire d'une journée entière. Il est possible de détecter un élément commun dans les deux séries: la détermination de l'artiste à capturer et à dépeindre chaque aspect des manières et des coutumes des femmes qu'il observait dans la cité d'Edo.

Dans cette série, Outamaro a utilisé une technique non conventionnelle qui omet les contours de la chair visible. Le renflement des seins et les contours des nez sont suggérés par la technique de la gravure en relief (*karazuri*) et les bouches des modèles représentées par des taches de couleur rouge (*beni*), ne sont que devinées. Encore plus audacieux est le traitement par Outamaro des visages des personnages, pour lesquels les contours sont complètement omis; les contours des visages sont suggérés de façon effective par contraste avec les arrière-plans jaune pâle. Cette expérimentation audacieuse de nouvelles techniques réussit à capturer la fraîche beauté de ces filles de bourgeois sans sacrifier la douceur tendre de la texture de leur peau et elle a produit une oeuvre qui suggère une image de la beauté féminine qu'il était précédemment impossible de réaliser dans le genre *ukiyo-e*.

Planche 12. *L'Heure du Dragon* (*Tatsu no koku*; 8 heures du matin). Ces deux jeunes femmes viennent de se lever et admirent des volubilis en pot, après être sorties dans le jardin pour se laver le visage et se brosser les dents.

Planche 8. *L'Heure du Serpent.* (*Mi no koku*; 10 heures du matin). Sur cette gravure, une jeune femme vient de finir son ménage matinal et elle s'essuie les mains, ses manches encore retroussées. Sa compagne vérifie, à l'aide d'un miroir qu'elle tient à la main les lignes de sa coiffure qu'elle vient de faire.

Planche 9. *L'Heure du Cheval* (*Uma no koku*; *midi*): la jeune femme qui se trouve à gauche tient des vêtements de rechange sous son bras et essuie de l'eau de son oreille. Le personnage assis tient entre ses dents serrées un petit sac rempli de son, appelée *mukabukuro*, qui était utilisé dans le bain pour brosser et stimuler la peau. Cette gravure illustre la coutume des jeunes femmes de cette période de prendre leur bain durant l'heure

du Cheval. Une inscription de la gravure précise que "dans l'ancien temps, lorsque les femmes prenaient leur bain durant l'heure du Singe, (4 heures de l'après-midi), cette scène aurait été vue plus tard dans la journée."

Planche 10. *L'Heure du Bélier* (*Hitsuji no koku*; 2 heures de l'après-midi). L'attitude prise par cette jeune femme, qui fume en s'appuyant légèrement contre un écran reflète l'atmosphère silencieuse de loisir tranquille d'une maison bourgeoise durant les heures du début de l'après-midi.

Planche 11. *L'Heure du Singe* (*Saru no koku*; 4 heures de l'après-midi): Cette gravure représente une jeune femme tout habillée, prête à sortir se promener, accompagnée par une servante. Son expression joyeuse suggère qu'elle va peut-être au théâtre.

13–16. *Hanaōgi d'Ōgiya: Takigawa d'Ōgiya; Komurasaki de Tamaya; Hanazuma d'Hyōgoya*, appartenant à la série "Un assemblage de beautés contemporaines au pinacle de leur popularité" (*Tōji zensei bijin zoroe: Ōgiya-uchi Hana; Takigawa; Tamaya-uchi Komurasaki; Hyōgoya-uchi hanazuma*). Format *Ōban*. Publiée par Wakasaya Yoichi, vers 1794. Musée national de Tokyo.
En 1794, Tōshūsai Sharaku, l'artiste extrêmement doué dont la carrière énigmatique semble avoir fini presque dès ses débuts, s'était assuré le patronage de Tsutaya Jūzaburō et il électrifia le monde *ukiyo-e* avec ses portraits d'acteurs de Kabuki (*Yakusha nigao-e*), superbement édités avec arrière-plans imprimés en poussière de mica (*kirazuri*). Il semble qu'Outamaro, qui était alors bien établi comme maître prééminent du *bijin-ga* fut énormément stimulé par l'apparition soudaine de cet artiste phénoménal, qui, tout comme lui, avait attiré l'attention critique de Tsutaya Jūzaburō. Outamaro publia presque immédiatement une série de *bijin-ga* intitulée "Un assembalge de beautés au pinacle de leur popularité" (*Tōji zensei nigao-zoroe*) qui indique assez clairement ses sentiments compétitifs envers le nouvel artiste. La déformation prononcée des personnages et la composition audacieuse des gravures dans lesquelles les caractères semblent presque trop grands pour l'espace qui leur est alloué, ainsi que les mouvements exagérés des mains des personnages par exemple, semblent témoigner clairement de l'influence de Sharaku. Après le départ de Sharaku du monde d'*ukiyo-e*, Outamaro, retrouvant son rythme de travail normal, élimina le mot "portrait" (*nigao*) du titre de la série, le remplaçant par "beauté" (*bijin*) pour nous donner le titre de la série tel qu'il est représenté par ces illustrations.

Quatre estampes de la série, qui en comporte dix en tout, sont reproduites ici; chaque estampe représente une des célèbres courtisanes des maisons de *geisha* également célèbres d'Yoshiwara: Hanaōgi et Takigawa d'Ōgiya, Komurasaki de Tamaya et Hanazuma d'Hyōgoya, toutes populaires durant les années 1790.

17–18. *Amour révélé; amour contemplatif*: appartenant à la série "Grands thèmes d'amour de la poésie classique." (*Kasen koi no bu: Arawaruru koi; Mono omou koi*). Format *Ōban*. Publiée par Tsutaya Jūzaburō, vers 1793. Musée des Beaux-Arts, Boston (Collection Spaulding).
Une femme amoureuse révèle ses sentiments par un changement d'expression, remarqué même par l'observateur le plus distrait. Dans la poésie japonaise classique, cet aspect de l'amour féminin était exprimé comme un amour qui "se révélait dans l'expression la plus discrète même lorsqu'une femme s'efforce de dissimuler ses sentiments." L'expression, et en fait, chaque mouvement, du modèle d' *"Amour révélé"*, suggère son bonheur de se souvenir de moments d'amour éphémères. L'emploi d'un bleu tendre, presque transparent, avec un arrière-fond de poussière de mica sur champ rose (*benikira*) est un bel exemple de l'ingéniosité d'Outamaro dans l'emploi des arrière-fonds et les tranformations habiles des styles traditionnels de représentation du visage et des mains, ainsi que des cheveux et des vêtements du modèle, sont des innovations inédites des gravures d'Outamaro de cette période.

Si on me demandait de choisir le plus grand chef-d'oeuvre d'Outamaro, je choisirais sans hésitation *"Amour contemplatif."* Cette estampe n'a pas de rivale dans la peinture japonaise, par la puissance avec laquelle Outamaro a exprimé la profondeur et l'intensité de réflexion de son sujet. De plus, il a capturé un état d'esprit très différent de la contemplation dépeinte dans des oeuvres occidentales telles que "Le penseur" de Rodin. Cet état est caractérisé par une qualité émotive uniquement orientale qui domine la culture japonaise traditionnelle. Au Japon, cette attitude était appelée *nasake* ou *mono no aware*, termes souvent traduits par "un sens raffiné de la tristesse des choses."

La femme dépeinte dans "Amour contemplatif" a rasé ses sourcils, ce qui suggère qu'elle est la jeune femme d'un marchant prospère. Son visage sans expression souligne l'effet de sa pose; elle appuie nonchalamment le poids de sa coiffure élaborée sur une main délicate, s'abandonnant aux rêves d'un amour impossible. Peut-être se souvient-elle d'un amour de jeune fille qui a pris fin avec son mariage ou souffret-elle de peur et de honte en pensant à une liaison illicite qu'elle poursuit actuellement.

19–20. *Tissus aux dessins audacieux nouvellement en vente à Kameya; Cotonnades fleuries de Shirokiya*; appartenant à la série "Beautés modernes en Kimonos d'été" (*Natsu ishō tōsei bijin: Kameya shiire no ōgata-muki; Shirokiya shiire no kafu-muki*). Format *Ōban*. Publiée par Izumiya Ichibē, vers 1805. Musée national de Tokyo.
Ces estampes font partie d'une série qui présentait les nouveaux tissus d'été offerts par les célèbres boutiques de kimonos d'Edo, qui comprenaient, en plus de Kamya et de Shirokiya, Echigoya, Matsuzakaya et Daimaru. Dans chaque estampe, avec le titre, se trouve représentée la bannière de tissu (*noren*) qui pendait à l'entrée des boutiques. Le *noren* de Kameya porte la représentation stylisée d'une tortue (*kame*), qui était l'emblème du magasin. Dans "Tissus aux dessins audacieux nouvellement en vente à Kameya," Outamaro a pris grand soin de capturer les détails du tissu, sur lequel un audacieux dessin de corde a été réalisé en laissant des parties du tissu sans teinture. La femme dépeinte ici constitue un mannequin de kimonos idéale, démontrant la grâce inconsciente requise pour conserver les lignes de son kimono parfaites même lorsqu'elle joue avec un enfant turbulent.

Shirokiya ouvrit dans l'élégant quartier Nihonbashi d'Edo en 1662. En 1805, ce commerce de kimonos était l'un des plus célèbres de la ville. Les cotonnades à fleurs (*kafu-muki*) dépeintes ici étaient des calicots décorés de dessins d'herbes et de fleurs, généralement appelés tissus in-kafu ou cotonnades de style indien. Le mannequin porte le kimono sur sa peau nue.

Une des fonctions de l'*ukiyo-e* a toujours été de garder les élégantes d'Edo au courant des dernières modes. Cette fonction semble ici se combiner à une publicité explicite de produits spécifiques de commerçants célèbres. L'emploi des couleurs dans ces gravures est frais et lucide et elles représentent la meilleure oeuvre d'Outamaro dans les dernières années de sa vie, durant lesquelles la qualité de son art diminua.

21. *Une scène sur le pont et au-dessous de celui-ci* (*Hashi no ue shita*). Format *Ōban*. Publiée par Ōmiya gonkurō, vers 1797–98. Musée national de Tokyo.
La zone entourant les rives du fleuve Sumida, qui coulait à travers la partie est d'Edo dans laquelle vivaient beaucoup de bourgeois devint le cadre de la culture urbaine vivace de cette ville. Le pont Ryogoku était le plus grand de plusieurs ponts qui traversaient le fleuve et les six estampes *oban* de cette composition ambitieuse dépeignent les habitants d'Edo profitant des rafraîchissantes brises du soir après une chaude journée d'été.

Sur le fleuve qui passe sous le pont, un groupe de femmes, au centre de la composition prennent le *sake* dans la cabine à toit d'un bateau. Les femmes qui se trouvent dans le bateau ouvert ont déplié leur parasol pour se protéger du chaud soleil d'été. Outamaro, quoique renommé comme peintre de belles femmes a néanmoins dépeint les deux bateliers comme deux galants jeunes et beaux, un penché sur le toit des bateaux, l'autre debout avec une perche à la main.

Sur le pont, Outamaro a représenté un groupe de jolies femmes de grande taille, aux parasols ouverts, se promenant sur le pont ou s'appuyant sur la balustrade pour regarder ce qui se passe sur le fleuve. Au coin d'extrême droite, derrière la femme debout qui tient un éventail rond, on peut apercevoir l'attirail d'un vendeur d'eau. Ces colporteurs tiraient profit du fait que l'eau pure et fraîche était rare dans cette partie de la ville, qui se trouvait sur des terres prises sur l'océan et ils apportaient de l'eau fraîche et limpide de sources distantes d'eau pure. Cette eau, qui était légèrement sucrée, était particulièrement la bienvenue durant les chaudes journées d'été.

Les six estampes qui constituent la composition peuvent évidemment être appréciées séparément ou ensemble. Les trois scènes situées sur le pont sont disposées horizontalement, surmontant les trois autres, ce qui produit une composition grande et harmonieuse. On peut dire que la conception ingénieuse des gravures individuelles et de l'ensemble de la composition est la caractéristique la plus frappante de cette oeuvre.

22. *Beautés dans la cuisine* (*Daidokoro bijin*). Diptyque *Ōban*. Publiée par Uemura Yohē, vers 1795–96. Musée national de Tokyo.
Ce diptyque présente une scène de cuisine dans le foyer d'une famille bourgeoise. Au centre de la scène, un grand pot destiné à faire bouillir

l'eau et un autre pot plus petit dans lequel mijote un ragoût ont été placés dans le large foyer; à l'arrière-plan, deux seaux d'eau reposent sur un grand tonneau d'eau. A droite, une jeune femme souffle sur les charbons avec un tube de bambou et une jeune fille essaie de tirer de l'eau chaude, en faisant la grimace dans la fumée. A gauche, une femme épluche une aubergine pour le ragoût et une femme plus âgée sèche un bol de laque qu'elle vient de laver. Cette dernière porte un petit enfant sur son dos et d'après cette gravure nous pouvons avoir une idée des rapports typiques qui existaient entre les femmes et leurs enfants durant la période Edo. (1600–1867).

Comme en témoigne cette oeuvre, les *ukiyo-e* ne se confinent pas aux portraits de courtisanes ou d'acteurs de *kabuki* ou à des illustrations des merveilleuses manières et coutumes des quartiers réservés. Ils produisent à l'occasion des tableaux de genre qui fournissent une vue réaliste des citadins ordinaires d'Edo. Dans le cas d'Outamaro, ceci semble avoir été surtout en réponse aux exigences de son éditeur et il a également publié un triptyque appelé *"Travaux d'aiguille"* (*Harishigoto*; fig. 17) pour Uemura. C'est un de ses chefs-d'oeuvre dans un style distinctif de peinture de genre.

23. *Okita, la serveuse de la maison de thé de Naniwaya* (*Naniwaya Okita*). Format *Hosoban*, imprimé recto verso. Editeur inconnu, vers 1793–94. Okazaki Heijirō.
Okita était une serveuse de maison de thé (*mizujaya*) appelée Naniwaya à Asakusa, un des quartiers les plus animés d'Edo. Les maisons de thé telle que la Naniwaya servaient du thé chaud et fournissaient une atmosphère élégante pour une pause lors d'une excursion à l'un des temples ou aux célèbres spectacles du quartier. Okita n'était ni une courtisane ni une *geisha* mais une jeune fille de la classe bourgeoise même et elle était connue pour sa grâce et sa bonne humeur autant que pour sa beauté. Avec Takashima Ohisa, autre serveuse (*mizujana musume*) dont la maison de thé bien connue, Senbeiya, était située dans le quartier ryogoku, Okita était l'une des beautés célèbres de l'ère Kansei (1789–1801).

Okita avait quinze ans en 1793 et il est supposé que ce tableau fut exécuté à peu près durant cette période. Elle est dépeinte dans une pose gracieuse, équilibrant une tasse de vert fin sur un plateau de la main gauche et portant une boîte d'ustensils pour fumeurs de la main droite, se préparant à servir un client. Une caractéristique technique spéciale de cette oeuvre est qu'Outamaro a capturé l'apparence d'Okita vue de devant sur un côté de la gravure et vue de derrière de l'autre côté, précisément selon les contours de la même silhouette. Outamaro a produit une gravure similaire dépeignant la rivale d'Okita, Takashima Ohisa, vue de devant et de derrière, dans une pose délicate, agitant doucement un éventail. Ces gravures portent le cachet de l'éditeur mais celui-ci n'a pas encore été identifié de façon satisfaisante.

24–25. *Oiran; Teppō*: appartenant à la série "Cinq nuances foncées d'encre dans le quartier nord" (*Hokkoku goshiki-zumi: Oiran; Teppō*). Format *Ōban*. Publiée par Isemago vers 1794–95.
Situé dans la banlieue nord d'Edo, le quartier d'Yoshiwara était populairement appelé le quartier nord (ou littéralement, le Pays Nord). Une des difficultés à comprendre les coutumes des quartiers réservés d'Edo est qu'il existait une hiérarchie précise des courtisanes, dont le rang dépendait de leur beauté et de leurs talents ainsi que de la situation sociale et de la richesse de leurs clients. Cette série de cinq gravures est unique parce qu'elle inclut des courtisanes de la classe la plus basse, qui n'étaient guère davantage que des prostituées.

Les *oiran* occupaient le rang le plus haut parmi les femmes dépeintes dans la série et par conséquent, l'*oiran* de la planche 24 est présentée dans une pose qui suggère son raffinement. Elle vient de se laver les cheveux, et avant de faire son chignon, elle vérifie la pointe de son pinceau à écrire car elle se prépare à écrire un billet doux à un client qui ne lui accorde pas assez d'attention. Alors qu'elle réfléchit à ce qu'elle va écrire, son expression semble suggérer l'artifice d'un acteur accompli du monde des quartiers réservés plutôt que la passion d'une femme amoureuse.

Des cinq courtisanes dépeintes dans cette série, *geigi* constituait le rang juste au-dessous d'*oiran* en ce qui concerne la beauté et les accomplissements. Au-dessous des *geigi*, les conditions de vie des courtisanes empiraient rapidement, les *kiri no musume, kashi* et *teppō* occupant des maisons délabrées sur les rives du canal qui traversait le premier et le deuxième quartier de Kyō-machi dans les quartiers réservés d'Yoshiwara.

L'origine de l'apellation *teppō* pour la classe la plus basse des prostituées nous donne un aperçu de la culture bourgeoise de cette époque. *Teppō* était une expression argotique pour une variété japonaise de poisson appelé *fugu* qui était, et qui est encore, un mets recherché par les gourmets. Cependant, certains des organes du *fugu* contenaient un poison mortel et le gourmet courait le risque d'être "frappé à mort" comme par un mousquet (*teppō*) même si le poisson avait été bien préparé. De même, il était bien connu qu'un homme qui fréquentait une prostituée de la basse classe, *teppō*, courait le risque de contracter une maladie vénérienne. Les parallèles entre ces deux plaisirs dangereux produisirent ainsi un des innombrables bons mots caractéristiques de l'éthos de la culture bourgeoise. Le portrait de cette prostituée de bas étage (Planche 25), aux larges seins négligemment exposés, tenant entre ses dents un morceau de papier hygiénique ne capture que trop vivemment le caractère sordide de la vie d'une femme à l'échelon le plus bas de la hiérarchie sociale.

26–28. *La courtisane saoûle; la paresseuse; la coquine*: appartenant à la série "Les lorgnons d'un parent attentif" (*Kyōkun oya no megane: Gutarabē; Namayoi; Bakuren*). Format *Ōban*. Publiées par Tsuroya Kinsuke, vers 1803.
Dès les premières années de l'ère Kansei (1789–1801) Outamaro avait perfectionné sa technique de l'*okubi bijin-ga*, c'est-à-dire la représentation de la seule partie supérieure du corps de ses sujets, et avait réalisé des portraits de beautés féminines sans parallèle quant à l'expression des qualités uniques de femmes d'âge, de classe et de personalité divers, ainsi que leur état d'esprit insaisissable. Toutefois au moment de la réalisation des dix gravures de cette série, Outamaro semble avoir porté son observation insatiable des femmes bien au-delà des limites expressives de la peinture, tout particulièrement en ce qui concerne la peinture sur bois et c'est au cours de cette période qu'il commença à se fier de plus en plus à une explication écrite de la personnalité et de l'état d'esprit de ses sujets.

En dépit de la frustration d'Outamaro devant son échec à développer le pouvoir descriptif de son moyen d'expression, les gravures de cette série peuvent être considérées comme des chefs-d'oeuvre des dernières années d'Outamaro.

Dans *La courtisane saoûle*, (Planche 26), Outamaro expose l'impropriété de permettre aux femmes de boire. Le passage écrit qui remplit la partie supérieure de la gravure note le monologue dénué de sens d'une courtisane complètment saoûle, qui tient sa tasse à l'envers et ne peut pas fixer son regard. Sa bouche est tordue et elle semble rabrouer quelqu'un mais, comme en atteste le texte, personne ne peut plus comprendre ce qu'elle dit. En dépit de l'explication importune, la représentation d'Outamaro d'une femme terriblement grise conserve beaucoup de pouvoir d'expression.

De même, dans "*La paresseuse*" (Planche 27), Outamaro a capturé une jeune femme indolente qui vient de se lever et se brosse les dents en vêtements de nuit. Sa chevelure décoiffée, les mèches folles de sa nuque ainsi que le manque de tenue de son maintien et son absence de modestie se combinent pour suggéer presque cruellement le caractère d'une femme paresseuse et négligée de sa personne.

Dans *La coquine* (Planche 28), Outamaro réprimande la femme qui a tendance à la coquinerie — sans culture, licencieuse et égoïste. Cette femme lampe du *sake* dans une attitude d'abandon complet, vidant son gobelet de style occidental, exposant son bras droit presque jusqu'à l'épaule. Son kimono est ouvert au cou et elle tient un crabe bouilli entier de la main droite. Outamaro représente vivement l'apparence d'une coquine qui, lassée de la vie, a renoncé à la modestie réservée exigée d'une jeune femme japonaise qui aspire au charme féminin.

29–31. *La classe supérieure; la classe moyenne; la classe populaire*; appartenant à la série "Manières des jeunes femmes des trois classes" (*Fūzoku sandan musume: Jōbon no zu; Chūbon no zu; Gebon no zu*). Format *Ōban*. Publiées par Wakasaya Yoichi, vers 1795–96. Musée national de Tokyo.
Les trois gravures de cette série divisent les jeunes filles des citadins en trois catégories: classe supérieure, moyenne et travailleuse, dépeignant leur vie quotidienne et leurs coutumes durant les mois chauds de l'été et elles ont été concues pour être regardées séparément ou comme triptyque.

Les deux femmes présentées dans *la classe supérieure* (Planche 29) sont sans doute une jeune femme et sa mère. La jeune femme tient un éventail rond et porte un kimono de soie légère avec de longues manches dans le style *furisode*, suggérant qu'elle n'a pas atteint l'âge adulte. La femme âgée qui se prépare à jouer du *koto* met des onglets. La boîte qui repose sur sa couverture en tissu qui a été enlevée contient les onglets et la petite cage que l'on voit à l'arrière-plan est destinée aux insectes, dont les bruits étaient considérés comme très agréables dans le vieux Japon. De facon assez appropriée pour une gravure qui

représente la "Classe supérieure," elles s'apprêtent apparemment à commencer une leçon de *koto*.

Dans la gravure intitulée "*La classe moyenne*" (Planche 30) deux jeunes femmes admirent des roseaux qui sont soigneusement cultivés dans un beau vase creux. Elles ont enlevé leurs veste en soie légère, qui sont pendues sur le crochet qui se trouve derrière elles et sont évidemment à l'aise. Leur pose modeste et leur expression modeste suggèrent le raffinement auquel aspiraient les femmes de cette classe.

Dans *La classe populaire* (Planche 31), le style de vie plutôt sans prétentions de deux jeunes femmes de la classe populaire est dépeint. Une d'entre elles s'est levée pour défaire son *obi*, l'autre a ouvert son kimono pour s'éventer. Les roseaux disposés sans art dans un seau en bois normalement utilisé pour port l'eau semblent un rappel de lumière approprié pour les silhouettes relaxées, décidément mutines de ces sympathiques jeunes filles auxquelles il est en même temps facile de s'identifier. Cette composition simple réussit bien à évoquer le plaisir de jouir de la brise fraîche du soir après une chaude journée à Edo.

32–43. *L'heure du Rat* (*Ne no koku*); *L'heure du Boeuf* (*Ushi no koku*); *L'heure du Tigre* (*Tora no koku*); *L'heure du Lièvre* (*U no koku*); *L'heure du Dragon* (*Tatsu no koku*); *L'heure du Serpent* (*Mi no.koku*); *L'heure du Cheval* (*Uma no koku*); *L'heure du Bélier* (*Hitsuji no koku*); *L'heure du Singe* (*Saru no koku*); *L'heure du Coq* (*Tori no koku*); *L'heure du Chien* (*Inu no koku*); *L'heure de l'Ours* (*I no koku*): *Série des douze heures lunaires dans les quartiers réservés.* (*Seirō jūni toki*). Format *Ōban*. Publiée par Tsutaya Jūsaburō, vers 1795–96. Musée national de Tokyo.
Comme dans la série intitulée "Un cadran horaire de jeunes filles" (Planches 8–12), cette série est disposée selon les douze signes horaires du calendrier lunaire. Dans la série présentée ici, Outamaro a dépeint des aspects des quartiers réservés et des vies des courtisanes durant chacune des douze périodes de temps lunaire (d'environ deux heures chacune) entre l'heure du Rat, minuit et l'heure de l'Ours, dix heures du soir, donnant des aperçus des quartiers réservés aux moments où ils étaient fermés aux clients ainsi que d'autres scènes plus familières. Sa présentation des courtisanes comme des beautés minces et de grande taille reflète l'influence de Chōbunsai Eishi, qui avait abandonné sa carrière de conseiller du shogounat pour devenir un artiste *ukiyo-e*. Cette représentation, ainsi que l'élégance et la grâce des mouvements et des poses des caractères exprime un aspect des courtisanes qui n'a pas été touché par la laideur et la tristesse intrinsèques de leur profession.

44. *Lecture d'une lettre*: appartenant à la série "Nouveaux dessins d'Outamaro pour la gravure *Nishiki-e* (*Nishiki-ori Utamaro-gata shinmoyō: Fumiyomi*). Format *Ōban*. Publiée par Tsuruya Kinsuke vers 1801–04.
Au début de l'ère Kyōwa, Outamaro jouissait d'une immense popularité à Edo en tant que maître inégalé d'estampes de belles femmes (*bijin-ga*), et il était naturel qu'une succession innombrable d'artistes de moindre talent tentent de produire des imitations de son oeuvre. Mis en colère par l'apparition de ces épigones, Outamaro exprima ses sentiments dans un colophon célèbre qu'il incorpora avec art dans le titre de cette estampe. Dans cette déclaration de son intention de produire une série de modèles représentant son style inimitable, on perçoit une conscience de sa propre position qui est très proche de l'arrogance.

Le *nishiki-e* d'Azuma est un des célèbres produits d'Edo. Cependant, des artistes inférieurs aussi nombreux et insignifiants que les feuilles des arbres ont cependant apparu l'un après l'autre. Ils ressemblent vraiment à une colonie de fourmis. S'appuyant uniquement sur la beauté lustrée de nos teintures rouge et bleue, ces imitateurs produisent des gravures hideuses. Ces médiocres imitations ont dernièrement fait leur chemin jusqu'à des endrcits situés à l'extérieur d'Edo et ceci ne peut qu'apporter de la honte à notre ville. C'est donc avec tristesse que j'ai décidé de produire ces gravures comme exemples de la véritable essence des *bijin-ga* d'Edo, pour la gouverne de ces minables créatures.

Les gravures de cette série représentent en fait l'expérimentation la plus audacieuse d'Outamaro avec des innovations sans précédent de sa propre création. Les contours des visages sont peints en lignes de vermillon et dans son traitement du kimono, Outamaro a abandonné les lignes produites par des traits de pinceaux dans un tableau oriental traditionnel, employant des techniques délicates d'ombrage pour suggérer la qualité du tissu. Ces innovations réussirent merveilleusement bien à capturer l'expression d'une femme perdue dans des songes d'amour, tout en suggérant le doux raffinement de sa posture et de sa toilette.

German Text

1. *Der Yoshiwara Sperlings-Tanz:* aus der Serie "Zeitgenössische Edo-Tänzerinnen in der Kleidung für das Yoshiwara-Niwaka-Fest" (*Tōsei odoriko zoroe: Yoshiwara suzume*). *Ōban*-Format. Veröffentlicht von Tsutaya Jūzaburō, *ca.* 1790–91. National-Museum Tokio.
Utamaro schuf das neue Genre des *bijin ōkubi-e,* ein Genre, welches mehr die Gesichtszüge und den Gesichtsausdruck seiner Modelle hervorhebt als lebensgroße Figuren, während der Kansei-Epoche (1789–1801). Auf den Drucken in diesem neuen Stil wird die Oberhälfte der Figur gegen einen Hintergrund aus hellem Glimmer-Staub geworfen; diese Arbeitsweise heißt *kirazuri.* Dies ist einer von fünf Drucken in einer Serie, die als das früheste Werk von Utamaro im *bijin ōkubi-e* gilt. Die Drucke stellen jeweils eine Tänzerin der Freudenviertel von Yoshiwara im Kostüm dar, das für eine der während des Niwaka-Festes aufgeführten Tanz-Komödien kennzeichnend ist. Bei den Drucken dieser Serie handelt es sich neben dem der Abbildung um den *Reiher-Mädchen-Tanz (Sagi musume),* den *Löwen-Mädchen-Tanz (Shakkyō),* den *Sanbasō-Tanz (Sanbasō)* und den *Dōjōji-Tempel-Tanz (Dōjōji).* Der Yoshiwara Sperlings-Tanz ist voll von Nuancen und historischen Anspielungen, in denen sich eine dünn verschleierte Beschreibung der Zustände in den Freudenvierteln mit der berühmten Liebesgeschichte von Minamoto no Yoshiie und Taka no Sei, einem Lieblingsthema des Kabuki sowie des herkömmlichen Tanzes, verbinden. Utamaros Verwendung gedämpfter Farben gegen einen hellen Hintergrund verstärkt die Wirkung der gewagten Komposition des Druckes.

2. *Der Ōmando-Tanz:* aus der Serie "Geisha auf dem Yoshiwara-Niwaka-Fest" (*Seirō niwaka onna geisha no bu: Ōmando*). *Ōban*-Format. Veröffentlicht von Tsutaya Jūzaburō, *ca.* 1783–84. National-Museum Tokio.
Das Niwaka-Fest, das während des achten Lunar-Monats jedes Jahres stattfand, war vielleicht das großartigste der in den Freudenvierteln aufgeführten zahlreichen Feste. In ihren prächtigen Aufzug gekleidet oder in den Kostümen der täglich aufzuführenden Tanz-Komödien glänzend, bildeten *geisha* mit männlichen Partnern einen Umzug durch die Hauptstraße von Yoshiwara, wobei sie unterwegs Halt machten für Aufführungen in Teehäusern.
   Wie im Text erläutert wird, tragen die Drucke dieser Serie kein Verleger-Siegel. Jedoch davon abgesehen, daß die Drucke aus der Tenmei-Epoche (1781–89) stammen, als die Beziehungen zwischen Utamaro und Tsutaya sehr eng waren, läßt der vorliegende Druck auf dem ein Exemplar von Tsutayas Buch *Yoshiwara saiken,* einem Führer durch Yoshiwara, auf den Boden geworfen wird, darauf schließen, daß diese Serie wirklich ein Projekt von Tsutaya war. In dieser Serie hat Utamaro, der unter dem Einfluß von Kiyonaga große Fähigkeiten in der realistischen Darstellung erreicht hatte, begonnen, seinen kennzeichnenden, eigenartigen Stil zu entwickeln, Dies hat sicherlich Tsutaya Jūzaburōs Hilfe und Verständnis ermöglicht.

3. *Elegante Unterhaltungen der vier Jahreszeiten (Shiki asobi hana no iroka).* *Ōban*-Diptychon. Verleger unbekannt, *ca.* 1783–84. Britisches Museum.
In diesem Diptychon wird eine Gruppe junger Edoiten kurz vor dem Besteigen eines Bootes zur Fahrt auf dem Sumida-Fluß dargestellt. Auf dem rechten Druck lehnt sich ein junger Samurai gegen das Dach des Ausflugbootes, während er sich fächelt und den Schweiß von seiner Brust wischt. Zwei *kyōka*-Beispiele, eins von Yomo no Akara (Ōta Nanpo), das andere von Akera Kankō, verzieren seinen Fächer. Der von Ōta hat folgende Aufschrift:

Haru no yo no	Ein Frühlingsabend,
Koko hitotoki mo	Hier, und nur eine Stunde lang
Senkin ni	Tausend in Gold
Kaemashi mono o	Könnte es dich kosten
Hana ga sanmon	Aber eine Blume kostet nur ein paar Pfennige.

Die Begleiterin des Samurais ist ein schönes junges Mädchen. Oder ist sie vielleicht eine *geisha?* Die Frau, welche die kühl-erfrischende Szene durch das durchscheinende Gewebe des *haori* der männlichen Gestalt hindurch genießt, dürfte, nach dem recht diskreten Muster ihres Kimonos zu urteilen, etwas älter als ihre beiden Begleiter sein. Links gehen zwei Frauen, die beide etwas zum Schutz des Gesichtes gegen die Sonne tragen, und ein kleiner Junge über einen Anlegepier zum Boot. Dieses Diptychon ist ein Beispiel des verhältnismäßig frühen Werkes Utamaros im Genre der polychromen *ukiyo-e* Drucke (*nishiki-e*), und der Einfluß von Torii Kiyonaga ist noch recht stark.
   Anmerkung des amerikanischen Übersetzers: Hier kommt ein witziges Wortspiel mit dem Wort *haru* vor, das sich während der Edo-Epoche (1600–1867) auf die erotischen Genüsse bezog, die man in den Freudenvierteln empfangen konnte, sowie auf seine übliche Bedeutung, "Frühling". Obwohl die Blume (*hana*) so vergänglich wie ein Frühlingsabend ist und daher ebenso kostbar, so stellt sie doch nur einen Bruchteil der Kosten weniger Augenblicke entfliehender Sinneslust dar. In diesem Gedicht wird auch die *honkadori*-Weise gebraucht, wobei die aus einem klassischen *waka*-Gedicht stammende Eingebung zu der des Neuen *kyōkas* wird. In der klassischen Dichtung verbindet sich ein Frühlingsabend oft mit einem entfliehenden Traum, der sich mit vornehmer Minne verbinden mag oder nicht.

4. *Der Hedonist:* aus der Serie "Zehn Studien der weiblichen Physiognomie" (*Fujin sōgaku juttai: Uwaki no sō.*) *Ōban*-Format. Veröffentlicht von Tsutaya Jūzaburō, *ca.* 1792–93. National-Museum Tokio.
Während im modernen Japanisch das Wort *uwaki* an Lüsternheit und Promiskuität denken läßt, hatte es nicht immer diese Bedeutung für Utamaro und seine Zeitgenossen. Vielmehr bezog es sich oft auf einen ziemlich unbeständigen, auffallenden Typ, welcher zur Erlangung des modernsten Stiles geneigt war, von einem Fimmel schnell zum anderen zu gehen. Utamaros wirksame Nutzbarmachung des Hintergrundes aus weißem Glimmer-Staub (*shirokira*) hebt die Gestalt mit dem nach dem Bade umgeworfenen leichten Gewand (*yukata*) hervor und erhöht den Effekt der feinen Farben, die auf wunderbarer Weise an die Beschaffenheit der Haut einer gerade aus dem heißen Bade kommenden jungen Frau denken läßt. In dem recht kokett halb-geöffneten Mund der Frau und ihrem verführerischen Augenausdruck, hat Utamaro das Wesen der auffallenden, hedonistischen jungen Frau des Zeitalters erfaßt. Der Druck bietet reichlichen Beweis für Utamaros Anspruch darauf, daß er die Physiognomie der weiblichen Typen vorzugsweise verstand.
   Die ursprüngliche Bezeichnung der Serie, "Weibliche Gesichtstypen von zehn Klassen" (*Fujo ninsō juppon*), wurde zur jetzigen Bezeichnung vor Abschluß der Serie geändert.

5. *Eine auf einem Poppin spielende Frau:* aus der Serie "Zehn Studien der weiblichen Physiognomie" (*Fujin sōgaku juttai: Poppin o fuku onna*). *Ōban*-Format. Veröffentlicht von Tsutaya Jūzaburō, *ca.* 1792–93. Kunstakademie Honolulu.
Diese frische, sorglose Schönheit war wohl die Tochter einer wohlhabenden Kaufmannsfamilie. Dieser Eindruck wird durch das ausdrucksvolle Muster ihrer *furisode* nahegelegt, eines von jungen unverheirateten Frauen getragenen Kleidungsstückes, auf welchem stilisierte Kirschblüten munter über ein hellrotes kariertes Muster verteilt sind. Sie spielt mit einem *poppin,* einem einfachen gläsernen Musik-Spielzeug, das sich während der Kansei-Epoche (1789–1801)

großer Beliebtheit erfreute. Wunderbar hat Utamaro sie gerade dann gefaßt, als sie sich zu einer reiferen, üppigeren Schönheit zu entwickeln scheint, aber doch noch die Unschuld und Weltabgewandtheit der Kindheit zu verlieren hat.

6. *Lippen-Bemalen (Beni-tsuke)*. *Ōban*-Format. Veröffentlicht von Uemura Yohē, *ca.* 1796–97.
Die hier dargestellte Frau hat gerade auf den Knieen vor ihrem Toilettentisch ihre Zähne geschwärzt und trägt nun rote Farbe (*beni*) auf ihre Lippen auf. Daß sie ihre Zähne geschwärzt, jedoch nicht ihre Augenbrauen rasiert hat, läßt darauf schließen, daß sie durchaus eine Kurtisane sein könnte. Mit dem Spiegel vor ihrem vorgebeugten Leib erreicht die Pose der Frau in gewisser Weise ein labiles Gleichgewicht, eine Andeutung über die Unsicherheit ihres Loses im Leben. Utamaro hat die Lustlosigkeit und die Traurigkeit der Szene mit außerordentlichem Geschick gefaßt, und diese Gemütsbewegungen gehen durch den gesamten Druck.

7. *Die Witwe von Hinodeya*: aus der Serie "Sechs berühmte Schönheiten fordern die Magnifizenz der sechs Dichter-Genies" (*Kōmei bijin rokkasen: Hinodeya no goke*). *Ōban*-Format. Veröffentlicht von Ōmiya Gonkurō, *ca.* 1796. National-Museum Tokio.
Utamaro liebte ganz besonders die reine Schönheit einer gerade aus dem Bade kommenden Frau und machte sie zum Lieblingsthema seiner schöne Frauen darstellenden Drucke. Die Witwe von Hinodeya war eine der berühmtesten Edo-Schönheiten, als der Druck erschien. Daß tatsächlich sie hier mit rasierten Augenbrauen dargestellt ist, muß dem "Rätsel-Bild" (*hanji-e*) in der oberen linken Ecke des Druckes entnommen werden. Die Morgensonne weist auf Hinodeya hin, (wörtlich "der Laden der aufgehenden Sonne"), während das *go*-Brett und das abgeschnittene Haar (*ke*) zusammen auf *goke* oder "Witwe" hinweisen.

Die Methode, die Persönlichkeit der Modelle des Künstlers in derartigen Rätsel-Bildern anzudeuten, war ein geschickter Kunstgriff zur Umgehung eines Shogun-Erlasses von 1796 (Kansei 8), nach dem es verboten war, die Namen von Modellen auf den eigentlichen Drucken zu verzeichnen. Gleichzeitig haben die Rätsel-Bilder sicher das Vergnügen der Kunden erhöht, denen eine neue Gelegenheit zum Denksport gegeben wurde.

8–12 *Eine Sonnenuhr von Mädchen (Musume hidokei)*, eine Serie von fünf Drucken. *Ōban*-Format. Veröffentlicht von Murataya Jirobē, *ca.* 1795–96. National-Museum Tokio.
Obwohl die mit den japanischen Ausdrücken *toki* oder *koku*, d.i. eine "Stunde" im Lunar-System, bezeichnete Zeitdauer nicht genau zwei Stunden lang war, war der Tag in zwölf Einheiten von etwa zwei Stunden eingeteilt, jeweils durch die zwölf Stunden-Symbole des Lunar-Kalenders dargestellt. In der Genre-Druck-Serie unter dem Titel "Eine Sonnenuhr von Mädchen" stellt Utamaro das tägliche Leben junger Frauen aus bürgerlichen Kreisen während jeder der "Stunden" dar, von der Stunde des Drachens (*tatsu no koku* oder 8 Uhr vm.) bis zur Stunde des Affen (*saru no koku*, 4 Uhr nm.). Außer der vorliegenden Serie schuf Utamaro noch eine Druck-Serie während derselben Zeit, "Die zwölf Lunar-Stunden in den Freudenvierteln" (*Seirō jūni toki*; Tafel 32-43), welche das Leben von Kurtisanen während jeder der zwölf "Stunden" darstellt, die den Lunar-Zyklus eines ganzen Tages bilden. Ein gemeinsames Element läßt sich in beiden Serien nachweisen: des Künstlers Entschluß, die Sitten und Gebräuche der von ihm in der Stadt Edo beobachteten Frauen in jeder Erscheinung zu erfassen und darzustellen.

In der vorliegenden Serie hat Utamaro durch den Verzicht auf Umrißlinien für blossgelegtes Fleisch eine nichtherkömmliche Methode angewandt. Das Wogen der Brüste und die Umrisse der Nasen werden durch Prägearbeit (*karazuri*) angezeigt, und die Münder der Modelle werden nur durch Tupfen roter Farbe (*beni*) angedeutet. Noch gewagter ist Utamaros Bearbeitung der Gesichter der Figuren, worin Umrisse gänzlich fehlen, und die Gesichtskonturen werden durch wirksamen Kontrast gegen den hellgelben Hintergrund angedeutet. Mit diesem gewagten Versuch mit neuen Arbeitsweisen gelingt es, die frische Schönheit dieser Töchter aus bürgerlichen Kreisen zu fassen, ohne auf die sanfte Weichheit der Hautstruktur zu verzichten, und das so geschaffene Werk gibt eine Vorstellung weiblicher Schönheit, wie sei im ukiyo-e Genre zuvor nie hervorzubringen war.
Tafel 12. *Die Stunde des Drachens (Tatsu no koku;* 8 Uhr vm.): Diese beiden jungen Frauen sind gerade augestanden und bewundern einige Topf-Winden, nachdem sie in den Garten hinausgegangen waren, um sich das Gesicht zu waschen und die Zähen zu bürsten.

Tafel 8. *Die Stunde der Schlange (Mi no koku;* 10 Uhr vm.): Auf diesem Druck ist eine junge Dame gerade mit ihrer morgendlichen Hausarbeit fertig, und ihre Ärmel sind noch hochgekrempelt, während sie sich die Hände abwischt. Ihre Begleiterin überprüft die Linien ihrer neugelegten Frisur im Handspiegel.

Tafel 9. *Die Stunde des Pferdes (Uma no koku;* 12 Uhr mittags): Die auf der linken Seite stehende junge Frau hält Kleider zum Wechseln unter dem Arm, während sie sich Wasser aus dem Ohr wischt. Die sitzende Figure hält, zwischen die Zähne geklemmt, einen mit Kleie gefüllten Beutel, einen sogenannten *nakabukuro*, welcher im Bad zum Scheuern und zur Anregung der Haut gebraucht worden war. Dieser Druck veranschaulicht die zu dieser Zeit herrschende Sitte, nach der junge Frauen ihr Bad während der Stunde des Pferdes nahmen. In einer Aufschrift auf dem Druck wird bemerkt: "In alten Zeiten, als Frauen ihr Bad während der Stunde des Affen (4 Uhr nm.) nahmen, wäre diese Szene später am Tag zu sehen gewesen."

Tafel 10. *Die Stunde des Widders (Hitsuji no koku; 2 Uhr nm.): Die Haltung dieser jungen Frau, leicht an einen Wandschirm gelehnt,* während sie raucht, gibt ein Bild der Atmosphäre unbeschwerter Gelassenheit und Ruhe in einem Bürgerhause während der frühen Nachmittagsstunden.

Tafel 11. *Die Stunde des Affen (Saru no koku;* 4 Uhr nm.): Dieser Druck stellt eine junge, formell gekleidete Frau dar, kurz vor einem Ausflug in Begleitung einer Bedienten. Ihr heiterer, fröhlicher Ausdruck läßt darauf schließen, daß sie vielleicht ins Theater geht.

13–16. *Hanaōgi des Ōgiya; Takigawa des Ōgiya; Komurasaki des Tamaya; Hanazuma des Hyōgoya*: aus der Serie "Eine Sammlung zeitgenössischer Schönheiten auf dem Höhepunkt ihrer Popularität" (*Tōji zensei bijin zoroe: Ōgiya-uchi Hana; Takigawa; Tamaya-uchi Komuasaki; Hyōgoya-uchi hanazuma*). *Ōban*-Format. Veröffentlicht von Wakasaya Yoichi, *ca.* 1794, National-Museum Tokio.
Im Jahre 1794 gelang es Tōshūsai Sharaku, dem hervorragenden Künstler, dessen rätselhafte Laufbahn anscheinend beinahe gleichzeitig begann und zu Ende ging, Tsutaya Jūzaburō zu seinem Mäzen zu machen, und er wirkte mit seinen in Prachtausgaben mit Hintergrund aus Glimmerstaub (*kirazuri*) gedruckten Porträts von Kabuki-Schauspielern (*Yakusha nigao-e*) elektrisierend auf die *ukiyo-e* Welt. Es scheint, daß Utamaro, der nun als überragender Meister des *bijin-ga* allgemein anerkannt war, wesentliche Anregungen aus der kurzfristigen Erscheinung dieses phänomenalen Künstlers empfing, der, so wie er, das scharfe kritische Auge Tsutaya Jūzaburōs auf sich gezogen hatte. Beinahe unmittelbar darauf veröffentlichte Utamaro eine *bijin-ga* Serie unter dem Titel "Eine Sammlung von Porträts von Schönheiten auf dem Höhepunkt ihrer Popularität" (*Tōji zensei nigao-zoroe*), woraus eine recht deutliche Verwirrung seiner Konkurrenz-Gefühle gegenüber dem neuen Künstler hervorgeht. Die starke Deformierung der Gestalten und die gewagte Komposition der Drucke, auf welchen die Gestalten fast zu groß für den Raum erscheinen, sowie die übertriebenen Bewegungen beispielsweise der Hände der Gestalten, treten als deutliche Beweise für Sharakus Einfluß hervor. Nach Sharakus Abgang aus der *ukiyo-e* Welt, entfernte Utamaro bei Wiedergewinn seines normalen Tempos das Wort "Porträt" (*nigao*) aus dem Serien-Titel und ersetzte es durch "Schönheiten" (*bijin*), um uns den Titel der in diesen Abbildungen dargestellten Serie zu hinterlassen.

Vier Drucke aus der Serie, die im ganzen aus zehn besteht, sind hier wiedergegeben, wobei sie jeweils eine der berühmten Kurtisanen der ebenso berühmten *geisha*-Häuser im Yoshiwara darstellen: Hanaōgi und Takigawa des Ōgiya, Komurasaki des Tamaya und Hanazuma des Hyōgoya, von denen alle in den 1790er Jahren populär waren.

17–18. *Erklärte Liebe; besinnliche Liebe*: aus der Serie "Große Liebes-Themen der klassischen Dichtung" (*Kasen koi no bu: Arawaruru koi; Mono omou koi*). *Ōban*-Format. Veröffentlicht von Tsutaya Jūzaburō, *ca.* 1793. Museum der schönen Künste, Boston (Spaulding-Sammlung).
Eine verliebte Frau erklärt ihre Gefühle mit einem selbst dem flüchtigsten Beobachter offensichtlich verklärten Ausdruck. In der klassischen japanischen Dichtung drückte sich diese Seite weiblicher Liebe als eine Liebe aus, die "sich im geringsten Ausdruck erklärte, selbst wenn die Frau ihr bestes tat, ihre Gefühle zu verbergen". Der Ausdruck, ja jede Bewegung des Modells in *Erklärte Liebe* deutet auf ihr Glücksgefühl hin, wie sie sich an die entfliehenden Augenblicke der Liebe erinnert. Die Verwendung eines klaren, fast durchsichtigen Blaus gegen einen Hintergrund aus Glimmer-Staub auf rosa Feld (*benikira*) ist ein schönes Beispiel von Utamaros Geschicklichkeit bei der Verwendung von Hintergrund, und die kunstvollen Abwandlungen überlieferter Stile für die Darstellung von Gesicht und Händen sowie

das Haar und das Gewand des Modells sind Neuerungen, die Utamaros Drucken aus dieser Zeit einzig eigen sind.

Hätte ich einen von Utamaros Drucken als sein größtes Meisterstück zu wählen, so würde ich, ohne zu zögern, *Besinnliche Liebe* sagen. Der Druck ist in der japanischen Malerei ohnesgleichen in der Kraft, mit der Utamaro die Tiefe und Intensität der Nachdenklichkeit seines Modells ausgedrückt hat. Außerdem hat er eine Geistesverfassung festgehalten, die sich völlig von der Kontemplation unterscheidet, wie sie in westlichen Werken wie Rodin's "Der Denker" dargestellt ist. Sie ist durch eine einzigartig ortienalische Gefühlsweise gekennzeichnet, welche die überlieferte japanische Kultur erfüllt. In Japan nannte man diese Einstellung *nasake* oder *mono no aware*, häufig übersetzt als "ein verfeinerter Sinn für die Traurigkeit der Dinge."

Die in *Besinnliche Liebe* dargestellte Frau hat ihre Augenbrauen rasiert, was darauf hindeutet, daß sie die junge Ehefrau eines wohlhabenden Kaufmanns, ist. Ihr ausdrucksloses Gesicht erhöht den Effekt ihrer Positur, während sie das Gewicht ihrer kunstvollen Frisur teilnahmslos auf zarter Hand trägt und sich Gedanken an unmögliche Liebe hingibt. Vielleicht ruft sie sich eine jungfräuliche Liebe ins Gedächtnis, die mit ihrer Heirat ein Ende nahm, oder leidet unter Betrachtungen von Furcht und Scham um eine andauernde unerlaubte Beziehung.

19–20. *Markante Muster, Neues Angebot in Kameya; Baumwollstoffe mit Blumenmustern in Shirokiya:* aus der Serie "Moderne Schönheiten im Sommer-Kimono" (*Natsu ishō tōsei bijin: Kameya shiire no ōgata-muki; Shirokiya shiire no kafu-muki*). *Ōban*-Format. Veröffentlicht von Izumiya Ichibē, *ca.* 1805. National-Museum Tokio.
Diese Drucke stammen aus einer Serie, zur Einführung der neuen Sommer-Stoffe, die in den berühmten Kimono-Läden von Edo angeboten wurden, zu welchen außer Kameya und Shirokiya auch Echigoya, Matsuzakaya und Daimaru gehörten. Auf jedem Druck steht neben der Bezeichnung eine Darstellung des Fahnentuchs (*noren*), das über dem Ladeneingang hing. Kameyas *noren* zeigt eine idealisierte Darstellung einer Schildkröte (*kame*), des Warenzeichens des Geschäfts. In *Markante Muster, Neues Angebot in Kameya* hat Utamaro sich sehr bemüht, die Kleinarbeit des Stoffes festzuhalten, in welchem ein markantes Schnurmuster dadurch zu Wege gebracht ist, daß manche Flächen des Tuchs ungefärbt gelassen worden sind. Die hier dargestellte Frau ist ein ideales Modell für Kimonos und trägt die nötige Grazie zur Schau, um die Linien ihres Kimonos in vollkommener Ordnung zu halten, während sie mit einem wilden Kinde spielt.

Shirokiya eröffnete seinen Handel im eleganten Nihonbashi-Bezirk von Edo 1662 und war 1805 einer der berühmtesten Kimono-Händler der Stadt. Bei den hier dargestellten Baumwollstoffen mit Blumenmuster (*kafu-muki*) handelte es sich um mit Gras- und Blumendessins verzierten Baumwollkattun, in der Regel als *in-kafu*-Stoffe oder Stoffe indischer Art bekannt. Das Modell trägt den Kimono auf der bloßen Haut. Es war stets eine von *ukiyo-e's* Aufgaben, elegante Edoiten über die letzten Moden gut unterrichtet zu halten. Hier scheint die Erfüllung dieser Aufgabe Hand in Hand mit unverhüllten Reklamen für bestimmte Waren berühmter Händler zu gehen. Die Verwendung von Farben in diesen Drucken ist frisch und klar; sie sind Utamaros bestes Werk seiner letzten verklingenden Jahre.

21. *Eine Szene auf der Brücke und darunter (Hashi no ue shita)*. *Ōban*-Format. Veröffentlicht von Ōmiya Gonkurō, *ca.* 1797–98. National-Museum Tokio.
Das Gebiet am Ufer des Sumida-Flusses, der durch den von vielen Bürgern bewohnten östlichen Teil von Edo floß, wurde der Mittelpunkt der lebhaften städtischen Kultur. Die Ryōgoku-Brücke war die größte einer Anzahl von Brücken über den Fluß, und die sechs *Ōban*-Drucke in dieser anspruchsvollen Zusammenstellung zeigen die Leute von Edo, wie sie die kühle Abendbrise am Fluß nach einem heißen Sommertag genießen.

Auf dem Fluß unter der Brücke genießt in der Mitte der Komposition eine Gruppe von Frauen den *sake* in der überdachten Bootskabine. Auf dem schattenlosen Boot haben die Frauen den Sonnenschirm aufgemacht, um der heißen Sonne des Sommers zu entgehen. Wenn Utamaro auch als Maler schöner Frauen bekannt ist, so hat er doch die beiden Rudermänner als junge, gut aussehende Kavaliere dargestellt, den einen auf dem Dach der Boote angelehnt, den anderen mit der Stange in der Hand stehend.

Auf der Brücke darüber hat Utamaro eine Gruppe großer schöner Frauen dargestellt mit offenen Sonnenschirmen, wie sie über die Brücke hin und her gehen oder sich gegen das Geländer lehnen, um die Szene am Fluß darunter zu betrachten. Auf der äußersten oberen Rechten ist hinter der stehenden Frau mit dem runden Fächer das Drum und Dran eines Wasser-Verkäufers zu sehen. Diese Trödler machten es sich zunutze, da frisches, reines Wasser in diesem Stadtteil knapp war, der auf vom Meer gewonnenen Land gebaut war, und brachten kühles, klares Wasser aus abgelegenen Süßwasser-Quellen. Dieses Wasser, welches leicht angesüßt war, war während der heißen Sommertage besonders willkommen.

Die sechs Drucke, aus denen sich die Gruppe zusammensetzt, könnte natürlich einzeln oder zusammen betrachtet werden. Mit den drei Szenen auf der Brücke oben nebeneinander und den übrigen unten werden sie zu einer großen, schön gebildeten Komposition. Die geschickte Konzeption der einzelnen Drucke und die Gesamt-Komposition sind tatsächlich das auffallendste Merkmal des Werks.

22. *Schönheiten in der Küche (Daidokoro bijin)*. *Ōban*-Diptychon. Veröffentlicht von Uemura Yohē, *ca.* 1795–96. National-Museum Tokio.
Dieses Diptychon zeigt eine Küchenszene im Hause einer Bürgerfamilie. In der Mitte der Szene auf dem großen Herd stehen ein großer Topf zum Wasserkochen und ein kleinerer, in dem Fleisch schmort, während im Vordergrund ein großes Wasserfaß zwei mit Wasser gefüllte Eimer trägt. Rechts bläst eine junge Frau durch ein Bambusrohr auf die Kohlen, und ein junges Mädchen verzieht ihr Gesicht vor dem Rauch, während sie versucht, etwas heißes Wasser auszuschöpfen. Links schält eine Frau eine Aubergine für den Fleischtopf, während eine ältere Frau eine Lackschüssel trocknet, die sie gerade ausgewaschen hat. Die ältere Frau trägt ein kleines Kind auf dem Rücken, und dieser Druck gibt uns einen Einblick in das landläufige Familienverhältnis zwischen Frauen und ihren kleinen Kindern im Edo-Zeitalter (1600–1867).

Wie aus diesem Werk hervorgeht, beschränken sich die *ukiyo-e* Künstler nicht auf Porträts von Kurtisanen oder Kabuki-Schauspielern oder auf Darstellungen der prächtigen Sitten und Gebräuche der Freudenviertel. Gelegentlich schufen sie Genre-Bilder, welche ein naturgetreues Bild davon geben, wie gewöhnliche Edo-Bürger lebten. In Utamaros Fall scheint es mehr darum gegangen zu sein, daß er den Forderungen seines Verlegers entsprochen hat, und er schuf auch ein Triptychon unter dem Titel *Handarbeit (Harishigoto;* Fig. 17) für Uemura. Dieses Werk ist eines seiner Meisterstücke in unverkennbarem Genre-Maler-Stil.

23. *Okita, das Teehausmädchen am Naniwaya (Naniwaya Okita)*. *Hosoban*-Format, beiderseitig bedruckt. Verleger unbekannt, *ca.* 1793–94. Okazaki Heijirō.
Okita war Kellnerin in einem Teehaus (*mizujaya*), namens Naniwaya in Asakusa, eine der lebhaftesten Gegenden von Edo. Teehäuser wie Naniwaya servierten heißen Tee und gaben eine elegante Umgebung zum Ausruhen auf einem Ausflug zu einem der Tempel oder den berühmten Sehenswürdigkeiten der Gegend. Okita war weder Kurtisane noch *geisha*, sondern Tochter aus echt-bürgerlichen Kreisen, und sie war für ihre Grazie und ihren Humor sowie für ihre Schönheit bekannt. Neben Takashima Ohisa, einem anderen Teehausmädchen (*mizujaua musume*), dessen bekanntes Teehaus, Senbeiya, im Ryōgoku-Bezirk lag, war Okita eine der berühmten Schönheiten der Kansei-Epoche (1789-1801).

1793 war Okita fünfzehn Jahre alt, und es wird angenommen, daß dieses Bild gerade um diese Zeit gemalt wurde. Sie wird in graziöser Positur gezeigt, wie sie eine Tasse grünen Tee auf einem Serviertablett mit der linken Hand balanciert und eine Schachtel mit Rauchzeug in der Rechten trägt, um einen Kunden zu bedienen. Ein besonderes technisches Merkmal des Druckes liegt darin, daß Utamaro Okitas Figur von vorne auf der einen Seite des Druckes und von hinten auf der anderen Seite genau innerhalb des gleichen Schattenbilds gefaßt hat. Utamaro machte einen ähnlichen Druck mit Okitas Rivalin, Takashima Ohisa, von vorne und hinten, wie sie eine zarte Positur einnimmt und einen Fächer vorsichtig benutzt. Diese Drucke enthalten ein Verleger-Siegel, dessen Identität jedoch noch nicht völlig geklärt ist.

24–25. *Oiran; Teppo:* aus der Serie "Fünf dunkle Schattierungen von Tusche im nördlichen Gebiet" (*Hokkoku goshiki-zumi: Oiran; Teppō*). *Ōban*-Format. Veröffentlicht von Isemago, *ca.* 1794–95.
In den nördlichen Vororten von Edo gelegen, sprach man im Volksmund von Yoshiwara als dem Nördlichen Gebiet (oder wörtlich dem Nordland). Was das Verständnis der in den Freudenvierteln von Edo herrschenden Sitten erschwert, ist, daß die Kurtisanen einer strengen Rangordnung nach ihrer Schönheit und ihren Talenten unterworfen waren und auch nach der Stellung und dem Reichtum ihrer Gönner. Diese Serie von fünf Drucken ist darin einzigartig, daß

sie die Kurtisanen niedrigsten Rangs umfaßt, welche nicht viel mehr als Straßenmädchen waren.

Oiran nahm den höchsten Rang unter den in dieser Serie dargestellten Frauen ein, und daher ist die *Oiran* in Tafel 24 in einer Positur gezeigt, die auf ihre Feinheit schließen läßt. Sie hat sich gerade das Haar gewaschen und, ehe sie es sich aufsteckt, probiert sie die Spitze ihres Schreibpinsels aus, in Vorbereitung auf einen verführerischen Brief an einen unaufmerksamen Gönner. Während sie über ihren Brief nachdenkt, erinnert ihr Ausdruck vielmehr an die Verschlagenheit eines vollendeten Schauspielers im Milieu der Freudenviertel als an die Leidenschaft einer verliebten Frau.

Von den fünf in dieser Serie dargestellten Kurtisanen, kam *Geigi* als nächste im Rang nach *Oiran* in Schönheit und Gewandtheit. Nach *Geigi* werden die Lebensbedingungen der Kurtisanen gleich viel schlechter, wie bei der *Kiri no musume, Kashi* und *Teppō*, die schäbige Häuser am Kanalufer im ersten und zweiten Kyō-machi Bezirk der Freudenviertel von Yoshiwara bewohnten.

Der Ursprung der Bezeichnung *teppō* für den niedrigsten Rang der Freudenmädchen gibt uns einen Einblick in die bürgerliche Kultur dieser Zeit. *Teppō* war ein Slang-Ausdruck für die japanische Pufferfisch-Sorte namens *fugu*, welche damals eine Delikatesse für Gourmets war und immer noch ist. Bestimmte Organe des *fugu* enthielten jedoch ein tödliches Gift, ind der Gourmet lief Gefahr, wie mit einer Muskete (*teppō*) "abgeschossen" zu werden, selbst beim Essen eines gut zubereiteten Fischs. Ebenso war es allgemein bekannt, daß ein Mann, der seine Zeit bei einer niedrigen *teppō*-Dirne verbrachte, Gefahr lief, sich Geschlechtskrankheiten zuzuziehen. Die Parallele zwischen diesen beiden riskanten Vergnügen brachte einen der zahllosen Witze hervor, die das Ethos der bürgerlichen Kultur kennzeichnete. Die Darstellung dieser niedrigen Dirne (Tafel 25) mit ihren liederlich entblößten großen Brüsten und einem Stück Toilettenpapier zwischen den Zähnen, gibt ein nur zu lebhaftes Bild des elenden Lebens einer Frau am unteren Ende der Gesellschaft.

26–28. *Die betrunkene Kurtisane; die Faulpelze; das Flittchen:* aus der Serie "Die Augengläser eines wachsamen Vaters" (*Kyōkun oya no megane: Gutarabē; Namayoi; Bakuren*). *Ōban*-Format. Veröffentlicht von Tsuruya Kinsuke, *ca.* 1803.
Um die Frühzeit der Kansei-Epoche (1789–1801) hatte Utamaro sein *okubi bijin-ga* vervollkommnen können, d.h. seine Darstellungen lediglich des Oberkörpers des Modells, und hatte Wiedergaben weiblicher Schönheit erreicht, ohnegleichen in ihrer Fähigkeit, die einzigartigen Eigenschaften von Frauen verschiedenen Alters und verschiedener gesellschaftlicher Schicht und Persönlichkeit sowie vorübergehende Geistesverfassung auszudrücken. Als Utamaro an den zehn Drucken dieser Serie arbeitete, scheint er jedoch seine unermüdliche Beobachtung der Frauen über die Ausdrucksgrenzen der Malerei und besonders des Holzschnitt-Druckes hinaus verfolgt zu haben, und in dieser Zeit machte er es sich mehr und mehr zur Gewohnheit, langatmige schriftliche Erläuterungen zur Persönlichkeit und Geistesverfassung seines Modells abzugeben. Trotz dieses Anzeichens für Utamaros Enttäuschung über seine Unfähigkeit, die Ausdruckskraft seines Mittels zu erweitern, sind die Drucke dieser Serie als Meisterwerk Utamaros späterer Jahre anzusehen.

In der *Betrunkenen Kurtisane* (Tafel 26) legt Uamaro dar, warum es falsch ist, Frauen das Trinken zu erlauben. Das den oberen Teils des Druckes ausfüllende Stück gibt den sinnlosen Monolog der hoffnungslos betrunkenen Kurtisane wieder, die ihren Becher verkehrt herum hält und außerstande ist, ihre Augen auf etwas zu konzentrieren. Sie hat ihren Mund verdreht und scheint auf jemand zu schimpfen, aber, wie die Schrift bezeugt, kann sie niemand mehr ihre Worte verständlich machen. Trotz seiner aufdringlichen Erklärung, behält Utamaros Darstellung der hilflos berauschten Frau starke Ausdruckskraft.

Ebenso hat Utamaro in den *Faulpelzen* (Tafel 27) eine schlampige junge Frau genommen, die sich die Zähne putzt im Nachthemd, wie sei gerade vom Bett aufgestanden ist. Ihre zerzauste Frisur, die losen Haarsträhnen im Nacken sowie ihre lässige Haltung und ihr Mangel an Sittsamkeit deuten fast grausam den Charakter einer faulen, sich vernachlässigenden Frau an.

In dem *Flittchen* (Tafel 28) gibt Utamaro eine Warnung für die Frau, die Neigungen zum Flittchen hat: unkultiviert, schamlos und ohne Gedanken für andere. Diese Frau schlürft *sake* in einer Haltung völliger Ungehemmtheit, während sie den Becher westlicher Art kippt und dabei den rechten Arm fast bis zur Schulter entblößt. Ihr *kimono* ist am Hals offen, und sie hält einen ganzen gekochten großen Krebs in der linken Hand. In der Darstellung faßt Utamaro lebendig das Aussehen

einer Dirne, welche lebensmüde den zurückhaltenden Anstand aufgegeben hat, wie er von einer jungen japanischen Frau, die nach weiblichen Reizen strebt, erwartet wird.

29–31. *Die obere Schicht; Die Mittelschicht; Die untere Schicht:* die Serie "Lebensführung junger Frauen aus drei Schichten" (*Fūzoku sandan musume: Jōbon no zu; Chūbon no zu; Geben no zu*). *Ōban*-Format. Veröffentlicht von Wakasaya Yoichi, *ca.* 1795-96. National-Museum Tokio.
Die drei Drucke dieser Serie teilen die Töchter der bürgerlichen Klasse in den oberen, mittleren und unteren Rang ein und stellen ihr tägliches Leben und Treiben während der heißen Sommermonate dar; sie waren dazu bestimmt, einzeln oder als Triptychon betrachtet zu werden.

Die zwei Frauen in *Die obere Schicht* (Tafel 29) könnten ganz gut eine junge Frau und ihre Mutter sein. Die junge Frau hält einen runden Fächer und trägt einen leichten Seiden-Kimono mit langen Ärmeln im *furisode*-Stil, was darauf hindeutet, daß sie noch nicht Erwachsenenalter erreicht hat. Die ältere Frau streift sich Finger-Plektrons auf, um dann auf dem *koto* zu spielen. Die auf ihrem abgenommenen Stoffdeckel stehende Schachtel enthielt die Finger-Plektrons, und der kleine Käfig im Vordergrund ist für Insekten bestimmt, deren Rufstimmen von alters her in Japan sehr angenehm empfunden wurden. Wie es für einen Druck über die "obere Schicht" sehr passend ist, scheinen sie gerade mit einer *koto*-Stunde anfangen zu wollen.

Auf dem *Die Mittelschicht* bezeichneten Druck (Tafel 30) bewundern zwei junge Frauen Wasserbinsen, die sorgsam in einer schönen flachen Vase gezogen werden. Sie haben ihre leichten Seidenjacken ausgezogen, die auf dem Ständer hinter ihnen hängen, und fühlen sich ganz offenbar wohl. Ihre anmutige Haltung und ihr zurückhaltender Ausdruck weisen auf die von Frauen dieser Schicht erstrebte Vornehmheit hin.

In *Die untere Schicht* (Tafel 31) wird der ziemlich anspruchslose Lebensstil zweier junger Frauen der unteren Schicht dargestellt. Eine von ihnen ist aufgestanden, um ihren *obi* locker zu machen, während die andere ihren *kimono* aufgemacht hat, um sich zu fächeln. Die Wasserbinsen sind einfach in einen Holzeimer gestellt, der sonst zum Wassertragen benutzt wird, und erscheinen als ein geeignetes Glanzlicht für die entspannten, entschieden kecken Gestalten der beiden Mädchen, die dem Zuschauer gleichwohl sympathisch sind und ihm liegen. Dieser einfachen Komposition gelingt es in hohem Maße, das Vergnügen an einer kühlen Abendbrise nach einem heißen Sommertag in Edo wachzurufen.

32–43 *Die Stunde der Ratte* (*Ne no koku*); *Die Stunde des Ochsen* (*Ushi no koku*); *Die Stunde des Tigers* (*Tora no koku*); *Die Stunde des Hasen* (*U no koku*); *Die Stunde des Drachens* (*Tatsu no koku*); *Die Stunde der Schlange* (*Mi no koku*); *Die Stunde des Pferdes* (*Uma no koku*); *Die Stunde des Widders* (*Hitsuji no koku*); *Die Stunde des Affen* (*Saru no koku*); *Die Stunde des Hahnes* (*Tori no koku*); *Die Stunde des Hundes* (*Inu no koku*); *Die Stunde des Bären* (*I no koku*): die Serie "Die Zwölf Lunar-Stunden in den Freuden-Vierteln" (*Seirō jūni toki*). *Ōban*-Format. Veröffentlicht von Tsutaya Jūzaburō, *ca.* 1795–96. National-Museum Tokio.
Ebenso wie in der Serie, *Eine Sonnenuhr von Mädchen* (Tafel 8–12), ist diese Serie entsprechend den zwölf Stundenzeichen des Lunar-Kalenders geordnet. In der vorliegenden Serie zeigte Utamaro, wie es in den Freudenvierteln während jeder der zwölf Lunar-Zeitspannen (von jeweils etwa zwei Stunden) zuging, zwischen der Stunde der Ratte, 12 Uhr Mitternacht, und der Stunde des Bären, 10 Uhr nm., und wie die Kurtisanen diese Stunden verlebten, wobei er einen Einblick in die Freudenviertel zu Zeiten gewährte, zu denen sie für Kundschaft geschlossen war, sowie bekanntere Szenen. Seine Darstellung der Kurtisanen als große, dünne Schönheiten wirft ein Licht auf den Einfluß von Chōbunsai Eishi, der seine Karriere als Rechtsberater des Shogunats aufgegeben hatte, um ein *ukiyo-e* Künstler zu werden. Diese Darstellung, im Verein mit der Eleganz und Grazie der Bewegungen und Haltungen der Figuren, drückt eine Seite der Kurtisanen aus, die von dem häßlichen und traurigen Wesen ihres Berufs unbefleckt bleibt.

44. *Beim Lesen eines Briefes:* aus der Serie "Utamaros neue Muster für den Nishiki-e Druck" (*Nishiki-ori Utamaro-gata shinmoyō: Fumiyomi*). *Ōban*-Format. Veröffentlicht von Tsuruya Kinsuke, *ca.* 1801-4.
Zu Beginn der Kyōwa-Epoche (1801-4) genoß Utamaro außerordentlich großes Ansehen in Edo als unübertroffener Meister der Drucke von schönen Frauen (*bijin-ga*), und es war natürlich, daß eine Reihe zahlloser geringerer Künstler versuchten, Imitationen seines Werks zu machen. Durch das Auftreten dieser Epigonen aufgebracht, ließ Utamaro seinen Gefühlen in einem berühmten Kolophon freien

Lauf, welches er in den Titel des Druckes geschickt einarbeitete. In dieser Erklärung seiner Absicht, eine Serie von Modellen in seinem unnachahmbaren Stil zu schaffen, spürt man das Bewußtsein seiner Stellung, das an Anmaßung grenzt.

Das Azuma *nishiki-e* ist eines der berühmten Erzeugnisse von Edo. In letzter Zeit sind jedoch minderwertige Künstler, so zahlreich und unbedeutend wie die Blätter eines Baumes, nacheinander erschienen. Sie gleichen förmlich einem Ameisenschwarm. Mit der glänzenden Schönheit unserer roten und blauen Farbstoffe als einzigem Mittel machen diese Nachahmer grauenhafte Drucke. Kürzlich haben diese schlechten Nachahmungen Zugang in Orten außerhalb von Edo gefunden; dies kann unserer Stadt nur Schande machen. So habe ich mit schwerem Herzen beschlossen, diese Drucke als Beispiele des wahren Wesens der *Do bijin-ga* zu schaffen, als Richtschnur für diese elenden Nachahmungen.

Tatsächlich stellen die Drucke dieser Serie Utamaros gewagtesten Versuch mit beispiellosen, von ihm selbst geschaffenen Neuerungen dar. Die Umrisse der Gesichter bestehen aus zinnoberroten Linien und in der Behandlung des Kimonos hat Utamaro die in der überlieferten orientalischen Malerie mit Pinselstrichen erhaltenen Linien aufgegeben und nun fein Schattierungsweisen gebraucht, um die Qualität des Stoffes anzudeuten. Diese Neuerungen hatten großen Erfolg und erfaßten den Ausdruck einer in Liebesgedanken verlorenen Frau, so wie sie die sanfte Vornehmheit ihrer Haltung und Kleidung andeuteten.